Feeling Unreal

Self-portrait by 22-year-old woman

suffering from depersonalization disorder

Feeling Unreal

Depersonalization Disorder and the Loss of the Self

Daphne Simeon, MD

Jeffrey Abugel

OXFORD
UNIVERSITY PRESS

OXFORD
UNIVERSITY PRESS

Oxford University Press, Inc., publishes works that further
Oxford University's objective of excellence
in research, scholarship, and education.

Oxford New York
Auckland Cape Town Dar es Salaam Hong Kong Karachi
Kuala Lumpur Madrid Melbourne Mexico City Nairobi
New Delhi Shanghai Taipei Toronto

With offices in
Argentina Austria Brazil Chile Czech Republic France Greece
Guatemala Hungary Italy Japan Poland Portugal Singapore
South Korea Switzerland Thailand Turkey Ukraine Vietnam

Copyright © 2006 by Oxford University Press, Inc.

Published by Oxford University Press, Inc.
198 Madison Avenue, New York, New York 10016

www.oup.com

First issued as an Oxford University Press paperback, 2009

Oxford is a registered trademark of Oxford University Press

Library of Congress Cataloging-in-Publication Data
Simeon, Daphne, 1958–
Feeling unreal : depersonalization disorder and the loss of the self /
Daphne Simeon, Jeffrey Abugel.
    p. cm.
ISBN 978-0-19-538521-2
1. Depersonalization.   2. Identity (Psychology)   I. Abugel, Jeffrey.   II. Title.
RC553.D4S56 2006
155.2—dc22   2005020558

9 8 7 6 5 4 3 2 1

Printed in the United States of America
on acid-free paper

To our parents

Acknowledgments

Many minds have contributed to the enormous amount of information we have synthesized within these pages. Some of them are well known; others have languished in obscurity for decades, waiting for their observations to be rediscovered. We wish to thank the many thinkers through the years who each have contributed in their own way toward solving the puzzle of depersonalization, a most enigmatic human experience. We have tried to include as many of them as possible within the text. In addition, permit us to add these personal asides:

Jeffrey Abugel: I would like to note the support and encouragement of the late Oscar Janiger, M.D. "Oz," as he was known, was a passionate explorer into the depths of the mind, and a strong motivating force during the embryonic stages of this book. As a doctor, friend, and teacher, he was living proof that curiosity and hunger for knowledge need not preclude a passion for life itself.

Daphne Simeon: I am deeply appreciative to all the teachers and mentors who have inspired and supported me, and to the many patients from whom I have learned and by whom I have been so touched.

Contents

Feeling Unreal

Introduction

This is the story of a mental condition that affects millions of people worldwide—yet few even know its name. Depersonalization has been well-documented in medical literature for more than 100 years, but this book, the first definitive work on the subject, is long overdue.

Everyone feels "unreal" from time to time. It may happen after a traumatic event, while in new or foreign surroundings, or in times of severe stress. As a defense mechanism, depersonalization serves a purpose—to mentally distance an individual from horrific or overwhelming circumstances. But this mechanism can go awry and exhibit a darker side, which manifests itself as depersonalization disorder.

For depersonalized people, the world within, or the world around, may seem strange and unreal for prolonged periods of time. They feel detached from the sense of self they once took for granted and struggle, often for many years, in fruitless searches for answers that are hard to come by.

Depersonalization can be transient or chronic. It may appear alongside other psychiatric disorders or completely on its own. It has been noted as the third most prevalent psychiatric symptom, after depression and anxiety, yet the average mental health professional usually knows little about it.

Imagine thinking without feeling, devoid of emotional connection to past or present. Imagine a heightened awareness of the thoughts parading through your head, or always watching yourself a step removed, interrupted periodically by a single emotion—the real fear of losing your mind. Living this way, feeling hollow, without familiar emotions, wreaks havoc on individuals' inner lives. Yet outwardly they may appear completely normal, even well adjusted. They know something is wrong, but they may not know what it is, so their lives often become facades of normalcy, masks to cover the unreality within. What is it? What causes it? What does it mean, and can it be cured? These are the questions examined herein.

This book is the culmination of more than a century of research and observation. It is the combined effort of a psychiatrist, recognized as the leading investigator of depersonalization in the United States, and a journalist who experienced the condition for more than a decade and explored its philosophical and literary implications for years to follow. The diversity of our backgrounds has assured a rich and balanced approach to the topic. Our intention is to present an accurate and unbiased distillation of the broad range of scientific material that has addressed depersonalization for the last century and earlier. We also examine the many philosophical and literary references to depersonalization-like states of mind. Sensations of unreality and the experience of "no-self" appear often in literature and religion, under different names and different guises.

Feeling Unreal is the result of countless hours spent seeking answers to questions that have eluded so many for so long. We offer it as a foundation—a solid ground on which patients and those who treat them alike can move forward, with greater knowledge of this baffling condition, and in turn, greater understanding of our individual selves.

1 Strangers to Our Selves

he mind is its own place," Milton reminds us. "And in itself can make a heaven of hell, and a hell of heaven." For most people, these lines from *Paradise Lost* are likely just the stuff of some long-forgotten English literature course. But for Ron, a 32-year-old magazine editor living in a coastal city, they ring true with profound insight. To his peers, Ron's life is practically heaven on earth. He's bright, funny, and successful at his job in publishing. With an apartment near the beach and plenty of friends, he is living a life that is envied by many. But Ron has a problem. And each day when he returns to his upscale neighborhood in time to see the sun setting, he wonders how long he can maintain what he has. He wonders if tonight will be the night he finally slips into the isolated hell of insanity.

Ron's problem is a mental one, and he knows it. Trapped within the confines of his mind, he is too aware of every thought passing through it, as if he were outside, looking in. At night he often lies awake ruminating endlessly about what's wrong with him, about death, and about the meaning of existence itself. At times his arms and legs feel like they don't belong with his body. But most of the time, his mind feels like it is operating apart from the body that contains it.

While he can interact with others who have no idea that anything is wrong, Ron lives without spontaneity, going through the motions, doing what he thinks people expect him to do, glad that he is able to at least *appear* normal throughout the day and maintain a job. He studied drama briefly while in college, and remains enamored of Shakespeare and literature, but an emerging self-consciousness eventually robbed him of his ability to act. Now he feels as if *all* of his life is an act—just an attempt to maintain the status quo.

Recalling literature he once loved, he sometimes pictures himself as Camus's Meursault, in *The Stranger,* an emotionless character who plods through life in a meaningless universe with apathy and indifference. He's tired of living this way but terrified of death. So he's settled into a predictable routine whereby work serves as a necessary diversion, and happiness is a dearly departed illusion. Dead people can't be happy, he thinks. To be happy, one has to feel, and Ron has not felt anything but fear, confusion, and despair for a long time.

This is the story of a baffling but very real condition of the mind that plagues Ron and millions like him. It isn't depression, or anxiety, though it can sometimes appear as a symptom of these better-known conditions. Often, it emerges with cruel ferocity as a chronic disorder completely unto itself. Its destructive impact on an individual's sense of self is implied in its very name—depersonalization.

In his autobiographical account of his battle with debilitating depression, *Darkness Visible,* William Styron writes: "Depression is a disorder of mood, so mysteriously painful and elusive in the way it becomes known to the self—to the mediating intellect—as to verge close to being beyond description." The writer's skills are tested when writing about what Styron calls "a howling tempest in the brain."[1] The wreckage caused by depersonalization is equally indescribable to anyone who has not experienced it. Phrases like "things feel unreal to me," "I feel detached from myself," and "my voice sounds different to me" are enigmatic to normal people yet clearly understandable to depersonalized individuals.

Most of us can imagine our darkest fear, such as being buried alive, or locked in a room full of rats or spiders. Most of us can remember moments of intolerable grief or unbridled terror, whether they occurred in waking life or in nightmares. We can remember being unable to "shake" some awful sensation in the conscious hours after a particularly bad dream occurs, or feeling "unreal" in the face of a sudden tragedy or loss. For the most part, depersonalized people are actually living everyday with the fear and unreality of a dream state come true. Inner and outer worlds seem strange and foreign, resulting in an altered sense of selfhood that dominates their mental lives.

Sarah, a 29-year-old graduate student from Long Island, New York, has dealt with depersonalization for most of her life. She explains the sensations to others in terms to which they can relate. "Most people have played little games with their minds at one time or another," she says, "like staring in the mirror so long that you no longer recognize your face, or repeating the same word over and over until it no longer sounds familiar—it sounds like something you've never heard before." These momentary impressions of strangeness that normal people can induce in themselves are quite similar to what Sarah feels much of the time, but cannot control, she says.

Our sense of familiarity with our selves, our sense of past, present, or future, who we are, and how we fit into the world around us enables us to live from day to day in relative stability, with purpose, sanity, and reason. But people with chronic depersonalization are never quite sure who they are in a sense. As such, they can find themselves in a life of going through the motions robotically, often attempting to appear "normal," wondering if others can see through their façade to the inexplicable disconnection that pervades their existence.

Tom, a 44-year-old sales executive, feels that he gets through his job using about "10%" of his brain capacity. "I'll sit in an important meeting and be asked crucial questions, and somehow I come up with the answers. But I'm not really there. It's as if nothing is real, myself or the meeting I am in. I look out the window 40 stories up and wonder where the sky ends. Or I see myself sitting in this meeting, discussing bottom lines and sales promotions as if they actually had meaning to me. It's more than daydreaming. It's like I'm too aware of certain larger aspects of reality. In the face of the infinite sky above me, or infinite time before and after my short existence, how could such things as my job have any meaning at all? Doesn't anyone else ever wonder about this stuff?" Tom's sensations of detachment from everything that is immediate and real in the day to day world, and his over-preoccupation with the nature of existence is something often experienced by depersonalized people.

"I sometimes feel like I'm from Mars," says Cheryl, a 33-year-old fabric designer. "Being human seems strange, bodily functions seem bizarre. . . . My thoughts seem separate from my body. At times, the most common, familiar objects can seem foreign, as if I am looking at them for the first time. An American flag, for instance. It's instantly recognizable, and immediately means something to everyone. But if I look at it for more than a moment, I just see colors and shapes on a piece of cloth. It's as if I've forgotten ever seeing the flag before, even though I'm still aware of what my 'normal' reaction should be."

This sense of strangeness about familiar objects outside of one's self is known as *derealization*, yet another aspect of the depersonalization phenomenon.

"What's so troubling to me is that if I were seeing these things for the first time, like a child, there should be some sense of wonderment, but there isn't," Cheryl adds. "I know that there's something wrong with me, and all it does is fill me with fear, especially the fear of being taken away screaming in a straight jacket."

Louise is a 24-year-old grade school teacher whose experiences of depersonalization permeate all the ways in which she relates to her body and her movements, as well as her whole visual experience of the world. Her depersonalization started when she was around 10, at which time she felt that whenever she lifted up her legs or arms, her body felt weightless and she began to float. She says: "For me, it can be a very visual experience. It's like I'm wearing glasses that I can't see through, like there is a zipper to unzip." She no longer feels much; she describes herself as numb, and it's rare for her to cry even when she feels like it. Her body does not feel like a part of her: "I sometimes smack my hand or pinch my leg just to feel something, and to know it's there." Louise often feels like one part of her is "acting." At the same time, "there is another part 'inside' that is not connecting with the *me* that is talking to you," she says. When the depersonalization is at its most intense, she feels like she just does not exist. These experiences leave her confused about who she really is, and quite often, she feels like an "actress" or simply, "a fake."

Greg, 42, owns a successful business and is the father of two. He first experienced depersonalization when he was 17, and in the beginning the episodes would come and go. For the past 15 years or so though, his depersonalization has been constant, at times more intense than at others. Like Louise, he eloquently describes the many facets of his self-experience that have become chronically distorted by depersonalization. He has thought about his condition a great deal, and has researched it on his own, as fervently as any doctor he has met to date. When he tries to explain his sensations to a professional, or to someone close to him, he does so in terms of the distinct domains of his selfhood that are affected:

Feelings: "I want to feel things like everyone else again, but I'm deadened and numb. I can laugh or cry but it's intellectual, my muscles move but I feel nothing."

Body: "I feel like I'm not here, I'm floating around. A separate part
   of me is aware of all my movements; it's like I've left my body.
   Even when I'm talking I don't feel like it is my words."

Mind: "My mind and my body are somehow not connected, it's
   like my body is doing one thing and my mind is saying another. Like my mind is somewhere off to the back, not inside
   my body."

Vision: "It's like glass over my eyes, a visual fog totally flat and
   two-dimensional."

Agency (feeling in control of one's actions): "I feel I'm not really
   here, I'm distant. I'm going through the motions like a robot."

People like Greg may suffer from chronic depersonalization for many
years, visiting a variety of doctors, psychiatrists, and therapists. Typically, health
professionals are not only unable to offer much relief—they rarely even offer a
reassuring label for the condition. Patients are commonly told that they suffer
from some kind of anxiety or depression and that what they feel is secondary
to their major problem.

The frightening absence of feeling often encountered in depersonalization
also can create a somewhat paradoxical state of mind. On one hand, selfhood,
and with it the individual's relation to the outer world, seems to deteriorate,
leaving the sensation of "no-self." Conversely, a heightened awareness of the
thoughts running through one's head can result in a distant heightened consciousness of the self, a self that no longer feels familiar or grounded. Strongly
held beliefs, vivid memories, strong emotions that were naturally sparked by
the senses now all seem like illusions, unfamiliar, without meaning, somehow
false. Familiar mental images are reduced to movie-screen pictures devoid of
the smells, sounds, and sensations that accompanied them earlier. Ideas or
memories that once had emotional meaning are now experienced with distorted awareness and little feeling, while the sufferer remains intellectually
very aware that this altered perspective is anything but normal. This lack of
"grounding" that accompanies a normal sense of self can leave one feeling
lost, vulnerable, and fearful.

"When I try to explain this it sounds like a complete contradiction." Says
Joanne, a 35-year-old mother of three. "Minutes can seem like hours to me
when every thought, no matter how insignificant, is weighed and overly present. It's like my thoughts are on a big movie screen in huge type, or shouted
at me in a loud unpleasant voice.

"Yet at the same time, my lifetime, and all the lifetimes before and after mine seem to last just seconds in the scheme of things. I try to recapture the feeling I had when I was young, that life was rich with promise. I looked forward to building memories to cherish in my old age. But now it all seems so short and empty, as if all the experiences I did enjoy to this point have been erased and I'm just existing in this very second . . . there is no past, no future. Instead of being rooted in this world, enjoying my children and my life, all I can think of is how transient it all is.

"I'd really rather have cancer than this," Joanne concludes. And she's not alone in this sentiment. Others who are chronically depersonalized have made the exact same statement. "With a disease that people know, you get some degree of empathy. But if you try to explain this, people either think you're crazy or completely self-absorbed and neurotic. So you keep your mouth shut and suffer silently."

Indeed, depersonalized individuals often say they would give anything to live their lives again with less scrutiny of existence and more spontaneity. While Socrates may have concluded, "the unexamined life is not worth living," the *overly* examined life, as experienced by the people we've met so far, is often too painful to endure.

Hardly a New Disorder

Depersonalization, as a human experience, is nothing new. It has traditionally been viewed as the mind's natural way of coping with overwhelming shock or stress, or intolerable living conditions such as life in a concentration camp. In such instances, the mind detaches itself from the surroundings for the purpose of sheer survival. But strangely, depersonalization can appear spontaneously, without any apparent trigger. Possible causes of onset have only been researched in depth in the last few years, though theories have proliferated for a century. (We'll cover these causes in detail later.) Some people can recall exactly how and when the problem began and whether or not it was tied to a specific event. For others, the condition may have begun so early in life that it is simply all they have ever known. In such cases, depersonalization becomes a safe void where nothing affects them, but at high price: when they'd like to feel they can't. They become what Ron and others have come to call "the living dead."

The word *depersonalization* itself, in a diagnostic sense, refers to both a symptom and a full-blown psychiatric disorder. Ludovic Dugas, a psychologist/philosopher who often wrote on the topics of memory and déjà vu, is most often credited with first using the term in its present context, in the late 1890s.[2] However, Dugas had first seen the word in a popular literary work of the era, *The Journal Intime*, by Henri Frédéric Amiel (1821–1881). This journal, the voluminous diary of an introspective and obscure professor, was published posthumously. One particular entry helped to define the nature of depersonalization for all time: "And now I find myself regarding existence as though beyond the tomb, from another world. All is strange to me; I am, as it were, outside my own body and individuality; I am depersonalised, detached, cut adrift. Is this madness?"[3]

Other, more renowned individuals later recognized depersonalization and derealization as very concrete human experiences. Sigmund Freud experienced a vivid encounter with derealization while visiting the Acropolis during a trip to Athens in 1904. "So all this really does exist, just as we learned at school!" he wrote some thirty years later, in an open letter to the writer Romain Rolland. In it, Freud explained that he had been seized that day by a "fleeting attack of derealization."[4] Even though he had read about the famous ruin for years and knew that it did exist, seeing the real thing had for some reason proven to be overwhelming. Freud realized his actual presence at the site, but found it oddly difficult to perceive it as being real.

In years that followed, renowned psychologists either touched on the subject of depersonalization in books or issued lengthy papers on the subject in nearly every major language. In the 1930s, a medical textbook entitled *Modern Clinical Psychiatry* first included depersonalization. Revised years later, it provided a particularly insightful description:

> Depersonalization, a pervasive and distressing feeling of estrangement, known sometimes as the depersonalization syndrome, may be defined as an affective disorder in which feelings of unreality and a loss of conviction of one's own identity and of a sense of identification with and control over one's own body are the principal symptoms. The unreality symptoms are of two kinds: a feeling of changed personality and a feeling that the outside world is unreal. The patient feels that he is no longer himself, but he does not feel that he has become someone else. The condition is, therefore, not one of so called transformation of personality. Experience loses emotional meaning and may be colored by a frightening sense

of strangeness and unreality. The onset may be acute, following a severe emotional shock, or it may be a gradual onset following prolonged physical or emotional stress. It is more frequent in personalities of an intelligent, sensitive, affectionate, introverted, and imaginative type. The patient may say his feelings are "frozen," that his thoughts are strange; his thoughts and acts seem to be carried on mechanically as if he were a machine or automaton. People and objects appear unreal, far away, and lacking in normal color and vividness. The patient may say he feels as if he were going about in a trance or dream. He appears perplexed and bewildered because of the strangeness of unreality feelings. He has difficulty in concentrating and may complain that his brain is "dead" or has "stopped working."[5]

To be completely accurate in terms of what's known today, the description should have ended there. But, in line with older theories about depersonalization, the textbook postulated that depersonalization was not a specific disorder outside of other neurotic and psychotic states, occurred more commonly in women and in puberty, and recommended electroshock therapy as the effective form of treatment.

It is now thought that the condition occurs about equally in both sexes, at many stages of life. Chronic depersonalization is now recognized as a unique disorder of its own standing, depersonalization disorder, rather than a condition secondary to depressive, obsessional or psychotic states.

Unlike the early days of studying the mind, today's field of psychiatry has developed a reference book, the *Diagnostic and Statistical Manual of Psychiatric Disorders* (*DSM*), revised periodically to stay current. These revisions list the latest criteria for making an accurate diagnosis of virtually any known mental illness based on more recently gathered evidence. Early versions of the *DSM* from the 1950s and 1960s mentioned depersonalization within the description of dissociative reaction, in the category of psychoneurotic disorders. As late as 1980, the *DSM* offered few specifics about the condition. But today that's changed. According to the latest edition, *DSM-IV*, depersonalization disorder, now listed under dissociative disorders, is covered in part, as follows:

The essential features of Depersonalization Disorder are persistent or recurrent episodes of depersonalization characterized by a feeling of detachment or estrangement from one's self. (Criterion A) The individual may feel like an automaton or as if he or she is

living in a dream or a movie. There may be a sensation of being
an outside observer of one's metal processes, one's body, or parts
of one's body. Various types of sensory anesthesia, lack of affec-
tive response, and a sensation of lacking control of one's actions,
including speech, are often present. The individual with Depersonalization Disorder maintains intact reality testing (e.g., awareness
that it is only a feeling and that he or she is not really an automaton) (Criterion B). Depersonalization is a common experience, and
this diagnosis should be made only if the symptoms are sufficiently
severe to cause marked distress or impairment in functioning.
(Criterion C).[6]

Detachment or estrangement from oneself, coupled with an awareness of this
detachment, is the essence of depersonalization, despite the multitude of associated symptoms that have been recorded over time. People may have difficulty describing their symptoms and may fear that their experiences signify
that they are "crazy," the *DSM* notes.

Additionally, the *DSM-IV* recognizes these other possible manifestations
of depersonalization disorder:

- Derealization, or experiencing the external world as strange or
  unreal,
- Macropsia or micropsia, which is an uncanny alternation in the
  size or shape of objects,
- A sense that other people seem unfamiliar or mechanical.

Other features common in depersonalization disorder include anxiety
symptoms, depressive symptoms, obsessive rumination, somatic concerns, and
a disturbance in a person's sense of time. In some cases, the loss of feeling
that is characteristic of depersonalization may mimic major depressive disorder and, in other cases, may co-exist with it. Depersonalization and derealization are frequent symptoms of panic attacks, *DSM* notes, but if depersonalization and derealization occur exclusively during such attacks, the individual
should not be diagnosed with depersonalization disorder.

The other major diagnostic reference used by physicians, the *International Classification of Diseases (ICD-10)*[7], lists depersonalization, but interestingly, places the condition in a category called "mental and behavioral
disorders: other neurotic disorders," rather than under dissociative disorders,
which are treated separately. This fuels an ongoing debate about exactly

which category is best suited for depersonalization. The *DSM-IV* and *ICD-10* describe depersonalization a little differently but they basically provide the same diagnostic criteria.

DSM-IV also recognizes that at some time in their lives, approximately half of all adults will experience a single brief episode of depersonalization, usually precipitated by severe stress. A transient experience of depersonalization develops in nearly one-third of individuals exposed to life-threatening danger and in close to 10% of patients hospitalized for mental disorders.

Transient depersonalization, lasting seconds, minutes, or even hours, can readily occur in "normal" individuals under extreme conditions of sleep deprivation, sensory deprivation, travel to unknown places, or acute intoxication with marijuana or hallucinogens. A high incidence of depersonalization has been found to occur transiently in one-third to one-half of student populations,[8] as well as among people who have been exposed to life-threatening danger.[9] The latter state has now been coined "peritraumatic dissociation," and is particularly interesting because it so often occurs after the extreme traumas that the Western world is now living in fear of and may predict how well or how poorly people fare long after the traumatic incident. As noted above, many people have had brief transient episodes of depersonalization, especially after a great emotional shock, use of certain drugs, or a period of tremendous stress. Depersonalization has been found to occur, at least fleetingly, in 50–70% of the population.[10] Research shows that approximately 1–3% of the general population might suffer from chronic depersonalization disorder.[11] Often, initial depersonalization goes away as mysteriously as it came, but sometimes it becomes more chronic, with an enigmatic life of its own.

Depersonalization is likely to make people think they're going insane. When it occurs after they've taken an illicit drug, they often think they've suffered brain damage. No longer grounded by familiar sensations or surroundings, they feel as if they're losing their grip on reality. But unlike people with psychotic conditions like schizophrenia, they are not going insane at all. They are, if anything, suddenly *overly aware* of reality and existence and of the ways in which their own experience is a distortion of a "normal" sense of a real self.

Depersonalization, in fact, resembles a sort of altered "awareness" or "awakening" that in some cultures is thought to be a level of spiritual growth. This is touched upon in the *DSM-IV*. But for most westerners, this abnormal sense of having no "self" is a state they'd prefer to leave behind. (In a later chapter, we'll take a closer look at philosophical interpretations of this state of mind.)

The Madness of the New Millennium?

Exploration of the nature of depersonalization, as a transient symptom or as a full-blown chronic disorder, is now taking on a new importance for several reasons. First, the use of illicit drugs, from the 1960s until now, has fostered an explosion of depersonalization cases in the last 30 years. Marijuana and many of today's "club scene" drugs are well documented as being specific triggers for chronic depersonalization. Second, there is evidence that more people are experiencing depersonalization, or at least making it known, than ever before, whatever the initial trigger. Many of these people suffered in silence, perplexity, and shame for years. Then, the advent of the Internet prompted the founding of several depersonalization support group websites. Consequently, thousands of people with strikingly similar experiences and symptoms began congregating in the late 1990s with a hunger for information and comfort through this new venue. One website, depersonalization.info, received more than 10,000 individual hits in a period of 3 months in 2001. The posting below is typical of the thousands who visit briefly, then return to their solitary worlds:

> I look at my mind from within and feel both trapped and puzzled about the strangeness of my existence. My thoughts swirl round and round constantly probing the strangeness of selfhood—why do I exist? Why am I me and not someone else? At these times, feelings of sweaty panic develop, as if I am having a phobia about my own thoughts. At other times, I don't feel "grounded." I look at this body and can't understand why I am within it. I hear myself having conversations and wonder where the voice is coming from. I imagine myself seeing life as if it were played like a film in a cinema. But in that case, where am I? Who is watching the film? What is the cinema? The worst part is that this seems as if it's the truth, and the periods of my life in which I did not feel like this were delusions.

This was written within an e-mail message, but the same articulate expression of the strangeness of depersonalization could have come right out of Amiel's journal, written with pen and ink, or from dozens of other philosophical or literary works through the ages. These cries for help have not gone unnoticed.

Finally, for the first time, a new awareness online and in doctors' offices has impressed several medical institutions enough to establish research programs singly devoted to the study of depersonalization disorder. These include the Depersonalization Research Unit at the Institute of Psychiatry, King's College, London, and the Depersonalization and Dissociation Research Program at the Mount Sinai School of Medicine in New York. These programs are devoted to studying depersonalization in depth in all its aspects, descriptive, cognitive, and biological, and to experimenting with new treatments that might offer relief to those who find depersonalization an unbearable mental condition.

In the next chapter we examine depersonalization through the stories several individuals from diverse backgrounds.

2 Expressions of the Inexpressible

Nobody realizes that some people expend tremendous energy merely to be normal.

—ALBERT CAMUS

Dissociative disorders in general are known to be founded in experiences of trauma or abuse. They are conceptualized as the human psyche's way of coping with intolerable circumstances—a means of escape to assure survival, no matter what the price. Depersonalization disorder (DPD) is classified by modern American psychiatry within the dissociative disorders, but its traumatic causes are more highly variable than those encountered in more severe dissociative disorders. Not only childhood trauma, but also later severe stress, frightening episodes of other mental illness, and even isolated drug use can precipitate the condition. In some cases of depersonalization disorder, there is even no apparent cause or trigger.

Sanity is sometimes described as little more than shared experience. If one person sees an angel hovering outside the window while no one else does, we think of them as either a religious visionary or, more likely, a person with schizophrenia. If 10 people see the same angel, it may be a mass hallucination, and if everyone sees the angel, then we safely assume the angel is really there, whatever the explanation for her presence. People with depersonalization have historically suffered in horrible isolation, fearful for their own sanity. But shared experience places their thoughts and sensations into perspective. Many with DPD have become momentarily elated upon reading or hearing their own thoughts and feelings, however bizarre, expressed by another.

In this chapter we discuss in more detail the stories of actual patients who suffer from DPD. The following excerpts from case histories present a profile of the experience of depersonalization and some of its subtle variations. These personal recollections do more to bring the experience to life than any medical textbook description could hope to. Remember, although short-lived depersonalization is not uncommon in the general population under conditions of sudden extreme stress, sleep deprivation, or drug intoxication, chronic depersonalization is more unusual (although by no means rare). This raises the question of whether a person might be suffering from what is known, according to the *Diagnostic and Statistical Manual of Mental Disorders*, 4th edition (*DSM-IV*), as depersonalization disorder.[1] We touched on the basic characteristics of this disorder in chapter 1, and in this chapter we describe and discuss them in much more detail.

In short, for an individual to be diagnosed as suffering from primary DPD by a doctor, the episodes of depersonalization must be recurrent or persistent, must not occur exclusively in the context of another psychiatric or medical condition, and must be associated with significant life distress or dysfunction. DPD also must be associated with "intact reality testing," meaning that an individual must know that these unusual subjective experiences of unreality are not normal. Here we describe five cases of people with distinctly different histories, who all suffer from DPD, and in their context we address questions and answers about this puzzling and frequently unrecognized disorder.

The Case of Sally

Sally K. is now 19 years old. She grew up as an only child, with a mother who suffered from schizophrenia. They lived in a small California town. Her mother did not work, and her father, a manager at a local supermarket, worked long hours and was hardly ever around. Despite some attempts to get her effective treatment, Sally's mother was largely untreated and never took medication regularly. Sally's earliest memories were of an erratic, unpredictable, and strangely behaving mother. Mrs. K. never had the capacity to keep a neat household. Sally recalls living in a messy, disorganized environment, with stacks of letters and clothing lying around everywhere. Her mother was unable to regularly cook meals, and Sally remembers from her early years having to scramble some semblance of a dinner from the half-empty refrigerator.

Despite loving Sally and never being abusive, Mrs. K was unable to provide any consistent warmth, nurturing, and guidance.

Often, Mrs. K. suffered attacks of some sort, Sally felt. She would become suspicious that neighbors were plotting against her to get her out of the neighborhood. So she would lock all the windows and doors of the house, turn off the lights, and ask Sally to take cover under a table or bed. The attacks could last for hours or days, although her mother's worst predictions never seemed to come true. Sally was terrified, both of the potential danger that her mother seemed to be sensing and, as the years passed, more of her mother's seeming craziness. She recalled innumerable instances of patiently waiting, for what seemed to be forever, for the crisis to pass and for her family to be able to return to some sense of normalcy. Sally at times tried to approach her father and tell him about what was happening in the home, but he remained largely uninvolved and seemingly unable to comprehend how serious things would get. Finally, Sally gave up on him as well.

Sally recalls typically coming home from school and having to brace herself for another evening of loneliness, pain, and bewilderment. She attended the local public school, and despite her deep yearning to have friends and to have fun with other kids, she never made lasting, good friends. Part of the problem was that her mother unwittingly hindered Sally's efforts at socialization. When Sally was invited to other students' homes, her mother often began to worry that somehow Sally would be hurt or mistreated and pleaded or demanded that she come back home. Friends sometimes asked to stop by Sally's home, but she was too ashamed to invite them over, fearing that they and their parents would catch on to her mother's peculiarities. Mrs. K. already had an odd reputation in the town, and people largely avoided her out of fear that she might unreasonably lash out or accuse them of imaginary wrongdoings.

Sally's isolated and deprived life continued throughout elementary, junior high, and high school. From those years, looking back now, she can recall a few instances of transient depersonalization. The first one occurred when she was about 8, when her mother had her first severe paranoid crisis, locked up the house in darkness in the middle of the afternoon, and demanded that Sally hide in the basement. Sally obediently did so, and remembers crouching in a corner feeling that this all was a dream; she no longer felt like the little frightened child that she was, but like a detached observer looking at Sally and appraising the situation. It was all unreal, she felt, happening but not really happening. The next time that she experienced depersonalization was around age 13, after another of her mother's horrible crises. Determined to do something about it, she stayed up late that night after Mrs. K. went to bed to discuss the matter with her father. When her father came home at 11 p.m. after his second shift, Sally eagerly described to him what her mother had been like that afternoon, trying to convince him that they could get help for her at the local hospital. Her father appeared exhausted and indifferent, saying, "Your mother is O.K., go to bed now." Sally again suddenly felt unreal; this could only be a dream. She remained in this state until she fell asleep, but the next morning she woke up "normal" again.

The third time Sally experienced fleeting depersonalization, she was 15. A friend from school, Tina, insisted on coming home with her one afternoon after class, so they could work on a homework assignment together. Sally felt great trepidation but said nothing as they walked to her home. When they entered the house Tina cried, "Sally, your home is a real mess!" The exclamation poignantly and painfully captured Sally's whole existence, and again she suddenly felt this was not real. It was as if she was no longer Sally. She felt deadened, and like an automaton went through the motions of the whole evening, even after Tina left. Tina never came back; as Sally found out months later by word-of-mouth, Tina's parents requested that she stay away from Mrs. K.'s house.

Sally graduated from high school with average grades, little ambition, and no sense of goals or direction. She then left home to attend junior college, two hours away, and lived in the dormitory. The first year of college was particularly tough for her. Classes were difficult, making friends was hard, and her mother often called her to warn her of unforeseen irrational dangers. Studying in the midst of noise and distraction had never been a problem for her. But now, everything from low-playing music to conversations in the hall to the sounds of the heating/ventilation systems seemed to make her feel flustered, confused, and unable to concentrate. Still, she found silent corners here and there.

Before long, she started dating for the first time and by the spring had a regular boyfriend, Ted. Ted did not treat her particularly well, and a couple months later she found out that he was having relationships with other women on campus. By April, she was immensely stressed out and felt she would just not make it through the first year. Finals were approaching, her midterm grades were mediocre, Ted was aloof, and she had a lot of studying in the next few weeks ahead. She kept trying to hang in. One week before finals, her father called late one night to tell her that her mother had another crisis. A disgusted neighbor had called the police and her mother ended up involuntarily in a hospital ward, screaming "If only Sally were here to protect me, this would not have happened." Sally started to fade in and out of a sense of reality. She began to feel foggy, absent, emotionless, and robotic. The feeling gradually and insidiously intensified over the next few weeks. She went to the mall to try to clear her mind, only to have the crowds there seem unreal and somehow nightmarish, as if they were all watching her. Inside a department store, fluorescent lights seemed to cast a ghoulish haze over everything and she began to feel lightheaded and detached from her body. Back home these feelings came and went to varying degrees, as if her very soul was seeping out of her body, little by little. By the end of her finals, Sally was in an unshakable depersonalized state.

Cognizant of her movements, watching herself as if she were in a movie with the sound turned down, she packed her things and left school to go home for the summer. She walked into her old home, visited her mother in the hospital, and talked with her father to find out the details of what was going on. But *she* was no longer there, for good. Alive but deadened, she felt, and she remained in this state all summer. In the fall, she returned to school and decided to seek help at the mental health clinic of the college. There was still the remnant of an attitude—a determination to tackle her problem and not let what happened to her mother happen to her, too.

Does Sally suffer from depersonalization disorder?

Sally does suffer from DPD. She had three transient episodes in her adolescent years, and in her first year of college she became chronically and continuously depersonalized for months. Although terribly stressed, she was not particularly depressed or anxious.

Could Sally be showing the first signs of some other disorder instead, such as her mother's psychotic illness?

It is true that there is a familial predisposition to schizophrenia, yet there is absolutely no evidence that Sally is becoming psychotic. She was never odd as a child, and even though she had few friends, she always longed for them, but her extenuating circumstances precluded her from cultivating lasting relationships. Although she felt unreal, she never in any way believed that she was becoming a robot or that her life was really a dream; this is just how it all started to feel. When reality became too painful, unreality somehow became a refuge. It was quite clear to her that her state was not "normal," and she opted to seek help. Her fear that she might be getting ill like her mother was normal: children often worry that they might somehow have inherited the conditions of their parents, but there is no evidence that Sally was becoming psychotic.

What were the precipitants of Sally's depersonalization?

Sally had an adverse upbringing, chronically and unremittingly. Although there was no abuse as we usually think of it, physical or sexual, and her parents cared for her as best as they could, Sally suffered serious emotional neglect. A child needs to feel safe, cared for, nurtured, guided, encouraged, and socialized, and these needs were essentially never met. Studies of DPD in recent years have shown that more subtle forms of childhood maltreatment appear to be associated with DPD; in particular, emotional maltreatment has been shown to be strongly predictive of the severity of DPD. Studies have also shown that having a seriously mentally ill parent, often psychotic from schizophrenia or some forms of manic depression, is not unusual in the histories of patients with DPD.

Is it common for depersonalization to occur transiently in the beginning, and later set in more permanently?

Transient depersonalization, followed by more permanent DPD, is not an uncommon pattern. Sally first experienced brief episodes of depersonalization at moments of intolerable distress. Then in her early adulthood she experienced new severe stress, with educational, social, and romantic demands that she felt she could not meet. This major role transition was the final straw that precipitated prolonged depersonalization. It is common for depersonalization to be triggered by a period of prolonged severe stress in early, or even later, adulthood, such as in Sally's case. Chronic depersonalization can indeed be triggered by severe stress that is not of the overwhelming life-threatening magnitude encountered in conditions such as posttraumatic stress disorder. More ordinary severe stress, to a vulnerable individual presumably prone to dissociating, can be enough to trigger the disorder.

The Case of Eric

Eric was 15 when he experienced his first episode of depression. Up to then he had been a happy and well-adjusted child. Those who knew him described him as introspective, thoughtful, deep, and mature beyond his years. By high school, Eric was an avid reader who loved to ponder the complexities of relationships, the human condition, life, death, and the question of an afterworld. At moments in his teenage years he had felt overwhelmed by thoughts of the vastness of the universe, the endlessness of time, and the minuteness of individual human presence. He wrote poignant essays in English classes, which he sometimes read out loud in class or in school competitions. He was in no sense pathologically troubled, however. He loved to have a good time, had several close friends, enjoyed tennis, and followed current events more closely than most boys his age.

His mother was a warm and reflective woman, who despite her interest and earlier career teaching English literature, decided to devote her time to raising her children, Eric and his younger brother by 2 years, Joseph. She was an involved and sensitive mother, whom both children felt comfortable talking to about their hurts and worries. Eric's father was a successful businessman who worked long hours but was at home often enough to be a good dad, always conveying deep affection for his children. The parents' marriage had, at moments, felt tense to Eric, but for the most part it was loving and harmonious.

Then, seemingly out of nowhere, the depression struck. In the winter of ninth grade, Eric felt a proverbial black cloud begin to enshroud him. He lost all interest in school, tennis, and his friends, and his usual pondering of the nature of existence took on a heavy, morbid weight. Like people of all ages, Eric had known brief moments of sadness, or discouragement, or self-doubt. But they had been fleeting and usually tied to a specific event. This was different.

"It was so much beyond anything I had ever felt that it was impossible to explain," Eric recalls. "It was like my ability to feel anything at all hopeful or positive had been taken away. Things I had loved and enjoyed were now meaningless, and it took too much energy to even think about them."

As the condition progressed, Eric lost his appetite and a considerable amount of weight over the next few months. Sleeping with any kind of regularity became impossible. Often, he would awaken with a start hours before the alarm was set to go off. He lay awake with eyes wide open, worrying about his illness, and the nature of his own place in the universe, until the alarm finally rang. Then he would want to shut it off and sleep for the rest of the day.

Eric continued going to school, though he wanted to just stay in bed hiding all day. His interest in his classes waned, and his homework was sloppy and hastily completed. Consequently, his grades began to drop.

Even more disturbing, his mind questioned who and what he was with relentless rumination. He felt unreal, like an actor in a play, going through the motions of daily life without any sense that he was an active participant in charge of his thoughts and feelings. Today, he vividly recalls sitting in English literature class, which he normally loved, and watching the whole scene like a spectator, totally removed:

"I began to wonder if this was what it was like to be dead. Although I was certain that whatever death held, it had to be better than this. Ironically, in English class we were going over Hamlet's 'to be or not to be' soliloquy. But I now saw it through changed eyes, because while I'd heard those lines a zillion times, like everyone else, now I really knew what Hamlet was saying."

This identification with a torn and troubled Hamlet brought little consolation at the time, however. By February, Eric was profoundly depressed; he wanted his life to be over. He dreaded the thought of the full lifetime of work and relationships that lay ahead. He wished he were an old man, near death, with nothing to look forward to but the bliss of eternal night. But even then, as Hamlet observed, within endless sleep lay the possibility of dreams, or nightmares.

"I was frozen in fear of life, and just as afraid of death." Eric recalls. "All I could do was try to feel normal, act normal, and pray that one day I would *be* normal."

Despite his attempts to conceal these thoughts from his parents, it was clear to them that something was dreadfully wrong. Ultimately swayed by his mother's persistence, Eric finally confided in her. He told her that he no longer felt like a person, but rather like some kind of "robot-like thing," painfully operating through each day while awaiting its end.

Eric's parents were rightfully alarmed and took him to see the school counselor. The counselor concluded that Eric was deeply depressed, but could not pinpoint any obvious trigger or reason. Eric's mother revealed that her own mother had a serious history of what must have been depressions, not diagnosed as such in those days, only to end up chronically institutionalized and ultimately dying in a mental hospital. Neither Eric's parents nor his brother had suffered from depressive episodes.

Eric began meeting with the counselor weekly, discussing how he felt and how he could strengthen his coping skills to make it through. The counselor explained to him the facts about clinical depression, including statistics inferring that it would lift in time on its own. But he did not pick up on Eric's specific depersonalization symptoms. By late March, indeed Eric's mood began to improve, and by May, he no longer felt completely incapable of feeling good.

"Somehow, the utter hopelessness began to lift. I started little by little to regain a sense of pleasure over little things and big things too," he recalls.

His concentration improved, as did his homework, and his grades picked up for his finals. He started going out with his friends again, his energy and appetite came back, and he began to look forward again to each day with hope of steady improvement.

Eric was still not completely himself, however. His own, private voice in his head seemed somehow louder, and somehow separate from his body. He continued to feel as if he were going through each day like a robot, watching himself as if from outside of his body, wondering who he really was. Before, he *knew* who he was. Now, inexplicably, the knowledge that he was an individual person was there, but not a clear feeling of "I."

He attempted to describe this funny feeling to his counselor in terms of *The Twilight Zone.* "I told him about an episode where a little girl fell through a wall into another dimension. I explained that I felt like I had fallen into another dimension, but hadn't come completely back out. I felt like most of me was back in the real world, but part of me was stuck on the other side, watching."

The counselor reassured him that this was just his depression getting better, and no longer met with him after school was dismissed in June.

During that summer, Eric continued to feel horrendously detached, even though he was not depressed. He gave up trying to describe this feeling to his family, as they only reassured him, with the best intentions, that he was on the path to recovery. By the fall and the start of the next school year, Eric started to feel more real again. He recalls walking to school one morning in October and distinctly feeling, in the crisp autumn air looking at the first yellowing leaves, that he was himself—the Eric he knew. It was as if his spirit had decided to reenter his body once again. From that day on, he felt "normal," free of psychological problems for the next few years. He did not forget it all, but he was able to put his dark time behind him, graduate from high school, and leave home excitedly for a prestigious college town.

From the outset, he loved college and did well. He was popular, and before long had a girlfriend. Life was good for a while. Then, halfway into his sophomore year, depression again began to resurface. The symptoms were just like the first time, and again, there was no apparent cause. Depersonalization accompanied the depression. Like a pair of thieves, Eric's worst enemies had returned together, attempting to steal his soul once more.

But this time Eric saw them coming. He sought help at the university's mental health service right away. He was diagnosed with clinical depression by the psychiatrist on staff. Medication was recommended to expedite his recovery, given his overall good adaptation, absence of major triggers, and serious family history of depression evidenced in his grandmother.

After about 4 weeks on antidepressant medication, Eric began to feel better, and within another month he was back to his usual nondepressed self. The cloud of despair lifted, he slept and woke up without much difficulty, and he felt hopeful about the future. However, the depersonalization remained as strong as ever. He continued not to feel solidly grounded in himself; he was Eric but he wasn't. His head felt hollow, as if it were full of air. Thoughts running through his brain again seemed somehow foreign and overly present, even though there was no real deviation in their content. Thinking just *felt* different, as if coming from somewhere else. And if the thoughts weren't coming from Eric, where were they coming from?

Praying for the day when this last unsettling disturbance would lift away as the depression had, he resumed a robotlike existence of going through the motions of his college life, getting up, going to classes, working out, meeting friends, and trying to show love and affection toward his girlfriend. When he described how he felt to his psychiatrist, his family, and his girlfriend, they all suggested that he might still be a little depressed. But he knew that the depression was one thing, and this was another. And there was no way to relay the difference to them.

The intensity of his depersonalization was relentless. In vain, he tried to describe how he no longer felt like a live person, but one of the "walking dead." Ultimately, realizing the pain it caused others to hear this, and the pain it caused him to not feel understood, Eric gave up on reaching out. Still on his antidepressant, he continued feeling depersonalized for the next year. When Eric came home for the summer, his parents recommended he see another psychiatrist. This doctor felt that Eric's depression might not be receiving adequate treatment, so he "boosted" his antidepressant regimen—to no avail. Eric continued to feel as depersonalized as ever. By August, he was losing hope, wondering if he would live like this for the rest of his life.

Then one night, Eric surfed the Internet looking for whatever he could find relating to experiences of unreality, and stumbled upon the term "depersonalization." Despite his numbness to everything lately, his eyes watered as he realized that he was, for the first time ever, encountering others like himself—depersonalized people suffering from a condition that most other people knew nothing about. He read everything he could about depersonalization and realized at last that he wasn't going insane, nor did he have some brain quirk that no one else in the world had ever had.

He returned to school in the fall, his symptoms unchanged, but a little more optimistic to know what was ailing him. He shared his research with his parents and girlfriend, who also felt very relieved to better understand what Eric had been talking about for so long, and they began to do their own research on the condition.

Does Eric suffer from depersonalization disorder or from depression?

Eric actually carries both diagnoses, according to the *DSM-IV.* He has had two clear episodes of what is known as major depression (i.e., serious clinical depression). But Eric also has depersonalization disorder. He did not feel depersonalized just during the time periods that he was depressed, but rather his depersonalization lasted for months the first time and for more than a year the second time, after his depression had clearly remitted. Some people can feel dissociated when they are depressed, but as the depression clears the dissociation may clear, too. In such cases, an additional diagnosis of DPD is not called for. According to the *DSM-IV,* the diagnosis of DPD can be made only when the symptoms have clearly been present outside of an occurrence of another disorder such as depression.

What was the trigger for Eric's ailments?

No triggers were uncovered later in Eric's case. Some people can become clinically depressed without any apparent major trigger or stress. This is more common if they have a family history of depression, like Eric's severely depressed grandmother. What about a trigger for his depersonalization? In Eric's mind the depersonalization was fueled by the depression itself. The depth of his despair and his incapacity to make any sense of what was happening to him, despite his deeply introspective nature, left him feeling like he no longer knew himself. He felt profoundly estranged from the self he had always known, a stranger trapped in his old body and mind that were now experiencing inexplicable thoughts, feelings, and physical symptoms beyond his comprehension. As he later explained to his doctor, he felt that the deep depressions themselves were the traumas that triggered his depersonalization.

Are there other cases such as Eric's?

There definitely are. For years, individual reports have appeared in the psychiatric literature of people who started out with a straightforward episode of depression, which left them chronically depersonalized after it resolved. In more recent times, studies that have systematically looked at large series of patients with depersonalization have found that in about 20% of cases, the depersonalization is initially triggered by a severe episode of mental illness, which presumably deeply disturbed a person's sense of selfhood as they had known it.[2]

Could there be other explanations for how the depression and depersonalization came together?

Possibly, another explanation might be that both DPD and depression have some common biological pathway or vulnerability that set them off at the same time. However, this may be an unlikely explanation because the vast majority of people with depression don't have depersonalization. Also, depersonalization is found not only in conjunction with depression, but with other mood and anxiety disorders. For many people, feeling depressed or anxious can make their depersonalization symptoms more pronounced, but for others the two can be totally independent.

Why did the medication treatment with an antidepressant help the depression but not the depersonalization?

Unfortunately, there is more and more evidence now that traditional antidepressants don't work for depersonalization. Some people with depression have been treated with many antidepressants and even electroconvulsive therapy, which has helped their depression but not made much of a dent in their depersonalization. Recently, a study of the antidepressant fluoxetine (Prozac) showed that it was no better than the placebo sugar pill for depersonalization.[3] Some patients felt slightly better, possibly less anxious or depressed, with the fluoxetine and described that their depersonalization bothered them a little less. However, their symptoms, based on both their subjective experience and objective scales measuring depersonalization, were not improved by fluoxetine. This doesn't mean that depersonalization cannot be treated pharmacologically, however. Later we'll look at a variety of treatment possibilities.

The Case of Evan

When he was 29 years old, Evan visited a psychiatrist for the first time. It was also the first time in his life that he was involved in a serious relationship with a woman. Holly, his girlfriend for about a year, had come to realize that Evan suffered when they were sexually intimate. In the beginning, her impressions were vague and unformed. Somehow, Evan seemed suddenly detached and uninvolved when in the midst of a sexual encounter. He lost his usual affection, acted distant and mechanical, and seemed almost relieved when it was all over. Later, or the next day, he seemed to revert to his usual self.

After a few months, Holly began to trust her impressions more. And because she also felt more comfortable with Evan, she decided to have a talk with him about her experience. She told him what she thought and felt, and to her surprise he readily, and with some relief, acknowledged that something very unusual always happened when they were intimate and also at other times that she had not been aware of.

Evan revealed to Holly that when they were intimate sexually, he would suddenly feel unreal and detached, as if he were leaving his body and observing the scene as a third party. He almost felt like he was floating over their bed, watching all that was transpiring without any emotional involvement. He knew very well that he was still himself, but his actions became perfunctory, and he merely went through the motions of intimacy without any sense of involvement or participation. Although very used to this scenario, he knew it wasn't normal. But it was all he had ever known since he first became sexually active at 17. Now it distressed him greatly because he wanted to feel and because he really cared for Holly. The detachment would typically stay with him until well after their encounters ended, often until he woke up the next morning, and sometimes for a few days after.

Sexual intimacy was not the only circumstance that made him feel detached, he confided to Holly. For many years, he had suffered episodes of depersonalization lasting from minutes to days in settings where he somehow felt threatened, closed in, or violated. He felt very guilty that being intimate with his loved one seemed to be such a circumstance. He described to Holly an incident that occurred about a year earlier, when his boss had become very angry and out of line with him. Evan was a competent computer technician, steadily employed with a large computer company for the past 4 years, and well respected. Once, his boss, whose behavior was unpredictable and erratic, became enraged at Evan because he had failed to promptly address a major software problem being experienced by an important client. He lashed out at Evan, telling him that "he knew what he was all about" and that "he had coming what he deserved." Evan suddenly felt out of this world, leaving the scene as it were and watching like a detached observer. He felt nothing, was too frozen to respond, and walked around like a zombie for a few days until the situation was cleared and his boss apologized for his coarse behavior.

"Other people I know would have lashed back, or at least taken the issue to a higher up. But I just disappeared inside. I went into a state of nothingness, no mood at all, as if I were dead," Evan recalls.

Holly asked Evan if he had any idea what these experiences might be all about. She had heard of nothing like them before and was frightened, although she did her best to be understanding and supportive. Evan agreed that his experiences were weird and that he had never heard of anyone complaining of such states. This caused him even more worry. With Holly's prompting and persistence, Evan agreed to see a psychiatrist. Reluctantly, he made an appointment with Dr. Krast, who had been highly recommended to him by a good friend.

Evan went to his first appointment, frightened but determined to get help. He described to Dr. Krast all that he had told Holly. The doctor listened attentively, encouraging Evan to go on whenever he stopped himself to reflect on the seeming absurdity of his experiences. The doctor then told Evan that there was a name for the condition he was describing: "depersonalization." Evan had never heard of the term and was relieved, almost joyous for a moment, to feel that not only was he not crazy or unique, but that his condition was known enough for this doctor to recognize his symptoms and give them a name. "Depersonalization" seemed a very befitting term for just what he felt: like he was not a person, his own person, every time "this state" came upon him.

Dr. Krast asked Evan when it had all started. Evan could not quite say, because he had had these experiences as far back as he could remember, even before starting grade school. As distressing as the condition was for him, it was terribly familiar to him: something he had lived with all his life. Dr. Krast then asked about his early life and memories. Evan had been an only child, who had never known his father. (The father had abandoned his mother when Evan was 3 months old and never saw either of them again.) Evan remembered growing up very isolated, alone with his mother. Her parents lived far away, and in his early years he had had little contact with any other adults or children. Dr. Krast then probed further into Evan's early years. With great shame, but little trouble remembering, Evan revealed that his mother sometimes did "strange" things to him. Every night when she gave him a bath, she would caress him and fondle his genitals. When she put him to bed, she did the same. She called him endearing names, which he recalled with a bitter taste—he knew she loved him in her way, and she had never been "bad" or violent. Sometimes his mother even told Evan, when he misbehaved, that he "had it coming" before engaging in her usual ritual. By the time Evan was 8 or so, his mother's rituals gradually diminished and ended. He never told anyone, and even though he recalled them vividly with a secret sense of shame, he had never given them much thought. He was not even sure how usual or unusual these happenings were.

Dr. Krast told Evan that they were unusual and could well account for his lifelong depersonalization symptoms. He explained that for some people, becoming detached from intolerable experiences and feeling as if they were not really partaking in them was a way of adapting to very disturbing circumstances that they otherwise could not control. Dr. Krast explained that it was not surprising that situations in his life reminiscent of threatening intimate interactions that he could not quite control still triggered depersonalization. The doctor recommended that Evan continue to see him in talking therapy to help him better understand and work through his early trauma and the symptoms it had left him with.

Does Evan have depersonalization disorder?

He does have DPD. Evan has experienced recurrent countless episodes of classic depersonalization symptoms his entire life. His episodes are short but predictably triggered by reminders of feeling closed in, degraded, or sexually exposed. They are clinically significant, meaning that they are clearly associated with marked distress for Evan, and his close relationships lack a genuine intimacy.

Could Evan be having psychotic episodes?

Evan is not psychotic. He has intact "reality testing" about his depersonalization: he knows he is still himself and that his unusual perceptions are just subjective experiences that are not "real" other than for his internal world.

A person with psychosis would not only feel as if he was leaving his body but would believe that this is in effect happening, and he or she might even have some magical and implausible explanation for it. For example, if Evan were convinced that his mother's spirit pulled him out of his body every time he attempted to be intimate with another woman, his condition would be more suggestive of a psychotic process.

Could Evan be suffering from another psychiatric disorder related to a traumatic history?

Evan certainly could be suffering from another psychiatric disorder, and that is why Dr. Krast took an exhaustive history to determine the full nature of Evan's symptoms. For example, he could be experiencing other dissociative symptoms in addition to depersonalization. The doctor asked Evan if he ever "lost time"—that is, could not account for time periods of minutes to hours. People with dissociative amnesia experience this core symptom: when they come to after an episode, they have no idea how the time elapsed and what they were doing during it. Evan denied this; although in his deepest depersonalized moments he may be almost "out," blanking with a content-less mind, he always has some basic awareness of time and its passing. Dr. Krast also asked him about identity shifts. People who have suffered early childhood abuse sometimes experience themselves in profoundly different ways at different moments, almost as if they are different people. At its extreme, these distinct states may have different names, appearances, ages, feelings, and behaviors, and are known as dissociated self-states or identities. If a person does not have amnesia for these different states, he or she is diagnosed as suffering from "dissociative disorder not otherwise specified." If, as in its more extreme form, a person has no memory for at least some of these states, then the diagnosis may be dissociative identity disorder (known to many by its old name, multiple personality disorder). Evan denies such altered states. No matter how depersonalized, he always feels he is himself, but a very unreal and deadened self. Evan thus does not appear to suffer from another dissociative disorder.

What about posttraumatic stress disorder?

Posttraumatic stress disorder (PTSD) has become much better known to the lay public in recent years, with the general growing awareness of the detrimental influences of traumatic events such as assault, rape, and domestic violence. PTSD became a part of everyone's awareness after the terrorist attack on the World Trade Center in September 2001 and the many writings about the posttraumatic symptoms that ocurred in its wake in those who were exposed to the horrific disaster. For a person to suffer from PTSD, they must have experienced a major trauma in response to which they suffer "reexperiencing" symptoms (bad memories, nightmares, flashbacks); massive avoidance of anything or anyone reminding them of the trauma and emotional numbness; and hyperarousal symptoms (trouble sleeping, excessive vigilance, and startling). PTSD is not uncommon after childhood abuse, especially if the trauma was frightening or violent and activated intense anxiety about safety and survival. Evan denied any of these symptoms, except for a general sense of emotional distress and sadness whenever reminded of how his mother treated him, a sense of detachment from others, numbness whenever his depersonalization was activated, and a certain "watchfulness" in relationships. He did not have PTSD, Dr. Krast concluded. Indeed, depersonalization disorder has a low co-occurrence with PTSD: about 3% in one large study.[4]

Could Evan be just anxious or depressed?

Countless people suffering from primary depersonalization are told, when they finally decide to seek help, that they are just "anxious" or "depressed." Evan was fortunate that Dr. Krast was quite familiar with his condition. Someone who is experiencing anxiety and depression should be able to admit to this, if not spontaneously, at least when asked the right kinds of questions by a professional. A person who has considerable anxiety will acknowledge feeling nervous, irritable, worried, tired, on edge, or wired when trying to fall asleep. He or she may describe physical symptoms such as shakiness, shortness of breath, or frequent urination. Someone who is depressed can usually acknowledge a very low mood and changes in sleep, appetite, energy level, concentration, and pleasure in day-to-day activities. Evan essentially denied any pronounced symptoms of depression or anxiety. He admitted to feeling down or anxious at times, but these symptoms were not pronounced or lasting enough to warrant a frank psychiatric diagnosis.

The Case of Trisha

Trisha was a 21-year-old college junior majoring in fine arts at a large state university. She was bright, attractive, ambitious, and sociable. She describes her upbringing as happy and uneventful. She was the second of four children raised in a small midwestern town, and her parents were still happily married. She got along well with both of them and was particularly close to her sister Jane, who was 2 years younger. Trisha always did well in school, was athletic, and had many friends. She had never felt particularly troubled, other than the ups and downs of normal teenagers. Prior to a fateful day that was to come, she had tried marijuana twice in her life. The first time she was in tenth grade, when she and her friends were at a party one Saturday and she took a few "tokes" of a friend's joint. She did not feel much of anything, and her friend told her she had to try it a few times to feel the effect. Trisha, however, was not particularly curious and did not try marijuana again until her second year in college. She was at the time dating a student who smoked pot regularly, and she tried it again one night at a party with him. After inhaling deeply a few times and holding the smoke as she had seen him do, she began to feel cloudy-headed, giggly, and quite hungry. Time seemed to move very slowly as well. She didn't feel particularly high nor enthralled with what she did feel.

A year passed and Trisha came on the occasion of smoking pot for the third time in her life, amidst a small gathering of friends. It was just a way of being sociable and joining the others. She smoked about a joint over the course of the evening, and felt "very stoned," oddly detached from her body and from everything happening around her. "It wasn't a pleasant sensation," she recalls. "My head felt too present, and hollow somehow. I felt like my mind had somehow disconnected from my body. I didn't panic because I knew it was temporary. At least I thought it was."

Trisha remembers going to bed much later that evening thankful that she still had Saturday and Sunday ahead of her to get straight and study some for her final exams coming up the following week. However, when she woke up the next morning she was feeling as strange and detached as the night before. Familiar objects around the room seemed somehow different in the morning light. Books, the alarm clock, a small trophy, a plant on the window sill—they had all been there each day, but now they looked less familiar, as if she were seeing them for the first time. She told her boyfriend that she was still stoned, by now feeling frightened. The pot must have been stronger than usual, he said, assuring her not to worry because it would gradually dissipate over the course of the day. He was back to his normal self, however, which did not reassure Trish at all. She tried to relax her mind by having breakfast, listening to some music and studying for her first exam. She found this terribly difficult to do, as it was very hard to focus on anything, and she absorbed very little of what she was reading. As the day unfolded, she felt she was in a dream, navigating through fog in slow motion, dazed and semi-aware of what was going on around her; time seemed eternal. She decided to go for a long walk, something that she often liked to do to relax whenever she felt stressed. She thought that the cold, fresh air might clear her head and help her feel more normal again, but it didn't. By bedtime that evening, Trish was starting to panic about her condition. She called several friends and her sister Jane and asked them whether they had ever felt stoned and hung over from pot for so long. Although no one wanted to give her too straight an answer, she sensed that no one had.

By the next morning, Trish woke up to find that nothing had changed, and she began to despair. In what turned out to be the most stressful few days of her life, she somehow managed to stick it out, take her exams, and return home for winter break. She then sobbingly confided to her parents what had happened to her. She now feared that she had somehow caused herself irreparable brain damage and hated herself for having smoked. Although her family tried to comfort her by reminding her that she had done nothing different from many other good kids her age, she could not stop worrying that she had permanently damaged her brain and had only herself to blame. Within a couple days the family arranged for their doctor to see Trisha. She tried to describe to him in detail exactly what she was feeling. He suggested that she was probably stressed by the high demands of the semester that had just ended. She did not say anything, but Trisha somehow knew this was not it. Although it had been a hard semester, she had been coping well with it, and she was not aware of feeling particularly stressed. She knew that this "physical" sensation had to be something different. She told the doctor that she was convinced the drug had somehow damaged her brain. To reassure her, he referred her to a neurologist.

Trisha saw the neurologist, who ordered a few tests to make sure she was undamaged by her brief experiences with drugs. Both the MRI scan of her brain and the electroencephalogram (EEG) test of her brain waves were normal. The neurologist then also told her that she appeared particularly stressed and anxious. So he referred her to a psychiatrist. Meanwhile, there had been no change in the severity of Trish's symptoms over 2 weeks, and fairly soon she had to return to school. She could not fathom going back and working hard with her head in a fog, a constant feeling that she was tripping or going insane. A few days later, she saw a psychiatrist who told her that her experiences had a name, depersonalization. She had never heard of it and felt vastly relieved to find out that there was a name for what she was experiencing. The psychiatrist told her that the syndrome might have been triggered by her drug use and acknowledged knowing little about how to treat it. Given that the next week she was preparing to go back to school, he referred her to the well-known psychiatry department of the university hospital of her school.

Does Trisha have depersonalization disorder?

Trisha does have DPD. She has suffered from unremitting depersonalization symptoms for about a month, without other emotional complaints, except for some secondary intense worrying about her condition that clearly followed its onset. Still, she is not clinically depressed, having panic attacks, or worrying extensively about anything other than her condition.

How common is it for marijuana use to trigger depersonalization?

It is not *considered* common, but it has now become well established that marijuana can trigger depersonalization. Given the very high prevalence of marijuana use in the general population, an outcome of chronic depersonalization is probably infrequent. Still, it is clear that it does happen. The first report of a few cases of chronic depersonalization induced by cannabis came out in the early 1980s.[5] At present, prominent investigators that specialize in researching DPD have found that about 10–15% of all cases appear to be triggered by marijuana use. Furthermore, they have found that the form of the disorder associated with this drug trigger is no different in its symptoms, severity, or course from the disorder as it appears in other circumstances.

Does depersonalization always manifest itself as it did with Trisha?

Not always. While some people become "stoned" and then find that they can never seem to "sober up," others encounter an initial intense panic attack after smoking marijuana or hashish. This can be terrifying to a person who has never heard of such attacks or experienced any higher-than-normal degree of anxiety. This may happen after smoking just once or after several times. Sometimes these panic attacks reoccur for several days, or even weeks, after which they subside and the person settles into a classic state of chronic depersonalization.

Did marijuana somehow cause irreversible brain damage to Trisha's brain?

There is no evidence for brain damage, and it would be premature to conclude there has been brain damage without evidence. Like any psychiatric condition, whether substance-induced or not, biological vulnerabilities are likely to play a role. That does not mean that the brain is permanently damaged, in the way that it may be in neurologic conditions like stroke, for example. Rather, this case suggests that Trisha's brain, and those of others like her, might have had some underlying neurochemical vulnerability that had previously laid dormant and unexpressed, only to be triggered by a drug that perturbed the particular neurochemical system. We will be discussing much more about neurochemical systems in depersonalization in chapter 6.

Was there some way to know that Trisha was more vulnerable to marijuana than others?

There is currently no method to detect neurochemical vulnerability to marijuana. Of the reported cases of marijuana-triggered chronic depersonalization, no preexisting patient characteristics or warning signs have been pinpointed.

Along with depersonalization, marijuana might sometimes act as the trigger for other chronic psychiatric conditions, such as schizophrenia or panic disorder. That does not mean that it caused them, but rather that it was the "last straw" in these particular cases that perturbed an already vulnerable biological system. Also, the kind of "trip" or "high" that a person experiences does not seem to be strictly related to developing chronic depersonalization. While some may report highs that were particularly frightening and thus triggered a stress-related fear response, others may report not being in quite their usual state when they got high but being highly stressed about something. Many report nothing out of the ordinary in association with their fateful trip.

Did Trisha really need an elaborate neurological work-up?

Trisha's neurological exam was probably not necessary. The sudden onset of DPD and its clear association with marijuana use are classic, and have never been found to be associated with neurologic lesions. When tests like brain scans or EEGs are done, they are usually conducted to look for brain lesions or conditions such as tumors and seizures. Trisha's history is not suggestive of these conditions, but her attending doctors were not particularly familiar with her symptoms. Some doctors may wish to be conservative and err on the side of safety with any new-onset unusual psychiatric condition to ensure that the problem is not physical in origin. For example, if Trisha's depersonalization had started more gradually, on and off, steadily increased over several months, and was associated with new-onset headaches, a doctor might be much more inclined to do a brain scan.

Is marijuana the only drug associated with chronic depersonalization?

Unfortunately, marijuana is not the only drug associated with DPD. Hallucinogens can also trigger it and are estimated to trigger about 6% of all DPD cases seen by one major medical center.[6] Ketamine, also known by its street name, Special K, and by its medical name as the "dissociative anesthetic," can also trigger chronic depersonalization—it is a much less commonly used drug of abuse. Ecstasy (MDMA) is increasingly being reported in the last few years in association with chronic depersonalization, which is something to keep in mind with the rapidly rising popularity of this potentially dangerous drug. Drugs that are not reported to be associated with depersonalization are opiates, like heroin, and stimulants, like amphetamines and cocaine. Alcohol does not typically lead to depersonalization, except with chronic, heavy use, which can be associated with a feeling of detachment and fogginess. Alcohol can, however, exacerbate concurrent depression or anxiety.

Does Trisha's vulnerability to depersonalization suggest that she must have been more stressed than she acknowledged or that she had other lifetime adversities that were underreported?

Not necessarily. Some individuals in whom chronic depersonalization was suddenly triggered by a drug clearly report earlier psychological troubles, such as varying degrees of childhood adversity or bouts of severe later stress. However, without studying this matter more conclusively, it is difficult to say to what degree and under what circumstances these adversities may have left them more vulnerable to the chemical triggering by drugs.

Since Trisha's depersonalization was marijuana-triggered, is a different kind of treatment indicated?

We talk more about treatment options in depersonalization in later chapters 8 and 9. However, there is no rationale for thinking that if a case was initially triggered by a drug, rather than a psychological circumstance, a different kind of treatment must be indicated. Medications could conceivably be helpful in both scenarios. The same goes for cognitive behavioral therapies that could help deal with the symptoms and their repercussions.

The Case of Alex

From his earliest years, Alex felt destined for a life at sea. Growing up in a bad neighborhood in New York, his greatest pleasures were regular drives to the beach or deep-sea fishing trips with his father or friends. His parents were strict and religious but also loving and fair. They successfully raised him with virtues of honesty and tolerance that would later be admired by many with whom he sailed. He excelled at school, and at home he devoured seafaring novels and textbooks on sailing and oceanography.

Alex graduated from the merchant marine academy with honors in the late 1960s and immediately found work as a third officer aboard a large tanker owned by a major oil company. Life at sea was exempt from many of the social changes taking place on land. Alex lived in a world of order, respect for authority, and a well-founded regard for the inherent power and danger of the oceans of the world.

While the culture he left on land was now obsessed with the Vietnam war, sexual experimentation, drugs, and long hair, there was nothing novel about any of this to men who sailed the ocean regularly. Alex had seen people in India with hair that had never been cut; he had witnessed bloody skirmishes, even an execution in Africa; and sailors ashore were known for their wanton disregard for conventional morality. Despite many temptations, however, Alex chose to remain morally upright, partly because of his religious beliefs and partly because of the status he needed to maintain in front of the crew. He felt that his faith in God, daily Bible reading, and regular prayer helped keep him on the right path. He was also married and believed in the union's sanctity.

He had met his wife, Teresa, shortly before graduating, at a Sunday night church service held near the academy. Long love letters between Alex and Teresa accumulated during his earliest voyages, and within a year they were married, despite his mother's protestations. They spent their honeymoon in Caracas, and when they returned to the states, Alex purchased a small house on Long Island to be their home.

Between voyages Alex had plenty of time at home and plenty of cash because his expenses had been minimal. It was his choice when he sailed again. But some of the major oil and shipping companies, where his friends and classmates worked, were beckoning. He had quickly earned a reputation as an officer with superior navigation and piloting skills, which better assured an uneventful voyage for the monolithic, costly company vessels. He had also been certified for increased responsibility. By his late 20s he was qualified to be a first mate on the largest vessels in the world with only the captain above him.

The first few stays at home with Teresa, after his regular 4-month voyages, were like extended honeymoons. But the downpayment on the house and subsequent furnishings soon diminished his cash reserves. In time, life on land seemed somewhat unsettling as well. At sea, an officer's authority was like that of a god. On land, people had little respect for authority, were detached from the real power of nature, and generally ignorant of the realities of life in the rest of the world.

Teresa, who had once promised to continue her education and finish college, also began to change. She no longer exhibited much ambition except for wanting to have children as soon as possible. The couple had talked of parenthood, but they had agreed to wait a few years. But Teresa was impatient; her other friends all had babies with fathers that worked in the city and came home each night. It became clear that this was what she desired as well.

After several voyages to Europe and South America, Alex began to feel increasingly uneasy during the months spent at home. Teresa watched too much television and talked on the phone to her parents and friends to an annoying degree. Alex often went to the beach to surfcast, and sometimes prayed for a sign of what to do next. The relationship was strained within the parameters of marriage; it was so different from the days of dating and dreaming of the future. Finally, under pressure from Teresa and her parents, he told her that he would complete one last voyage, then look for maritime-related work on land. An infusion of cash and a break from each other seemed to be what both of them needed.

Alex's last voyage was on Lake Superior, serving as first mate aboard a moderately sized tanker. The money was good, and Teresa was glad that he was still within the borders of the United States, instead of the North Atlantic or China seas.

For Alex, the trip was uneasy. He didn't know any of the officers or crew and the waters were rough much of the time. He had never worked for this company before and sensed some tendencies to take shortcuts with maintenance and safety. Still, he did his job, remained businesslike, and kept to himself.

On the return voyage, with only days to go, Alex felt inexplicably uneasy again, though some of his distress could be pinned to concern about the future. He was at the moment tired of being on ships, but life on land held little appeal. Perhaps his marriage had been a mistake. His mother had discouraged it; maybe she, as usual, had been right. But, with God's help it would all work out, he reasoned.

Then, in the early morning hours after his 4-hour watch, Alex stood outside on the deck to think and pray. The lake was now placid and glasslike, uncharacteristically still. A fog had rolled in so that the water blended with the horizon to create a single, indeterminate mass. An unsettling stillness overtook Alex as well. His mind was a complete blank, as if awaiting a thought, or a vision. Then, in an instant, he felt something he had never experienced before—an intense sense of panic and fear that seemed to physically begin somewhere in the interior regions of his body and work its way up through his spine into his head. A sharp, blinding fear that he could never have imagined had him looking at the rail before him with a complete and all encompassing urge to jump over the side.

Stories of madness have always been part of the lore of the sea. Such anecdotes were common in sailing times, when scurvy, poisoning from tin cans, or year-long voyages would trigger serious mental illness in many sailors. Even today, Alex can recall instances of seamen going berserk, having "the fits" or jumping overboard to commit suicide.

His immediate thought on the deck was that this was "his turn." This was what it was like to go insane. The fear was so inextricably intense that his only desire was complete obliteration. It was a fear not of anything that existed before him, nor in the past or future of a life that was unfolding. It was a fear of existence itself.

"It was something like waking up to find that you're in a coffin, buried alive," he recalls. "Only the coffin is your body, your very existence."

Physically shaken, Alex raced to his cabin, only to find himself frantically looking around in all directions as if to search for some anchor upon which he could hook his sanity.

He sat on his bunk and glanced at the pictures of his wife and parents. He took deep breaths, and after some time the absolute panic began to subside. Was he going insane? Was this what it was like? Had he been poisoned or given LSD by this suspect crew? His mind raced for explanations until, exhausted, he feel asleep.

Alex would never completely be the same again, though he would know some periods of normalcy, or something close to it, in time. He returned home safely and was glad to be in his own house with Teresa by his side. But his head did not feel right. He felt anxious and fearful of having another attack like the one he'd had on deck. His confidence and self-esteem were gone, and he lay awake all night thinking endlessly about infinity of time and space, the nature of God, and the strangeness of his own existence. All the things he had accomplished, all the places he had been now seemed like dreams, acted out by someone else. He was a fearful, lost, nonperson—the *real* Alex, who had existed beneath the façade of faith, courage, and action for so many years.

Teresa noticed a difference, too. He couldn't make love and had difficulty showing interest in anything she said. Before long he went to see an internist whom he had known for years.

A complete physical revealed nothing out of the ordinary. The doctor said it sounded like some kind of depression and anxiety and after going through his *Physician's Desk Reference*, prescribed one of the older class of antidepressants.

Over a period of weeks, the medicine did have some effect. At first Alex was sleepy most of the time and took long naps, looking forward to escaping life in dreamless slices of nonexistence. In time, the free-floating anxiety was quelled, and Alex felt he was actually somewhat better. The beginnings of hope began to emerge, but still his thinking seemed somehow separate from the rest of his body. He was able to smile and begin to plan for the future, but he felt like his mind was a radio that was not quite tuned into a station—noise and static and confusion often filled his head with an exhausting overaware-ness of every small thing that went on within it.

"In the very beginning, even when the panic had subsided, I never had a mood," Alex recalls. "Everything felt was moment to moment, with every thought overly conscious in my head. I went through numerous variations of this for about a year," he recalls. "I was able to function again, but only in the daily hope that I would wake up one day and be myself again."

Alex's sense of time seemed somehow altered as well. Minutes sometimes seemed like hours; yet his whole life now seemed to have raced by him in sec-onds. In the midst of this, time continued on its own pace and a decade came and went. On the surface, life looked good. Teresa got the boy and girl she had wanted, and Alex joined up with an old classmate to start a charter fishing boat service on Long Island. The family moved to an established middle-class neighborhood on the South Shore and everyone appeared happy and prosper-ous. But inside, Alex's private world, hellish at times, continued.

When he felt better from the antidepressants, he stopped taking them with no apparent ill effects. He was no longer the person he once was but tried to somehow be content within the context of what he had become. If things got rough again he could always go back to the medicine and sleep a few days away and make another comeback of sorts.

On the heels of that first attack his mind had gone through a constellation of thoughts and "symptoms." He feared that this would continue indefinitely, that there would always be new terrors, new mad thoughts that would forever make it worse and worse. This wasn't the case, however.

For more than 10 years, well into the 1980s, Alex kept an encrypted diary documenting what he felt and thought. Over the course of time, there seemed to be some pattern to his condition. If his ailment had specific symptoms that ap-peared regularly, there might actually be a name for the condition, he reasoned.

With the analytic nature that he had not lost, he determined that he was indeed human and, as such, could only be susceptible to known human ailments. After all, even though he often felt like it, he wasn't from another planet.

To explore this reasoning and also seek something even more effective than the one antidepressant he had tried, he visited a psychiatrist. Unfortunately, he learned little more than he had from the internist he had seen years earlier. The psychiatrist also suggested long-term psychoanalysis, which Alex viewed with skepticism, if not outright contempt. So he decided to continue on his own.

In his diary he broke down his specific symptoms and concluded that they were sometimes predictable, even cyclical. This is how he described his symptoms:

> Free floating anxiety that comes and goes, and a constant fear of The Panic. This is the direct antithesis of how I once felt, when I was filled with a sense of adventure, confidence, and willingness to go anywhere, do anything.
>
> Circular, pointless rumination about everything from existence itself, to something someone said, to the reasons for my illness.
>
> Detachment of my inner voice from my body. Almost constantly, the thoughts running through my head are loud and visible and completely detached from my head. They seem up high in my head, somewhere else. The act of thinking seems strange and foreign.
>
> The Aloneness. An acute awareness of being alone in my thoughts, a prisoner in my own head. With this is a shattering realizing that no one, ever, has shared my thoughts with me. I have heard them alone since I was born and will hear them alone until I die.
>
> Fear of not controlling my actions. I drive and wonder what prevents me from intentionally crashing. I play with my children and wonder what keeps me from slaughtering them. How is it that I still know right from wrong and would kill myself before harming another?
>
> Over self-consciousness. In crowds, at the mall, at parties, virtually anywhere, I am flustered by noise and crowds and feel that I stick out like an ogre to be mocked in some way. My legs and arms move awkwardly and feel foreign sometimes.

The Voice. Aside from outright panic, this can be most unsettling of all. The exaggerated self-consciousness mentioned above initially felt like I was seeing *through* myself all the time, as if someone was watching my every move and making fun. In time, for whatever reason, this feeling came on even when I was alone, and ultimately manifested itself in the form of an actual voice in my head. For everything I thought on my own, this little voice would make comments, usually derisive ones. If I was talking to someone else it would interrupt my thoughts and mock the words coming out of my mouth, or mock something about the person I was talking to. This "voice" persisted for about a year and seemed to replace all the other symptoms. Everything was refined into the voice, which made my life miserable, despite the fact that I told myself a hundred times a day that it was me doing it. I knew there was no demon, no other voice in my head. Yet it was there, and I couldn't get rid of it.

These core symptoms that Alex experienced sometimes appeared concurrently, but most often, a single one of them would manifest itself to the exclusion of all others. When he was panicky, there was no voice. When he felt the aloneness most, anxiety was minimal, except as a direct result of fearing the aloneness. And through it all, he never considered himself depressed. He dealt with that particular annoyance any way he could until either a degree of normalcy or the next symptom took its turn. In time he also learned something quite amazing. In periods of severe stress or heartache, such as when loved ones died or catastrophic events hovered near, he became the "strong one" and dealt far better with it than others around him. In contrast, the smaller daily stresses of life—financial problems, screaming kids, house or car problems, bills and noise—were difficult to handle, and whenever they were compounded, one or more of his symptoms was sure to emerge.

It's now been decades since that fateful morning on Lake Superior when a first officer's life was changed forever not because of something outside, but rather something deep within. Alex worries little, but feels little. A kind of emotional deadness inside seems to be the end result of a thousand mental blows through the years. And with it, a philosophical interpretation, of sorts.

"That sailor and everything he believed in so strongly no longer exists,"

Alex says. "And neither do I. I feel like the 'I,' for lack of a better term, is now somehow situated across many moments. My identity is scattered everywhere; as if I am everyone, and everything, and the spaces between things. And there is a sense of loss, because if this feeling is true, I ought to know everything, feel everything, but I don't. It's like the reflection of the sun being split into shards of light on the sea. I have dissolved, into a kind of 'oneness' with all that exists, but it's a fragmented oneness. It isn't yet complete."

Does Alex suffer from depersonalization disorder?

Alex does suffer from DPD, and the symptoms he describes fall into a category that has been called the "phobic anxiety-depersonalization syndrome." Alex's symptoms parallel those described in some of the literature dealing with depersonalization that had appeared in the late 1950s and early 1960s. Unfortunately, Alex never encountered a doctor who had even heard of his specific symptoms, and at the time it was extremely unlikely that he would have.

Could Alex have benefited from further treatment?

It surely would have helped Alex enormously if someone had explained in detail what he already suspected—that he had a recognized disorder with an actual name. Some of the medications that have been used to treat depersonalization effectively were available during the time period of his case history. So aside from having no clear diagnosis, or even a name for his condition, he was never given the option of exploring additional medicinal treatments that may have proved helpful. Alex might also have benefited from exploring in psychotherapy the complex meanings of the life-changing moment that triggered his depersonalization.

What might have caused that initial panic attack?
Was the depersonalization that followed a result of it,
or part of some overall condition?

There are many reasons that people may have a panic attack or panic disorder. Whether Alex had a preexisting tendency toward panic or DPD is unknown. There was no evidence of mental illness in his immediate family and no records existed for his grandparents. What is likely, however, is that the "blow" of the panic was severe enough to eventually throw him into anxiety-depersonalization syndrome with all of its seemingly bizarre manifestations. In Alex's case, it may have been a continuous build-up of small stresses on the tail of major ones. For other people, drugs like marijuana can sometimes have the same effect, with symptoms quite similar to what Alex described.

How common is the "voice" Alex mentioned?

In the Mount Sinai study of 117 individuals with DPD, the vast majority (over 80%) reported no voices at all.[7] However, a minority did experience an inner voice, a single one, best likened to an out-loud thought inside one's head, accompanied by an awareness that the voice is the person's own thoughts experienced in an intense yet disconnected fashion as a distinct "voice." This voice typically sounds like the person, is not experienced as alien, and is a commentary on the person's thoughts, feelings, or actions as if coming from a detached other, the dissociated part of the self. This infrequent experience of a voice in DPD distinctly differs from that of individuals with dissociative identity disorder or its variants, who have multiple internal voices, often experienced as less owned by the individual and more alien, representing intrusions on the conscious self by the various alternate personalities.

Other Voices

These case histories have shown various manifestations of depersonalization within the context of individual lives. They by no means cover the full range of possible scenarios that can and do appear within depersonalization disorder. It has taken more than a century of study for psychiatrists, psychologists, and philosophers to disseminate the symptoms described by thousands of people. In the next chapter, we take a closer look at that process and its results.

3 The Path of Understanding

A Century of Exploration

Depersonalization is the neurosis of the good looking and intelligent who want too much admiration.

—PAUL SCHILDER, 1939

People suffering with depersonalization disorder and their families face a difficult task when trying to learn more about the condition. Someone dealing with cancer, diabetes, depression, or bipolar disorder can find many sources of information readily available. Libraries, bookstores, the Internet, and even newsstands provide venues for research material. But this is still not the case when it comes to depersonalization.

Although in recent years the Internet has offered a ray of hope by providing at least some readily accessible information about depersonalization disorder (DPD), most people suffering from it remain in the dark, struggling to determine what could be wrong. In years past, time-consuming, exhaustive searches in university or hospital libraries, or a visit with one of the few savvy psychiatrists who really knew about the condition, could reveal some answers and provide some direction to the road to improvement and recovery. But even then, problems in achieving the correct diagnosis sometimes arose. Of the dozens of clinical papers that exist, using just one at random could result in a wrong or misleading interpretation of the condition. For instance, taking Paul Schilder's highly subjective comment leading off this chapter[1] out of context, from a galaxy of other observations, would not be particularly helpful. Visiting a clinician unfamiliar with all the literature, or at least the most recently published findings, could be equally fruitless, and sometimes even harmful.

This chapter provides an overview of how the definition of depersonalization disorder has become what it is today, after having undergone its own evolutionary process for more than a century. Through a slow but fairly continual stream of patient group studies and their published results, certain "core symptoms" of depersonalization have emerged with great prevalence. Other symptoms, while as valid as they were 50 or 100 years ago, have periodically receded into the background only to resurface and receive renewed attention. Some conclusions drawn from different studies have been subject to debate or later revision by those who initially drew them. Some were downright wrong. Yet certain aspects of the disorder have been agreed upon almost universally.

We are fortunate in that depersonalization enjoys a surprisingly long history of documentation in the medical and psychological writings of Europe, beginning in France and Germany. Much of this material developed in the mid- to late nineteenth century, when dramatic social changes gave rise to intellectual and philosophical explorations the world had not yet seen.

The earliest writings specifically dealing with depersonalization as a unique disorder emerged from Maurice Krishaber, who in 1873 was the first to look at DPD as a possible "cérébro-cardiac" malfunction,[2] and psychiatrist Ludovic Dugas, credited with coining the term "depersonalization."[3] Aside from case histories of patients they observed, these writers drew from the knowledge and anecdotes, and likely some of the biases, of a variety of European doctors, philosophers, and intellectual dilettantes. Despite the differences between modern medical practice and that of the nineteenth century, many of the earliest observations remain valid with few, if any, modifications, largely because what was being described by patients then is described so similarly today. Depersonalization is what it is, then and now.

Sensory Distortion Theories

Records of patients suffering from "thinking without feeling," a sense of detachment, incompleteness, or total lack of feelings began accumulating in medical circles as early as the 1840s. Then, in the 1870s, Krishaber, a Hungarian eye, ear, nose, and throat specialist, reported on 38 patients showing a mixture of anxiety, fatigue, and depression. More than one-third of these patients complained of baffling and unpleasant mental experiences consisting of the loss of feeling of reality.[4] Krishaber theorized that these feelings were the result of pathological changes in the body's sensory apparatus. Multiple sensory distortions would therefore lead to experiences of "self-strangeness."

"One patient tells us that he feels that he is no longer himself, another that he has lost awareness of his self," Krishaber wrote.[5] Although the term "depersonalization" was not used until 26 years later by Dugas, Krishaber's 1872 case histories marked the first true scientific study of the experience of DPD.

Another prominent theorist, Théodule Ribot, agreed with the sensory-distortion theory when he reported of patients describing feelings of "being separated from the universe, or feeling as if their bodies were wrapped in an isolating substance that interposed itself between themselves and the external world; underlying these experiences there were physiological abnormalities whose immediate effect is to produce a change in coenesthesia" [bodily sensations].[6]

Krishaber's sensory hypothesis was later challenged by others, like Dugas and Pierre Janet, a major figure in nineteenth-century psychology. Janet pointed out that many patients with clear sensory pathology, such as double vision (diplopia) or the loss of joint sense caused by neurosyphilis, did not complain of any sensations of unreality, while many patients suffering from depersonalization were in fact normal from the purely sensory viewpoint.[7]

Dugas wrote of a patient whose own voice sounded foreign to him:

> Although he *knows* that it is his voice, *it does not give him the impression* of being his own. . . . Acts other than speaking are also involved. . . . Everytime the subject moves he cannot believe that [he] is doing it himself. . . . The state in which the self feels that its acts are strange and beyond its control will be called here *alienation of personality* or *depersonalization*.[8]

Thus Dugas provided this condition with a name for the first time.

Dugas saw depersonalization as a blurring of what Blaise Pascal centuries earlier defined as two distinct elements of our being: "the willing mind and the automaton."[9] This blurring between the separation of the two renders all voluntary actions automatic.

"Depersonalization behaviors not only seem automatic; to an important extent, they are," Dugas wrote. "By automatic I mean any behavior to which the self feels indifferent and foreign, and which it produces without thinking or wanting, as might happen in states of total distraction or absent mindedness."[10] This "apathy," a term which appears often in the literature that followed, marks the emotional deadness that is one of the hallmarks of depersonalized people. It is not a decision to be indifferent or unfeeling. It is automatic and unstoppable.

"Depersonalization is not a groundless illusion," Dugas concluded. "It is a form of apathy. Because the self is that part of the person that vibrates and feels and not what merely thinks or acts, apathy can be truly considered as the *loss of the person*."[11]

Memory, True and False

Nineteenth-century thinkers were also intrigued by the concept of false memories. Understandably, the mystery of depersonalization emerged amid the prevalent theories about "déjà vu" phenomena (literally meaning "already seen"), and their opposite, "jamais vu" phenomena ("never seen"). Dugas initially regarded the presence of depersonalization as evidence for the view that déjà vu was a form of "double consciousness," a popular term of the era used to describe dual or alternating personalities. But he changed his mind completely when he took a closer look at depersonalization all by itself. Still, the compelling similarities between strange phenomena like hypnotic suggestion, dreaming, déjà vu, and depersonalization kept these mysterious mind states swimming together in the same fishbowl, so to speak, as observers watched, took notes, and tried to determine their possible connection. But all along, they sensed that there was something singular and different about depersonalization.

Pierre Janet, who, as noted earlier, challenged the sensory distortion theory, is also well known for introducing the words "dissociation" and "subconscious" into psychology terminology. He attributed the nineteenth-century affliction "hysteria" (later known as "conversion disorder," in which a psychological conflict manifests itself in the form of some bodily dysfunction such as hysterical paralysis or blindness) to imbalances in "psychic energy" and "psychic tension." (The use of the word "psychic" in this instance simply means psychological, relating to the mind.) Janet considered depersonalization to be a manifestation of "psychasthenia," an antiquated term for any nonspecific condition marked by phobias, obsessions, compulsions, or excessive anxiety.[12]

Certainly, phobias, obsessions, and excessive anxiety often accompany depersonalization or mark the beginnings of it. But Janet also stressed the presence of a *sentiment d'incompletude*, an experience of incompleteness that many observers found well-represented in Dugas' source for the term "depersonalization," Frédéric Amiel's diary, *The Journal Intime*.[13] "What characterizes the feeling of depersonalization . . . is that the patient perceives himself as an incomplete, unachieved person," Janet states.[14]

This feeling of being incomplete is indeed part and parcel of the experience of depersonalization, in terms of one's being out of sync with one's normal self. It can also be a secondary feeling, referring to reflections of what life "used to be" or "might have been" that can emerge in people who have been depersonalized for many years. As we will see in chapter 7, Amiel's journal graphically depicts both of these attitudes.

Overall, however, Janet's theories brought about a shift in the predominant thinking on depersonalization. Janet believed that all psychic activity was either primary or secondary. Primary psychic activity encompassed everything that was evoked by external stimuli—from knee jerks to memories. Secondary psychic activity was a background echo elicited by representations of primary acts. By conferring upon primary experiences a feeling of vividness (*l'impression de vie*), this secondary echo creates the illusion of a continuous flow of psychic activity: "thousands of resonances, constituted by secondary actions, fill the spirit during the intervals between external stimuli, and give the impression that it is never empty."[15] Disconnectivity between these primary and secondary brain processes could result in depersonalization-like symptoms. Janet's language was different, but his theory remains surprisingly contemporary.

Further Inquiries

As the twentieth century emerged, existing theories about depersonalization still seemed inadequate because there were simply too many aspects of the condition that remained unexplained. Depersonalization began to be viewed in terms of the loss of some brain mechanism that causes the *feeling* of mental experiences and attribution to the self as the agent who experiences them—the sense that "my experiences are mine."

In the 1930s, Heidelberg psychiatrist Wilhelm Mayer-Gross's now-famous paper, "On Depersonalization," reviewed the theories, case histories, and subsequent speculations up to that time in an attempt to elucidate the nature of the disorder.[16] Mayer-Gross was first to highlight the distinction between depersonalization and derealization, two manifestations of what is probably the same disorder. Much of what Mayer-Gross said was referenced again and again by other writers in succeeding decades, up to the present.

Mayer-Gross believed that depersonalization was an expression of a "preformed functional response" of the brain, analogous to delirium, catatonia, or seizures. He took exception to theorists who focused on isolated symptoms of the disorder, such as increased self-observation, loss of emotional response, or impairment of memory:

> It is a characteristic form of reaction of the central organ, which
> can be set going by different causes. . . . The difficulty of descrip-
> tion by means of normal speech, the defiance of comparison, the
> persistence of the syndrome in the face of complete insight into its
> paradoxical nature—all these point to something more than purely
> psychic connections. Such a disturbance cannot be explained by
> the loss of a little wheel out of the clockwork.[17]

Mayer-Gross recorded another important observation, which holds particularly true for people who can remember the exact moment of onset of their depersonalization, especially when the trigger was marijuana or some other drug: "depersonalization and derealization often appear suddenly, without any warning. A patient sitting quietly reading by the fireside is overwhelmed by it in a full blast together with an acute anxiety attack. In some cases it disappears for a short period, only to reappear and finally persist."[18]

This sudden psychic blast from seemingly nowhere has appeared not only in the annals of medicine, but in literature and philosophy as well. (We examine this further in chapter 7.) Years before Mayer-Gross's 1935 account, there was a description of a similar type of panic onset in William James's classic work, *The Varieties of Religious Experiences*, published in 1902. In the chapter entitled "The Sick Soul," James relays the words of a French writer who has captured the flavor of the kind of panic that can sometimes trigger chronic depersonalization:

> I went one evening into a dressing-room in the twilight to pro-
> cure some article that was there; when suddenly there fell upon
> me without any warning, just as if it came out of the darkness, a
> horrible fear of my own existence. Simultaneously there arose in

my mind the image of an epileptic patient whom I had seen in the asylum, a black-haired youth with greenish skin, entirely idiotic, who used to sit all day on one of the benches, or rather shelves against the wall, with his knees drawn up against his chin, and the coarse gray undershirt, which was his only garment, drawn over them enclosing his entire figure. . . . This image and my fear entered into a species of combination with each other. That shape am I, I felt, potentially. Nothing that I possess can defend me against that fate, if the hour for it should strike for me as it struck for him. There was such a horror of him, and such a perception of my own merely momentary discrepancy from him, that it was as if something hitherto solid within my breast gave way entirely, and I became a mass of quivering fear. After this the universe was changed for me altogether.[19]

For some people, this narrator describes with uncanny precision the moment that marked the onset of their own depersonalization. The inexplicable panic that the writer attempts to explain goes well beyond the clichéd images of sweaty palms or rapid heartbeat associated with spontaneous panic or anxiety attacks today. The certainty of imminent insanity, which, unknown to the victim, passes with the attack, lies at its heart.

While James does not tell us what happened to this particular person, the inclusion of this experience in "The Sick Soul" seems particularly appropriate. Depersonalized people, who sometimes say they have "lost their soul," may well recall a single episode like this as the very moment when their soul departed. Of course, others can experience this kind of incident once, or repeatedly, without the end result of chronic depersonalization.

James refers more specifically to feelings of depersonalization and unreality in the chapter titled "The Reality of the Unseen," where he writes: "Like all positive affections of consciousness, the sense of reality has its negative counterpart in the shape of a feeling of unreality by which persons may be haunted, and of which one sometimes hears complaint." Drawing from other sources, he then quotes the French poet Louise Ackermann, who wrote in *Pensées d'un e solitaire*: "When I see myself surrounded by beings as ephemeral and incomprehensible as I am myself, and all excitedly pursuing pure chimeras, I experience a strange feeling of being in a dream. It seems to me as if I have loved and suffered and that erelong I shall die, in a dream. My last words will be, 'I have been dreaming.' " This sense of the unreality of things, James comments, "may become a carking [perplexing] pain, and even lead to suicide."[20]

James the psychologist does not suggest any treatment for the condition he explored only briefly, and ultimately, convinced that depersonalization was founded in some cerebral dysfunction, Mayer-Gross did not see a lot of point in psychoanalytic attempts to treat the condition: "Writers make abundant use of hypotheses about narcissism, libido-cathexis, etc.," he wrote. "I have found it difficult to gain any fruitful idea from such suggestions or from the suggestions of psychoanalytic writers about depersonalization. The disagreement between them is rather discouraging." This did not discourage psychologists from continuing to propose new theories for decades. But Mayer-Gross concluded that depersonalization should be regarded as a physiological disorder, a "non-specific pre-formed functional response of the brain."[21] While most of Mayer-Gross's assessment of depersonalization has stood the test of time, today's thinking draws from both physical and psychological explanations, with fresh understanding of the fact that they are not necessarily incompatible with one another.

Psychological Theories

Psychoanalytic thinkers have issued their own theories about the origins of depersonalization for many years. The majority of these writers have agreed on one point: that depersonalization serves a purpose as a defensive strategy ("defense mechanism" as described in stricter psychoanalytic lingo) of some sort. Our purpose here is to illustrate the diversity and richness of the theories, not necessarily to agree or disagree with them. Even if flawed, or not generally applicable to all depersonalized patients, these psychological theories might still give us insights into the processes of depersonalization in individual patients. Clearly, a lot of thought has gone into trying to figure out the nature of what many people, including physicians, have long perceived as an obscure condition, or merely a part of some other disorder.

As we touched upon in chapter 1, Freud had something to say about depersonalization after he had experienced intense, fleeting derealization while viewing the Acropolis up close and in person. As he analyzed his experience at 80 years of age, in the now-famous letter to Romain Rolland, Freud wrote:

"These derealizations are remarkable phenomena which are still little understood. . . . These phenomena are to be observed in two forms: the subject feels either that a piece of reality or that a piece of his own self is strange to him. In the latter case we speak of 'depersonalizations'; derealizations and depersonalizations are intimately connected." Their positive counterparts, Freud adds, "are known as *fausse reconnaissance, déjà vu, déjà raconte* etc., illusions in which we seek to accept something as belonging to our ego, just as in the derealizations we are anxious to keep something out of us."[22]

According to Freud, "naively mystical" and nonpsychological attempts to explain déjà vu interpret it as being evidence of a former life. "Depersonalization leads us on to the extraordinary condition of '*double conscience*' which is more correctly described as 'split personality.' "[23]

Freud also referred to the defensive characteristics of depersonalization when he wrote about feelings of unreality in a famous case history that came to be known as the "Wolf Man."[24] Considered one of Freud's most complex and detailed accounts of the psychotherapeutic process, the subject of the story was a wealthy young Russian who sought Freud's help because he felt that there was a "veil" between himself and the real world. This was coupled with intense fear of wolves, specifically the fear of being eaten by them. While little is told of his specific symptoms, the mention of the "veil" does sound like depersonalization. The case centers largely around a dream the man had as a child, of white wolves perched in a tree, staring at him as he observed through an open window. The man's early childhood was rich with material for his doctor to explore. He had either actually, or within his imagination, walked in on his parents having sex, his genitals had been fondled abusively by his older sister, and she, aware of his wolf phobia, further tormented him by periodically surprising him with pictures of the animals.

Freud's lengthy analysis dissected each of these and other events that happened to the young Russian before the age of 5. Probing the man's memories deeply and methodically, Freud was able to build his case for "infantile neurosis," a notion that at the time (1918) was being challenged by other analysts like Adler and Jung.

In the end, the young Russian apparently recovered, in part from the revelations about his subconscious relayed to him by Freud, and perhaps partly, as Freud himself noted, because his fortunes and family were lost after the revolution of 1917, assuaging his long-endured feelings of guilt.

Ultimately, Freud knew that there was much to be explored in depersonalization/derealization. He interpreted his own intense derealization before the Acropolis as his mind's defense against the guilt he himself felt about succeeding in life so beyond his own father, who had died in obscurity.

While Freud's comments on depersonalization specifically were rather limited, his followers have often attempted to explain the condition within the context of his theories, specifically the structural theory of the mind, which divides the psyche into three parts: id, ego, and superego. Ego is the concept of one's self, the mediator between the id, the primitive part of the self containing all our drives, and superego, the seat of our conscience.

One approach to understanding the psychology of depersonalization has been to focus on the ego, or "self" in plain English, and on how well integrated an individual's overall sense of self is. Within such a framework, depersonalization has been linked to a poorly integrated ego or sense of self, resulting from the presence and activation of conflictual and inadequately integrated parts of the self (known as partial identifications or self-representations). This explains the higher frequency of dissociative experiences among adolescents, for example, where the developmental task of identity formation has not been fully completed. Indeed, the onset of depersonalization often occurs in adolescence, possibly triggered by the overwhelming developmental task of consolidating a relatively well-integrated sense of self.

Although there is no single accepted theory among psychodynamic authors, most perceive depersonalization as a defense against a variety of negative feelings, conflicts, or experiences, when the individual's more adaptive defense mechanisms fail. "Defense mechanism" is yet another tricky term that is still controversial as far as dissociation is concerned. Most contemporary theorists would probably agree that dissociation is more than a defense mechanism, (i.e., a largely unconscious way of processing internal conflict); instead, it is a subjectively experienced self-state or state of being.

Sometimes suggestions made in the broad range of analytical papers ring true to a depersonalized individual who may encounter them in their search for answers or upon a visit to a psychologist. Some of these commentaries are speculative and now dated but still remain a part of the evolution of thought about the condition. For instance, Paul Schilder, in a well-known paper on the treatment of depersonalization, stated: "I am inclined to stress the fact that the patient with depersonalization has been admired very much by the parents for his intellectual and physical gifts. A great amount of admiration and erotic interest has been spent upon the child. He expects that this erotic inflow should be continuous. The final outcome of such an attitude by the parents will not be different from the outcome of an attitude of neglect."[25]

In its original terms, the formulation is rather antiquated, but translated into more contemporary thinking, this formulation could have something to offer. Schilder goes on to say that the parental attitude of considering the child a "showpiece" rather than a complete human being eventually results in deep dissatisfaction. Initial self-adulation, stemming from an identification with parental attitudes, will ultimately be followed by emotional emptiness, even though intellect remains intact and the person may appear quite normal or even successful to others. Again, in more modern terms, emotional neglect and its detrimental impact on the development of the self comes to mind—a person who was never known to others may never know himself.

Schilder also had something to say about the self-scrutinizing component of depersonalization: "All depersonalized patients observe themselves continuously and with great zeal; they compare their present dividedness-within-themselves with their previous oneness-with-themselves. Self-observation is compulsive with these patients. The tendency to self-observation continuously rejects the tendency to live."[26]

Schilder made some astute observations about the "automaton" aspects of depersonalization, which he called "negation of experiencing." He says,

> In clear cut cases, the patients complain that they no longer have an ego, but are mechanisms, automatons, puppets—what they do seems not done by them, but happens automatically. . . . raw materials of their somatic [body] sensations is unchanged. . . . Their lack of memory images is not a *loss* of imagery, but rather an *inhibition* of existing memories. Such patients fight, defend themselves against their perceptions; they negate internally their entire experience, and prevent themselves from experiencing anything fully.[27]

Nonetheless, many patients may remain capable of complex achievements, which, however, are experienced as fake and without deeper meaning—part of the false, showpiece self.

Other psychologists, before and after Schilder, either concurred with his views, put their own spin on existing ego psychology theories, or forged new ones. Fritz Wittels, in 1940, saw depersonalization as resulting from identification with a large number of phantom images (unintegrated identifications), the ego being unable to accept any one of them as the real self, due to superego condemnation of each of them. Along similiar lines, psychologist Edith Jacobson became interested in depersonalization after studying female prisoners who depersonalized in response to being imprisoned by the Nazis in World War II. In a 1959 commentary, she stated that depersonalization always represents an attempt to solve a narcissistic conflict, and she viewed depersonalization as a struggle between conflicting identifications. Unacceptable identifications are defended against by disowning and denying those undesirable parts of the self, and these shifts between the various conflicting identifications result in feelings of depersonalization.[28]

Another psychologist, C. N. Sarlin, also conceptualized depersonalization as defending against conflicting ego identifications. The disorder may occur, he said, when a conflict between the individual's mother and father becomes internalized as two conflicting aspects of the child's ego. The struggle between simultaneous hostile identifications with both parents may cause the individual to lose his or her identity.[29]

Jacob Arlow, one of the better known ego psychology theorists, agreed with the thinking that depersonalization represents the outcome of intrapsychic conflict, "in which the ego utilizes, in a more or less unsuccessful way, various defenses against anxiety. The split in the ego which results in the dissociation between the *experiencing* self and the *observing* self takes place in the interest of defense." Depersonalization, he believed, boils down to a specific set of reactions of the ego in the face of danger. These reactions consist of a split into a participating self and an observing self—the danger is experienced pertinent to the participating self, and can thus be distanced from the observing self. Arlow, who also wrote about déjà vu and distortions in the sense of time, said in the 1960s that depersonalization and derealization represent a "dissociation of the function of immediate experience from the function of self observation."[30]

Arlow took the view that the essential ego alteration in depersonalization is a dissociation of two ego functions that are normally integrated: the function of self-observation and the function of experiencing or participating. In depersonalization, he said, the participating self is partially, but not completely, repudiated. The patient is still able to maintain some sense of connection and some feeling of identification.

Arlow was one of the few psychologists to bring up the similarities between dreaming and depersonalization. Indeed, feeling as if in a dream is one of the more common complaints among depersonalized patients. Two characteristics of depersonalization, feelings of unreality and the split of the sense of self into an observing self and a participating self, are prominent in dreaming.

All of these psychological hypotheses followed Mayer-Gross's 1935 statement that such theories were devoid of any "fruitful" ideas. Certainly, the person who can trace his or her onset of depersonalization to a specific event seemingly devoid of meaningful psychological content (marijuana smoking, for example) would not be interested in the possibility of deep-rooted psychological causes. In contrast, excessive conviction about a seemingly "obvious" cause, or no cause at all for that matter, can certainly obscure more subtle yet powerful dynamics that can trigger uncontrollable psychological processes in anyone. In this light, a person's initial conviction that his or her depersonalization, or any other symptom for that matter, is not driven by specific psychological processes should not be taken at face value before being thoroughly explored.

Altered Sense of Time

Distortion of time perception is a frequent complaint of depersonalized individuals; it is often mentioned today on depersonalization-themed websites and in personal stories. In a 1946 paper, "The Depersonalization Syndrome," H. J. Shorvon reviewed aspects of his study of 66 patients. One-third of these complained of changes in time perception. Shorvon cited a statement by Aubrey Lewis that time consciousness "is an aspect of all conscious activity; it is essential to all reality. In *déjà vu* there is a brief inability to actualize the present, which in consequence is projected into the past."[31] Of time disturbance in depersonalization, again Shorvon quoted Lewis, who said:

> They [time disturbances] illustrate many of the outstanding features of the disorder; the inability to evoke the past readily or clearly, to distinguish the present from the past or future; there is paradoxically the increased quickness with which time passes though it seems to drag along, the seeming remoteness of the recent past, the unconfirmed feeling of the inability to judge the length of time.

Paul Schilder adds that "the present is a concept which has meaning only in relation to experiencing personalities. The inanimate has no past, present or future. . . . Cases of depersonalization, whose total experience is splintered, all have an altered perception of time. In extreme cases, time seems to them to be at a standstill, or the present seems to be like the distant past."[32]

"The only reason for time is so that everything doesn't happen at once," said Albert Einstein in his disarmingly understated way.[33] Yet to depersonalized people, time often does not unfold in the normal manner; past, present, and future can seem indistinguishable, as if they were indeed all happening at once.

Obsessiveness

The obsessional aspects of depersonalization have not been ignored through the years, though Sir Martin Roth in 1960 pointed out the major difference between obsessional states, such as contemporary obsessive-compulsive disorder (OCD), and the kind of obsessiveness present in depersonalization. Roth identified a particular subgroup among depersonalized individuals that included patients fraught with ongoing free-floating anxiety and excessive rumination. Depersonalization, in any context, does not involve classic obsessive rituals, like hand washing, or outwardly eccentric compulsive behavior. Roth remarks: "Obsessional features commonly present, though rarely in the forefront of the picture, are a compulsive self-scrutiny and preoccupations with fears of disease, insanity or loss of self-control."[34]

Roth also pointed out the distinction between DPD and classic phobic states, which involve fears of specific acts like flying, or objects or creatures, such as snakes or spiders. "The free floating anxiety which is said to be characteristic of anxiety neurosis proper, is very common in the phobic-anxiety-depersonalization state," Roth observed.[35] But these patients are unable to suppress their anxiety altogether by avoiding feared objects or situations in the way a person with a phobia might. If the center of the fear is the self, or existence itself, escape or avoidance is impossible.

The obsessional components of depersonalization were further explored by Evan Torch, MD, who observed that there is a particular type of patient whose obsession is observing himself or his "vegetative functions." Torch wrote, "Even in a typical case of hypochondria, conversion neurosis or depression, *in the background of an obsessional personality* it is not hard to see how continual, repetitive preoccupation with one's self can lead to a feeling of unreality, based in no small way on the fact that even to a philosopher . . .

the question of just where to locate centrality of 'self' or 'being' is an uncomfortable one to face."[36]

Among patients with DPD, Torch, like Roth, also noticed a particular subtype of the disorder, which he called the "intellectual-obsessive depersonalization syndrome." This subcategory, Torch said, is composed of a complex combination of alternating states of depersonalization and obsessive self-scrutiny. The end result is the "burned out" depersonalization patient, who, "although still fully in touch with reality, refuses to acknowledge its intrinsic meaning."[37]

Viewing One's Self

One of the many intriguing metaphors used by depersonalized people is that they feel as if they are viewing themselves, as if watching a movie. Depersonalization involves an unpleasant sense of self-observation, an exaggerated hyperawareness of one's self. The split between the observing and the acting self can, at its most extreme, become an out-of body-experience, although for most people it is not. Noyes and Kletti explored this split when discussing partial or complete depersonalization among accident victims. For the 66% of the normal subjects who suddenly depersonalized, the condition appeared to be "an adaptive mechanism that combines opposing reaction tendencies, the one serving to intensify alertness and the other to dampen potentially disorganizing emotion."[38]

Social Factors

Depersonalization means different things to different cultures. In Western culture, we seem to be witnessing a rise in the number of reported cases of depersonalization disorder. This may in part be attributable to the widespread use of illicit recreational drugs, as well as improved communication via the Internet. But the question also arises of whether or not modern society is, in itself, a cause of depersonalization. Writing about depersonalization and its relation to society in the 1970s, James Cattell and Jane Schmahl Cattell said, "People working under centralized bureaucracies are routinized, humiliated, and thereby dehumanized. The economic system prevents involvement and fosters detachment. It generates competition, creates feelings of inadequacy and fear of human obsolescence. It creates hostility and suspiciousness."[39]

Quoting the French writer Simone de Beauvoir, Cattell agreed that the basic characteristic of the American value orientation is that the source of one's value and truth is perceived in things and not in oneself. Consequently, material comfort has a high place in the value hierarchy. Success puts its emphasis on rewards. "The success system, which William James has colorfully described as 'the bitch Goddess success,' is comprised of money, prestige, power and security."[40]

For the majority of people, the safest road to success lies within the embrace of a corporation, usually the bigger the better. Corporations bind their employees through job security, wage scales, health insurance, sick leave, and retirement plans, making it difficult to leave no matter how dehumanizing a particular job may become. Such perks are especially attractive to the individual who tries his or her hand at their own enterprise and fails. The desire for security is particularly strong in those who have taken risks and lost.

The impact of bureaucratization is a movement from an "inner-directed" individual to "other-directed" individual, Cattell suggests, characterized by (1) orientation toward situational rather than internalized goals; (2) extreme sensitivity to the opinions of others; (3) excessive need for approval; (4) conformity on internal experience as well as on externals; (5) loss of achievement orientation; and (6) loss of individualism. The clear ramifications are that if a person defines his or her self in terms of occupation or works purely for increased wealth and social status, the loss of a job or a sudden social change could easily result in alienation and the loss of a sense of self. The self had been rooted in shallow ground to begin with.

Some of Cattell's observations may now seem out of date. Certainly, more people are able to work independently today, even if they have to invest a few years of conformity to corporate life in order to gain experience. People change jobs and locations far more often as well. But other factors of today's society may contribute to an altered sense of the self and its place in society in other ways. The post 9/11 world is increasingly insecure. People were incredulous when they viewed the Twin Towers collapsing on live television, and in an unprecedented way, real life "seemed like a movie" to the national consciousness. Certainly, our shared sense of security and reality was shaken as never before.

Today's cyber culture may also contribute to a blurring of reality, particularly in young people who, spending countless hours in cyberspace, have learned how easy it is to be anyone at any time while online. In addition, the media's obsession with celebrity lifestyles seems to send the message that fame and fortune are admirable in and of themselves. If you're not a celebrity, you're nobody, one might conclude. So where does the obscure individual fit in? While these scenarios could more broadly be classified as experiences of modern-day "alienation," and may not bear directly, in many cases, on the clinical syndrome of depersonalization, they do raise questions about the societal influences on the individual self and how it adjusts to the culture in which it must function.

Family Influence

Cattell and other writers on the subject believe that the self is largely a product of culture, in that the individual picks up reactions of others and incorporates them into a meaningful, coherent self-structure. The true self begins at home, where in infancy having an attentive mother leads to basic trust, satisfaction, and a sense of security in the child, who begins to recognize itself as a distinct being. So what processes can bring about a miscarriage in self-identity development, leading to depersonalization? Distorted messages, mixed messages, or nonmessages, and the relationships of the individual's perceptions of these to his or her concept of self and the world are particularly relevant, according to Cattell. "To the extent that there is a disturbance in the normal separation-individuation phase of development (sense of autonomy), the perception of the mother is distorted and, therefore, perception of the self is distorted. Thus, there is interference with reality contact—difficulty in distinguishing between self and objects."[41]

An example Cattell cites is artificial (arbitrary) feeding times, which prevent the infant from feeling that its actions will result in being fed. "When we feel that we cannot influence the important things that happen to us but that they follow the dictates of some inexorable power, then we give up trying to learn how to act or change them."[42] When development miscarries in this manner, the self can split into two parts, the true self and the false self, or the subject and the object, according to Cattell.

Cattell explains that the true self is the unembodied self that functions as observer, controller, and critic of what the body is experiencing and doing. The true self translates into action what one wants to be. Only the true self feels real. The false self, in contrast, is built on compliance. The false self arises in compliance with the intentions or expectations of the significant others or what one imagines these to be. The body is perceived more as an object among other objects in the world than as the core of one's individual being. The individual feels that he or she is a spectator of what the body is doing rather than a participant observer.[43]

Cattell summarized that vulnerability to depersonalization comes about through deficiencies and distortions of the patient's experiences with nurturance in infancy and in subsequent stages of personality development. These include exposure to double-bind messages, rejection of the true self, and fostering of the development of the false self. In essence, the infant is programmed to deny satisfaction of his needs and expression of his emotions in order to avoid extreme anxiety. Such repudiation leads to repression of unacceptable needs and emotions that are not consciously recognized. This is the intrapsychic programming that must be dealt with in treatment.

The Question of Structural Dissociation

Van der Hart, Ninjenhuis, and colleagues have put forth a structural model of dissociation, which proposes that dissociative symptoms fall into two broad categories: positive and negative.[44] Positive symptoms represent dissociative "intrusions," such as hyperamnesia (intrusion of traumatic memories) and various somatoform (bodily) dissociative symptoms like sensory flashbacks. Negative symptoms represent dissociative losses of various functions such as memory (amnesias) or motor control (paralysis). This model proposes that simple dissociative symptoms such as absorption, trance, and depersonalization/derealization are not dissociative symptoms at heart because they do not reflect a structural dissociation of the personality, but rather they are simple alterations of consciousness. An exception is made in the case of depersonalization when it presents as a structural symptom (i.e., a split between observing and experiencing ego). In this structural dissociation model, in its simplest form, two aspects of the personality are stipulated, an "apparently normal part of the personality" (ANP) and an "emotional part of the personality" (EP). The ANP is that aspect of the personality that is dedicated to daily life functioning, whereas the EP is the segregated portion of the personality that is fixated on past trauma and responds to perceived danger.

Does this structural model of dissociation fit DPD well? Can an ANP and an EP be defined in all cases of DPD? If so, the ANP would undoubtedly be the depersonalized self, whereas the EP would be the prior "feeling" state. The analogy initially seems apt, in at least some people with DPD. People with DPD may relate to distinct states reminiscent of an EP and an ANP, such as the "old" and the "new" self, the "real" self and the "unreal" self, the "participating" self, and the "observing" self, the "live" self and the "dead" self. However, this may be more of a metaphor than a realistic model for DPD. Unlike the ANP and EP of disorders such as dissociative identity disorder (DID) and its variants, the two states of DPD do not contain distinct experiences, memories, or emotional states that are not known to one another. Rather, the two states reflect more of what was and what no longer is. Simply put, everything that is accessible to the EP is also accessible to the ANP, at least intellectually, even though it does not feel the same. In this fashion, DPD could be likened to the distinction between the "depressed" self and the previously "happy" self, the "anxious" self and the previously "relaxed" self, or, for that matter, the "psychotic" self and the previously "sane" self. Also, unlike other disorders characterized by structural dissociation, DPD typically does not present with transitions and fluctuations between the various self-states, but rather by a stable alteration in consciousness.

An exciting new theoretical model about the nature of dissociation by Elizabeth Holmes and Richard Brown is more on target in capturing the dissociative essence of depersonalization.[45] These authors proposed two basic types of dissociation: "detachment " and "compartmentalization." The detachment category of dissociation incorporates depersonalization, derealization, and similar phenomena such as out-of-body experiences. In each case, the subject experiences an altered state of consciousness characterized by a sense of separation (or detachment) from certain aspects of everyday experience, be it the body (as in out-of-body experiences), the sense of self (as in depersonalization), or the external world (as in derealization).

Compartmentalization phenomena are characterized by a "deficit in the ability to deliberately control processes or actions that would normally be amenable to such control."[46] As a result of this compartmentalization, these functions and the information associated with them are no longer under voluntary control. The compartmentalization category of dissociation includes dissociative amnesia as well as the medically unexplained neurological symptoms encountered in conversion disorders such as conversion paralysis, sensory loss, seizures, and pseudo-hallucinations, also referred to as "somatoform dissociation."

In this model then, depersonalization comprises the quintessential experience of detachment, which is not associated with true compartmentalization, but rather a pseudo-compartmentalization between the nondetached self and the detached self. Is this distinction important, or is it simply a theoretical technicality? It is important, because there is accumulating evidence from descriptive, cognitive, and brain imaging studies that the information-processing pathways that relate to detachment versus compartmentalization are quite distinct from each other. To give one example, in chapter 4 we talk about how the memory-processing difficulties in dissociation are of two major types. In depersonalization (detachment), there can be difficulty with attention and encoding so that new memories, especially emotional ones, are not formed as effectively. In contrast, in dissociative amnesia (compartmentalization), memories are stored in the brain but cannot readily be retrieved.

Symptoms Compared and Clarified

So far we have presented many theories. The consensus of most of them is that depersonalization can be viewed as a response that is intended to distance the self from overwhelmingly painful or conflictual impulses or feelings. Conclusions drawn in some of the psychological papers may seem enigmatic, frightening, or right on target for different depersonalized individuals, and this ultimately illustrates the broad range of symptoms persons might feel during the disorder as well as the variations in how it has affected their inner lives, their work lives, or their sexual tendencies.

The concept of depersonalization as a defense mechanism against overwhelming traumatic stress makes good sense. The subsequent lack of feeling and emotionless automaton behavior seem completely reasonable, even valuable.

"The data presented suggest that depersonalization is, like fear, an almost universal response to life threatening danger," say Noyes and Kletti. "It develops instantly upon the recognition of danger and vanishes just as quickly when the threat to life is past."[47] This description certainly describes the purpose and usefulness of transient depersonalization, which Noyes and Kletti were discussing in the context of accident victims. In the face of life-threatening danger, normal depersonalization is an adaptive, even life-saving mechanism that is considerably more useful than this process gone awry, which locks a person in heightened awareness and dampened emotions long after any perceived danger has past.

Clearly, time and again, the variety of internal and external stressors to which depersonalization may be a response have been amply illustrated and discussed. But reliance on a single premise may result in a limited formulation that may do little to help the patient. Depersonalization ultimately involves a constellation of unpleasant symptoms that have been discussed in earlier chapters and theorized on by the writers we've mentioned here.

To set things right and clarify the real nature of this complex and multi-layered disorder, in 2001 psychiatrists Mauricio Sierra and German E. Berrios reviewed the constants and stability of the older writings describing depersonalization against more recent material.[48] While doing so, they made some important points.

By using the year 1946 as a dividing line, Sierra and Berrios reviewed 200 cases of depersonalization appearing in the medical literature since 1898, dividing them into pre- and post–World-War-II groups. In addition to descriptions of unreality, the other key symptoms that emerged throughout the literature include:

- emotional numbing[49]
- heightened self-observation[50]
- changes in body experience[51]
- absence of body feelings such as hunger, thirst, and so on[52]
- changes in the experience of time and space[53]
- feelings of not being in control of movement (i.e., loss of feelings of agency); having the mind empty of thoughts, memories, and images[54]
- inability to focus and sustain attention.[55]

After analyzing all the data from the two time periods and the broad range of symptoms discussed, Berrios and Sierra were able to draw some interesting conclusions, supported by strong evidence:

Current operational definitions restrict depersonalization to the experience of unreality. This is likely to neglect clinical features of potential neurobiological relevance. . . . The phenomenology of depersonalization has remained stable over the last hundred years. In spite of this, the clinical profile of published case reports has been found to vary in specific ways. These variations are likely to have been determined by changing theoretical views on depersonalization. Guided by theory, clinicians were sensitized to perceive and report the same clinical phenomena in selective ways.[56]

In other words, certain biases developed that may have caused an undue emphasis on certain aspects of depersonalization, such as the feeling of unreality, or loss of agency, to the neglect of others. Instead of becoming more on target in terms of the whole disorder, the clinical papers may well have fallen short of presenting the true richness and diversity of DPD as a century of observation unfolded. Researchers, it seemed, fell into the habit of honing in on patients' loudest complaints, sometimes leaving physicians uncertain about the validity of more subtle symptoms that received less notice, but were important nonetheless.

Still, two clusters of symptoms emerged. The nonchanging core symptoms include visual derealization, altered body experience, emotional numbing, loss of agency feelings, and changes in the subjective experiencing of memory. The distress caused by these particular problems is probably why they are reported most frequently. The second cluster of symptoms, including unreality experiences not related to vision, mind-emptiness (subjective inability to entertain thoughts or evoke images), heightened self-observation, and altered time experience, are less likely to be reported by a patient first and foremost. Various theories may well continue to be forged in an effort to explain these symptoms, but, "the identification of theoretical biases is essential to the understanding of both the structure and the frequency of symptoms and for current neurobiological research on depersonalization."[57]

All of this information, the theories formulated over a century, and the more recent inventory of the ongoing essential core symptoms, has laid the groundwork for a new era of research about, and treatment of, depersonalization. In the next chapter we look at how some new diagnostic tools, new biological research, and new technology have come together with the goal of effective treatment of DPD.

4 Diagnosing Depersonalization Disorder

The finest words in the world are only vain sounds if you cannot understand them.

—ANATOLE FRANCE

L ike any other psychiatric condition, the diagnosis of depersonalization disorder (DPD) is made clinically, by meeting with the patient and conducting a thorough evaluation interview. Descriptions of the symptoms, as we have described throughout this book, and as spelled out in the *Diagnostic and Statistical Manual of Mental Disorders*, 4th edition (*DSM-IV*), serve as the point of departure—symptoms that are not just fleeting, but recurrent or persistent. The symptoms must also not be occurring exclusively and only in the context of some other condition, be it psychiatric, medical, or related to substance use. If, for example, the depersonalization happened only when the person was deeply depressed, or during a panic attack, or a seizure, or because a person has a brain tumor, he or she would not be diagnosed as having DPD. Likewise, regular substance users (daily drinkers or marijuana users) who experience depersonalization only in that context would not be diagnosed with DPD.

In a healthy young persons without any known medical risks or conditions, who can be trusted when they state they are not using substances, limited medical testing is required before making the DPD diagnosis. It is wise to first obtain an electroencephalogram (brain wave test) and a brain imaging scan (such as a CT scan or an MRI) to ensure that an individual is not suffering from a seizure disorder without other manifestations, or from a brain lesion such as a tumor that has not yet otherwise become apparent.

Distress and Dysfunction

In addition to the presence of symptoms, the *DSM-IV* requires that a person must suffer significant distress or dysfunction as a result of these symptoms to be diagnosed with various disorders, including DPD. Indeed, many people with DPD suffer tremendously. Depersonalized individuals will typically describe that they function suboptimally or barely at all in school or at work because they feel so foggy, spacey, or obsessively preoccupied with trying to figure out their condition. They also typically say that their personal relationships, especially intimate ones, are very disturbed because of the abnormal sense of selfhood and the distorted sense of connectedness with others. The pervasive sense of distance and unreality may or may not be sensed by others when engaging in interpersonal interactions. The partners or close friends of those with DPD are sometimes highly aware of how cut off, flattened, or disengaged the patient is. At other times, they are surprised, dismayed, or frustrated to hear of the condition and how it affects the patient's relatedness since, as far as they can tell, everything seems fine on the surface. Still, some individuals with DPD feel so socially impaired that they live in virtual seclusion.

Some people find depersonalization so distressing that every living moment is a nightmare, often expressed in terms like: "I have no soul," "what is the point of killing myself, I'm already dead," or "I'm not alive any more, nothing makes a difference." Notably, these devastating feelings can be present even in the absence of depression.

Paradoxically, there are some people with DPD, especially those who have had it as far back as they can recall, who do not find depersonalization so distressing. Some may have adapted to it in their own way. They describe that the dissociation is a safe, comforting place for them to retreat, which shields them from being overwhelmed and envelops them in a state of nothingness. This is not to imply that DPD doesn't cause dysfunction in these patients, however. Others may find similarities between DPD and altered states of consciousness that are actively sought through meditation and other consciousness-altering practices (see chapter 7 for more on philosophical interpretations). But for the person who finds DPD unbearably unpleasant, the sense that something about them is terribly out of kilter makes a lot more sense than any interpretations pointing toward a higher consciousness or an enlightened state. For many, these realms are something they never sought and something from which they would like to escape.

Interviews and Questionnaires

The diagnosis of DPD can be assisted by the use of various interviews and scales. One that is widely used, especially in research settings, is Marlene Steinberg's Structured Clinical Interview for DSM-IV Dissociative Disorders (SCID-D).[1] Steinberg, the well-known author of the popular book *Stranger in the Mirror*,[2] did extensive work to develop a thorough and standardized interview quantifying the different kinds of dissociative symptoms and leading to the diagnosis of the various dissociative disorders. After appropriate training, a clinician needs about 30 minutes to 1.5 hours to complete this interview with a patient, depending on how many experiences are endorsed by a particular individual. The SCID-D inquires specifically about five types of dissociation: depersonalization, derealization, amnesia, identity confusion, and identity alteration. It scores the severity of each one of these, based on set criteria, as absent, mild, moderate, or severe. If this interview is given to persons suffering from DPD, they will typically have high scores for depersonalization and derealization, and possibly for identity confusion if they experience a sense of confusion about who they are, which may be part-and-parcel of the depersonalized condition. However, individuals with DPD do not have amnesia or identity alteration, as encountered in other dissociative disorders such as dissociative amnesia, dissociative fugue, or at their most extreme, dissociative identity disorder (DID), formerly known as multiple personality disorder.

A very simple, quick, self-administered questionnaire that has been widely used for 20 years to measure dissociative symptoms is the Dissociative Experiences Scale (DES), originally developed in 1986 by Eve B. Carlson, Ph.D., and Frank Putnam, MD, two well-known experts in the field of trauma and dissociation. Since its introduction, the DES has been used in hundreds of studies of dissociation. But while it can be used to detect depersonalization disorder, it is not an ideal instrument for that purpose. Out of its 28 questions, only a few relate to depersonalization and derealization experiences. So it is very possible for a person to suffer from troubling depersonalization and still score quite low on the DES, which had been designed with the more "severe"

dissociative disorders in mind. However, a few items of the DES, when examined individually, can be much more specifically suggestive of the presence
of DPD, especially when the remaining items are scored low. Such items have
to do with classic symptoms like watching oneself from a distance, feeling
outside of one's body, perceiving one's surroundings as unreal, or looking at
the world through a fog.

More recently, the Department of Psychiatry at the University of Cambridge developed a self-administered questionnaire called the Cambridge
Depersonalization Scale, which specifically measures only depersonalization
and derealization experiences and contains a wide range of questions cover-
ing such experiences. The Cambridge Depersonalization Scale, given in its
entirety in table 1, has proven to be a more reliable measure for quantifying
the severity of pure depersonalization in the absence of other dissociative
symptoms. Each of the 29 questions in the scale is rated for both frequency
(how often it occurs) and duration (how long it lasts). To obtain a total score,
the frequency and duration of all the items are added up.

Let's now think about the types of questions included in the Cambridge
Depersonalization Scale questionnaire. First, the questionnaire includes a few
queries about a variety of derealization experiences, related to a sense of
unfamiliarity and estrangement about the surrounding world, which often accompany depersonalization (items 2, 13, 19, 29). But mostly the questionnaire
covers many different kinds of depersonalization experiences: a detachment
from one's body (items 3, 23, 27), from one's thoughts (items 10, 26), from
one's sensations such as vision, hearing, smell, taste, and touch (items 2, 11,
7, 20, 25), from internal sensations such as hunger and thirst (item 28), and
from pain, a symptom known as analgesia (item 22); an altered sense of time
(item 14); difficulty evoking past memories (items 16, 21); and what is known
as hypoemotionality or emotional numbness, a dampening of one's feelings,
positive and negative, such as sadness, anger, love, and happiness (items 4,
5, 9, 18).

Some patients experience symptoms from many or most of the above domains, others from only a few. Some will even say that they suffer from only
one or a very limited number of symptoms, such as just being numb (not feeling), or having just sensory-type symptoms, like everything looking visually
distorted, or just having an altered relationship to their physical self as if they
are somewhat removed, watching themselves from "somewhere behind the
eyes." Patients therefore ask, and sometimes have trouble believing, whether
all these experiences are encompassed under the same disorder. Yet, there is

Table 1.

Cambridge Depersonalization Scale[4]

Frequency	Duration—In general, it lasts
0 = never	1 = few seconds
1 = rarely	2 = few minutes
2 = often	3 = few hours
3 = very often	4 = about a day
4 = all the time	5 = more than a day
6 = more than a week	

Symptoms: Frequency   Duration

1. Out of the blue, I feel strange, as if I were not real or as if I were cut off from the world.   _____   _____

2. What I see looks "flat" or "lifeless," as if I were looking at a picture.   _____   _____

3. Parts of my body feel as if they didn't belong to me.   _____   _____

4. I have found myself *not being frightened at all* in situations which normally I would find frightening or distressing.   _____   _____

5. My favorite activities are no longer enjoyable.   _____   _____

6. Whilst doing something I have the feeling of being a "detached observer" of myself.   _____   _____

7. The flavor of meals no longer gives me a feeling of pleasure or distaste.   _____   _____

8. My body feels very light, as if it were floating on air.   _____   _____

9. When I weep or laugh, I do not seem *to feel* any emotions at all.   _____   _____

10. I have the feeling of *not having any thoughts at all*, so that when I speak it feels as if my words were being uttered by an "automaton."   _____   _____

11. Familiar voices (including my own) sound remote and unreal.   _____   _____

12. I have the feeling that my hands or my feet have become larger or smaller.   _____   _____

13. My surroundings feel detached or unreal, as if there was a veil between me and the outside world.   _____   _____

14. It seems as if things that I have recently done had taken place a long time ago. For example, anything which I have done this morning feels as if it were done weeks ago.   _____   _____

(continued)

Table I. *(continued)*

Symptoms:	Frequency	Duration
15. Whilst fully awake I have "visions" in which I can see myself outside, as if I were looking at my image in a mirror.	_____	_____
16. I feel detached from memories of things that have happened to me—as if I had not been involved in them.	_____	_____
17. When in a new situation, it feels as if I have been through it before.	_____	_____
18. Out of the blue, I find myself not feeling any affection toward my family and close friends.	_____	_____
19. Objects around me seem to look smaller or farther away.	_____	_____
20. I cannot feel properly the objects that I touch with my hands for it feels *as if it were not me* who were touching them.	_____	_____
21. I do not seem able to picture things in my mind, for example, the face of a close friend or a familiar place.	_____	_____
22. When a part of my body hurts, I feel so detached from the pain that it feels as if it were "somebody else's pain."	_____	_____
23. I have the feeling of being outside my body.	_____	_____
24. When I move it doesn't feel as if I were in charge of the movements, so that I feel "automatic" and mechanical as if I were a "robot."	_____	_____
25. The smell of things no longer gives me a feeling of pleasure or dislike.	_____	_____
26. I feel so detached from my thoughts that they seem to have a "life" of their own.	_____	_____
27. I have to touch myself to make sure that I have a body or a real existence.	_____	_____
28. *I seem to have lost* some bodily sensations (e.g., of hunger and thirst) so that when I eat or drink, it feels like an automatic routine.	_____	_____
29. Previously familiar places look unfamiliar, as if I had never seen them before.	_____	_____

no evidence, at least to this day, to the contrary. All these patients appear to have similar triggers, onset, and course to their condition. Additionally, the few biological studies of depersonalization that have been conducted have not described subtypes in which different brain circuits are disrupted. However, given the small numbers of patients in these research studies to this day, we are probably not at the stage where we would be able to reliably begin to delineate different subtypes. Many psychiatric disorders are characterized by some variability in symptoms in different patients, but still constitute the same core disorder. For example, some patients with schizophrenia hear voices, others have visions, others are convinced of false ideas, and yet others have all of these symptoms. Some patients with depression cannot eat or sleep, while others overeat and oversleep when depressed.

Ultimately, scales such as those discussed here are not quick tests to determine whether or not a person has depersonalization disorder; in and of themselves they cannot "make" a diagnosis. They are simply valuable tools to be used in the process of diagnosis, in which person-to-person interviews by a knowledgeable, professional clinician remain a crucial element.

Understanding the Language

People suffering from the varied symptoms of depersonalization can be quite adept at communicating with each other. Certain words and phrases seem immediately recognizable to them, while to friends, family, and even clinicians what they are attempting to describe may seem nothing less than crazy. It is important, therefore, that professionals not only familiarize themselves with the existing literature and case histories of depersonalization, but also pay attention to and understand the many catch phrases that may emerge during the diagnostic process.

Some cultures have many different words to describe the subtle variations of a single concept, experience, or phenomenon. The Inuit language's multitude of words to signify "snow" is a classic example, and is understandable considering the snowy Alaskan climate where Inuit is spoken.

The vast terrain of depersonalization would benefit from a broader lexicon to help find words for the unspeakable. But to date, to communicate their condition, depersonalized people must rely on the subtle nuances of simpler words or phrases often used as metaphor to capture the experiential with language. The word "unreal" is *the* key word for depersonalized people. To describe "unreality" they must often use metaphors for comparison to other sensations that may or may not be more understandable to everyone else.

Key phrases can be misinterpreted, and they often are. An expression like "I feel nothing" may easily be attributed to depression. "I feel detached from myself" may seem as much a cognitive or philosophical complaint as an experiential one referring to a subjective self-state. Concerned listeners may wonder if the term "unreal" means the same as "*not* real."

In an article in the Johns Hopkins University publication *Philosophy, Psychiatry, and Psychology,* Filip Radovic and Susanna Radovic recently explored some of the terminology of depersonalized patients, including the term "unreal."[6] The authors pointed out that, considering the broadness and prevalence of the word "unreal" in our culture, people can often express that things feel unreal without reflecting an underlying depersonalization experience; rather, they are talking about something way out of the ordinary. Life seems unreal to someone who is depersonalized, yet it also may seem unreal to someone who has just won the lottery. The latter person may be having an intellectual experience of unreality, as in "this cannot be happening to me," because of his "unbelievable" good fortune. Less likely, he may be actually experiencing an episode of genuine depersonalization, essentially for the very same reason, triggered by the overwhelmingness of the extreme event.

According to Radovic and Radovic, in everyday language, the term "unreal" has three primary usages:

1. not existing (as in the case of an imaginary friend or mythological being),
2. fake, made up, or artificial (such as a toy bear, which, of course, is not a real bear),
3. not normal, atypical, or nonoptimal (as in "he is not a *real* or *true* friend").

When depersonalized people say "life seems unreal," their meaning can involve any or all three of these usages. Ultimately, however, the experiential change of depersonalization goes beyond what is meant by any of these definitions. Radovic and Radovic liken this change to that of a dream state: it cannot be described satisfactorily within the existent *real* and *unreal* parameters. You may know that a dream is not real, but it may feel real.

"Dreams are often accompanied by a varying degree of a sense of reality (or unreality) that has no obvious correlation with the amount of strangeness or atypicality present in the dream,"[7] Radovic and Radovic explain. "This particular feeling of unreality may be a salient and distinct feature of a dream and is often reported by subjects after awakening."[8] This point about dreams is particularly interesting because so many depersonalized people describe their state as "dreamlike," yet any relationship between dreaming and DPD remains unexplored to date.

The "as if" aspect of DPD also comes into play quite often. Words like "mechanical," "dead," and "lifeless" enter the picture, as well as the use of metaphors such as "I feel like a robot." Such phrases reflect how the typical depersonalization experience is difficult to capture with literal vocabulary. "The only way to give an approximate account of one's subjective experiences is then to paint a picture in words."[9] The "as if" prefix, therefore, reflects the uncertainty about the adequacy of a proposed description—it is simply the best verbalization a patient can come up with.

There is a second important aspect of the "as if" feature that shows that a patient is nondelusional—that is, he or she has intact reality testing as a required criterion for the diagnosis of depersonalization. The patient doesn't believe that he *is* a robot but feels *as if* he is functioning like one.

The word "feel" is also fraught with its own mysteries. A person may suffer immensely from lack of feeling, yet the suffering itself is a feeling—a negative one. But suffering only is a very constricted emotional world, and some people describe feeling nothing at all.

The language of the *DSM-IV* itself can be subject to interpretation, despite the care that is put into the wording. For example, part of the manual's depersonalization description mentions "a sensation of lacking control of one's actions."[10] Does this mean that someone is fearful that they might act on impulse and harm someone or themselves, like a person with obsessive-compulsive disorder? Does it imply a sense that one's arms or legs will give way involuntarily, like a person with tics and twitches? Or does it mean they do things robotically, without a clear awareness of their actions? Even "normal" people can sense a lack of control from time to time, under the influence of intense emotions or new and unpredictable circumstances.

Discussion about the precise meaning of words and the true intent of the person saying them inevitably leads down a long and winding road. Ultimately, describing certain symptoms of depersonalization is akin to describing the taste of an orange or a peach. You can say it's tart, tangy, sweet, semisweet, or comparable to something else, but no words can truly describe the taste.

Yet despite the limitations of words, depersonalized people have shown themselves to be quite capable of relating to each other's descriptions of symptoms, as evidenced by the burgeoning communication that has evolved in forums and chat groups on the Internet. Through all venues, certain core symptoms have been identified, and the ways of describing these symptoms usually involves the same intuitively understood language.

To further explore the types of descriptions that clinicians are likely to draw on in assessing depersonalization experiences, let's look in more detail at some of the primary complaints voiced by depersonalized people, through a general list of symptom categories. Each category includes statements made by varied individuals, all drawn from diagnostic manuals, clinical papers, case studies, and patient interviews over the last few decades. These symptom categories are overlapping—people may experience one type of symptom, several combined, or all of them at different times. We include these categories not as just clinical data, but to capture the experience of depersonalized people through the breadth and richness of their own statements. The following passages are composites of things said by several patients.

Detachment from the self

My thoughts are separate from my body, as if my mind exists in one place and my physicality in another. I see myself doing things, like I'm in a movie. I go through the motions as if I'm in a play. How can I be inside myself while watching myself at the same time? Words come out of my mouth, but they don't seem to be directed by me. They just come out, and sometimes I become flustered and begin to stammer or slur. My arms and legs don't feel like they're mine. How do I control them? What makes them move? I look in the mirror to try to recenter myself, but I still feel like I'm in the "twilight zone." I have no sense of time: a thousand years can seem like an hour, a few seconds can seem like days. My memories of my past life feel like they did not happen to me. Remembering my past is like looking at photographs of someone else's life. My most treasured memories are now so dulled—dreams feel more real than waking life.

Detachment from the world

Familiar things look strange and foreign. I feel like an anthropologist from another planet, studying the human species. I look at things that once meant a lot to me, and I don't understand what I saw in them that made me love them.

They're just shapes, objects, things, with no personal connection to me. My old coffee mug looks no more familiar than a baby with two heads. It's all just there and it's all strange somehow. I see everything through a fog. Fluorescent lights intensify the horrible sensation and cast a deep veil over everything. I'm sealed in plastic wrap, closed off, almost deaf in the muted silence. It is as if the world were made of cellophane or glass. I feel like Alice in Wonderland. The world is inside out, upside down, and unpleasantly strange, like being trapped in a carnival fun house where mirrors distort everything.

Hypoemotionality

I have no moods. Things that used to cause a response in me do nothing. A beautiful painting or a vivid sunset that once moved me no longer arouses me. I wanted to cry when my mother died but didn't. Not because I didn't love her, I just could not evoke how it should feel; I knew she's no longer in the world, but neither am I. I remember once feeling the change of seasons in my stomach, filled with memories and nostalgia. I can't feel all that anymore. Nothing sparks any kind of emotion in me, except possibly fear. I feel as if I am dead. I have no sense of humor but fake false smiles when necessary. I cannot feel sex. I am deceiving my loved ones pretending to feel for them, to be connected and to care. My soul has been stolen from me. All I feel is a strange void. It is like a biblical curse—my wine has turned to vinegar, food to dry, tasteless powder—my soul has departed.

Anxiety and ruminations

My thoughts about the depersonalization lead me on a perpetual tortured journey of questions without answers. I am always watching and analyzing everything about me, trapped in my brain, with every thought encircled by a million other thoughts about that thought. Each thought, no matter how insignificant, seems magnified. I am overly aware of all the voices in my head, my out-loud thoughts, and I almost "see" everything I think as if it were spelled out on a billboard. I feel as if I am on the verge of panic all the time because of the ever-present sense of the strangeness of the thoughts running through my head, like a radio caught between stations. I can't stop thinking about thinking. Thinking itself feels strange and unnatural; it has lost all spontaneity. I can never relax and stop thinking. I think and think in circles until I am exhausted, and I long for the escape of sleep.

What am I? Where did I come from? Where will I end up? I thought I knew once, but I feel that my answers were all illusions. Everyone is sleepwalking through life, deluded with their own sense of purpose and meaning. But I have died, and with this lack of feeling comes a strange unification with the cold, unfeeling night that lasts forever. I'm ready to move on, but always wonder about those who kill themselves—I am already dead. When I was very young, I had fleeting moments of awe and terror pondering my puny existence, the infinity of time and space, my moment of living and the forever of what came after. Are we alive or is it all a dream that never happened?

Back now to making the diagnosis of DPD. After inquiring about a persistent history of the types of symptoms such as those described above, and ensuring that their occurrence is not simply part of another condition, whether psychiatric, medical, or substance-related, a person with the diagnosis of DPD can be expected to meet a number of clinical characteristics regarding its onset, course, precipitants, and co-occurring conditions. In the next chapter, we examine these in greater detail.

5 Unraveling the Enigma

Clinical Research on Depersonalization Disorder

Mountains cannot be surmounted except by winding paths.

—GOETHE

The human brain, the only organ capable of studying itself, has in the last century turned its attention toward the mysterious phenomenon of depersonalization, examining it from many perspectives. Depersonalization disorder (DPD) remains one of the most frequently misdiagnosed or underdiagnosed conditions in modern psychiatry. Why? Likely for several reasons. DPD is often accompanied by anxiety, depression, or other disorders, and patients may have trouble or hesitation expressing its vagaries in words that anyone but fellow sufferers can understand. Patients often wind up being treated for depression or anxiety, even though they have tried to make clear that they were depressed or anxious only initially in their depersonalization course, or only well after depersonalization had set in. The patients are often clear that what they are struggling most with are feelings of "unreality," "deadness," or "no self" and that they know the difference from being solely depressed or anxious. Clinicians, however, do not always agree, possibly because they have solid training in—and are more comfortable dealing with—the domains of anxiety and depression.

One telling distinction between DPD and depression or anxiety lies in how depersonalization symptoms fare alongside depression or anxiety symptoms. Does the person still feel depersonalized, even during periods when not anxious or depressed? If depression and anxiety wax and wane, does depersonalization follow along, or does it have a life of its own?

In the general population, the majority of people have had at least a fleeting moment of depersonalization or derealization. In other words, the symptom of depersonalization is not an unfamiliar one to many. Yet, DPD is still not adequately recognized as the singular and independent disorder that the latest research suggests it is. Clinicians experienced in the diagnosis and treatment of dissociative disorders can recognize depersonalization symptoms without much difficulty. Individual professionals are likely to tailor treatment to the needs of individual patients with a combination of drugs and psychotherapy, based on their knowledge and experience with patients expressing similar complaints. But specific interviews and questionnaires helpful in differentiating DPD patients from those with other disorders have been nonexistent until fairly recently. These new tools can help clinicians pinpoint a condition that was often previously overlooked. Such instruments have also proven useful to research units created specifically for the study of DPD.

Since the 1990s, the Department of Psychiatry, Mount Sinai School of Medicine, New York, and the Institute of Psychiatry, King's College, London, have investigated DPD through volunteer participants in their programs who meet the diagnostic criteria for the disorder. In 2003, both centers published articles in leading journals describing by far the largest series of patients suffering from DPD to be systematically studied to date. The Mount Sinai Research Unit's report, published in the *Journal of Clinical Psychiatry*, was based on a sample of 117 patients suffering from primary depersonalization disorder.[1] Each of these patients received an extensive psychiatric interview in person. The Institute of Psychiatry's report, published in the *British Journal of Psychiatry*, reported on 204 patients with chronic depersonalization; 124 were interviewed in person, while the rest were assessed by phone or Internet by completing a set of questionnaires.[2] In other words, the British study included all responders who had depersonalization *symptoms*, of whom 71% actually suffered from primary DPD (as defined by the 4th edition of the *Diagnostic and Statistical Manual of Mental Disorders* [*DSM-IV*]), whereas the American study only included those with primary DPD.

Despite the somewhat different approaches and assessment tools used in the two groups' studies, they yielded strikingly similar findings in many respects. In this chapter we summarize these cutting-edge findings about the disorder. Together, they offer a reliable and comprehensive profile of people with DPD, based on more than 300 cases combined. This number might not appear large to the general public, but it is actually a huge step forward in the field of psychiatry for examining in great depth the characteristics of a previously uninvestigated disorder, traditionally assumed to be rare.

How Rare Is Depersonalization Disorder?

In order to determine the true prevalence of any psychiatric or, for that matter, medical condition in the general population, a large "epidemiological" study is needed. Such a study randomly samples the population in different parts of a country, with well-established instruments and well-trained interviewers, so that the presence of particular conditions can be detected and measured with accuracy. Such epidemiological studies have been conducted for numerous psychiatric conditions, such as depression, anxiety disorders, schizophrenia, and even posttraumatic stress disorder (PTSD), but not for the dissociative disorders (including DPD). Therefore, our estimates of the prevalence of dissociative disorders in the United States or elsewhere in the Western world are, of necessity, approximate.

The few studies that have looked at dissociative symptoms in the general population have generated conservative estimates in the range of 3–10%. Studies that have looked at the lifetime occurrence of depersonalization or derealization, even transient, in general population samples (mostly students) have reported rates in the very broad range of 20–70%.[3]

In 1995, Aderibigbe and colleagues conducted a survey of the prevalence of depersonalization and derealization over a 1-year period in rural eastern North Carolina.[4] A random sampling of 1008 adults was conducted by telephone. Each person was asked about depersonalization and derealization experiences over the past year. It was found that 19% of the interviewees acknowledged depersonalization experiences, 14% said they had experienced derealization, and 23% said they had encountered both. This is quite a high rate for experiencing a psychiatric symptom over a 1-year period. Women and minorities reported higher rates.

Before we begin calling North Carolina the "depersonalized state," a look at how the answers were assessed will shed some light on the results. People were asked the following question: "Sometimes people feel as though they are outside themselves, watching themselves do something; feel as if their body doesn't quite belong to them, like a robot, or feel like they are in a daze or a dream. Have you had any of these feelings within the last year?" A simple "yes" put 19% of the respondents into the depersonalized category.

Similarly, to assess derealization, the interviewees were asked: "Sometimes people feel as though other people or objects around them appear strange or changed in some way: that their surroundings are not quite real. Have you had any of these feelings in the last year?" As stated earlier, about 14% of the people called said "yes," and on average these people experienced derealization about 26 times over the course of a year, ranging from just one time to once every day. About 19% of the total sample had depersonalization and/or derealization experiences that were defined as more substantial, lasting at least 1 hour or occurring at least 3 times during the year. In other words, one in five people had depersonalization/derealization experiences. But was this all depersonalization disorder? The answer is almost certainly no. Psychiatric disorders per se were not assessed, so it is not possible to know which of these people might also have suffered from clinical depression, anxiety disorders including posttraumatic stress disorder, or disssociative disorders other than depersonalization disorder. There was also the possibility that some of them were chronic drug or alcohol users.

However, when asked when their depersonalization and derealization tended to happen, their answers concurred with the trends found in more thoroughly conducted research. The most commonly reported associations were

- when under severe stress (78%),
- when nervous or depressed (66%),
- when having upsetting memories of past events (45%),
- when in danger (25%),
- for no particular reason (35%).

These associations are nothing new, and they confirm what we already know about the contexts in which depersonalization and derealization are most likely to occur.

From the Aderibigbe et al. study, one can safely infer that the 1-year prevalence of depersonalization disorder is certainly less than 20%, but the study cannot really tell us how much less. For example, the 45% of subjects who dissociated when having upsetting memories were likely to be suffering from posttraumatic stress disorder or dissociative disorders other than DPD. The 25% who dissociated with danger might have been having an acute stress reaction, at its extreme known as "acute stress disorder." The 66% having dissociation when nervous or depressed might or might not have suffered from primary depersonalization disorder. (As stated earlier, people who only experience depersonalization during a bout of anxiety or depression are not diagnosed with depersonalization disorder. In contrast, those who also dissociate outside of marked anxiety or depression bouts might have had the disorder.) Finally, it is pretty safe to say that most of the 35% who had depersonalization and derealization "for no particular reason" are quite likely to have had the disorder, although this cannot be stated conclusively because medical, neurological, and substance use conditions were not assessed.

Ultimately, even if only a portion (let's say one third) of the 35% who reported depersonalization for "no particular reason," out of the 19% of the total surveyed sample who reported *any* depersonalization experiences, really did suffer from DPD, we can derive a very rough estimate for the disorder of around 2% in this rural population, over a 1-year period. Of course, lifetime prevalence would presumably be higher than the 1-year prevalence. This estimate concurs with two community surveys carried out in the United Kingdom in the 1980s and again in the 1990s, which reported a 1.2–1.7% one-month prevalence of depersonalization, briefly assessed among many other symptoms.[5]

Finally, Colin Ross, a well-known expert in dissociative disorders in North America, conducted a community survey of about 1000 randomly selected residents of Winnipeg, Canada, in the late 1980s, using the Dissociative Experiences Questionnaire, followed by an interview for those with elevated scores on the questionnaire.[6] He estimated a 2.4% prevalence of current depersonalization disorder.

In summary, then, it seems safe to say that although there has not yet been a conclusive study of the population prevalence of dissociative disorders, several studies converge on a conservative estimate for depersonalization disorder around 1–2% of the population. This may sound like a small number in the scheme of things. But if you consider that the United States population was 281 million people in 2000, the estimate of just 1% establishes that roughly 2.8 million people suffer from full-blown depersonalization disorder right now. If the 2.4% figure is more accurate, more than 6.7 million people suffer from the disorder. This is more than double the number of people with schizophrenia and virtually equal to the figures for bipolar disorder or for obsessive-compulsive disorder. Yet these other conditions are certainly more widely known and granted considerably more attention and research funding.

Patient Profile

Both the Mount Sinai and the Institute of Psychiatry research teams studied adult DPD patients with an average age in their mid-30s.[7] Many participants, of course, were considerably younger or older. Gender distribution was about half men and half women in this very large combined sample, and we can now say definitively that this disorder seems to affect the two genders equally. People suffering from chronic depersonalization disorder typically describe great dysfunction in their daily living. Only a few said that the depersonalization did not interfere with either their occupational or their social functioning. It was not unusual for people to function in their jobs better than in their relations with others. However, often there was both occupational and interpersonal dysfunction. Sadly, individuals with DPD described that even within close relationships with loved ones, they often felt like they were just "going through the motions"; feelings were not accessible to them, and they experienced a pervasive sense of detachment and distance from their loved ones. A substantial number were not able to hold full-time jobs. Among those who did, many felt that they were struggling because they had failed to realize their full potential for better jobs or to succeed in ways they might have before the disorder set in. Those in more achieving and demanding jobs often felt that they were barely holding on, finding it very difficult to focus, process, and remember information because of the cloud of detachment and fog that enveloped them or because of the preoccupation with their symptoms, including fears of going insane.

The average age of onset of DPD was around 16 years in the Mount Sinai sample and 23 years in the Institute of Psychiatry sample, ranging from very early childhood, as far back as some people could remember, to late onset in very few people in their 40s, 50s, or 60s.[8] Interestingly, although the London study found that the people with earlier onset had more severe dissociative symptoms,[9] the U.S. studies did not replicate this finding. In the Mount Sinai sample, 80% of people described onset by age 20 and 95% by age 25. In other words, this is very much a disorder of adolescence; onset in middle or late age appears to be quite unusual. This means that it is not uncommon to find someone seeking treatment for DPD in their 30s after having suffered from depersonalization for about half their lifetimes. The people who participated in these research programs had experienced DPD from as little as 3 months to as long as 6 decades.

Onset and Course

The way that depersonalization disorder begins is highly variable. In some people it happens very suddenly, and such individuals can typically recall the exact day and circumstances of how it started. For example, Bob will never forget the moment his depersonalization set in. He was 20, sitting in a college junior-year class in chemistry. The year had been highly stressful for him on a number of counts. His girlfriend of 2 years had broken up with him 1 month earlier; his grades had taken a plunge after his recent decision to pursue medical school and to complete his pre-med requirements; and his mother had just been diagnosed with metastatic cancer. On a fateful morning in early March, as he was sitting in the packed classroom and taking notes on the lecture, he suddenly felt as if he were floating upward; everything around him seemed intensely unreal; the teacher looked like a far-away performing robot; and his own scribbling hand felt strangely disconnected. He experienced a disturbing sense of stillness, as if his ears were plugged or he were under water, and he began to feel strange in his own skin. A sense that something terribly wrong was about to happen added to his discomfort. There seemed to be a kind of separation between his mind and body—something he had never experienced before.

Bob attributed his weird sensations to his fatigue and stress and reassured himself they would go away later in the day when he went home and took a nap. Perhaps he had a fever or was coming down with something. However, he later woke up feeling just the same, and the experience did not leave him for years.

For other individuals the onset of depersonalization can be very insidious, setting in over a period of weeks, months, or even years, or it may have started so far back that a person really cannot recall how it started (research shows about a 50/50 ratio of insidious versus acute onset). Miriam had only hazy memories of her disturbing childhood; she suddenly lost her mother to a car accident when she was just 3. She was an only child, and her overwhelmed father distanced from her, soon remarried, and had more children. Miriam became the outcast in the new family, a lonely and emotionally deprived child, deeply longing to be felt and heard by others. Her depersonalization dates as far back as she can remember, and she has no recollections of her mother. This gives rise to the frequently asked question: If this is the only subjective state that she can remember, how can she know there is something "off" about it?

Some people report being sad or anxious as far back as they can remember, yet they also assume that what they feel isn't normal or right. Presumably, we all somehow know, even without conscious memory or comparisons, that there are other ways of feeling and being that may no longer be accessible. Perhaps it is instinct, remote hidden memory, or momentary glimpses into what is being missed during rare, fleeting moments of wakefulness or during dreams. Almost invariably, lifelong sufferers do seem to know the difference.

James had never experienced depersonalization until the age of 12. On the day when his beloved father gathered his three kids and announced that he was leaving their mother, James felt unreal for a few hours and then recovered. He vividly recalls feeling at the time that this must be a dream; it cannot really be happening. Three years later, when James fractured his arm in a frightening skiing accident, he felt depersonalized for 2 days. By the end of high school and early college, he started to experience longer bouts of depersonalization, lasting days or weeks, whenever he felt very stressed. Gradually and insidiously, before he knew it, the depersonalization set in for good; looking back he thinks that it was probably sometime in the midst of his junior year in college that he no longer ever felt real.

The course of the condition in the majority of people is continuous. Shockingly, such individuals are chronically in a depersonalized state without a break. They may barely remember what it felt like not to be depersonalized, or they may refer to themselves as the "old" self and the "new" self, or as a "no self." In about a third of people, the course of the disorder is episodic. In this scenario, the depersonalization comes and goes, lasting from minutes to hours, days, or even months at a time, then subsiding until the next episode. Although episodes can differ greatly from person to person, it is not unusual for an episode to start abruptly but to fade very gradually. About 10% of people, like James, start out with discrete episodes of depersonalization which eventually, after weeks, months, or years, become continuous.

What Triggers Chronic Depersonalization?

As with any psychiatric disorder, one foremost question is what brings it on. Why does it happen when it happens? Depersonalization disorder, along with other psychiatric conditions such as depression, anxiety, and schizophrenia, likely involves genetic predispositions, followed by early life events that enhance vulnerability, and subsequently later life occurrences that trigger the onset of chronic symptoms. (This likelihood is not a certainty, however.) Unlike some of the better understood psychiatric disorders, much less is known about these components when it comes to DPD.

Heritability

When questioned informally, only a few people (5% in the Mount Sinai study and 10% in the Institute of Psychiatry study) described some known family history of depersonalization, although relatives were not formally interviewed in either study.[10] It seems safe to say that there is no marked heritable component to depersonalization, although on rare occasions one encounters individuals suffering from the condition who describe that it runs in their families. It's likely that previous generations simply didn't know what to call their condition or were ashamed to discuss it. Others may have masked their feelings and their fears of being insane through drinking or drugs, legal or otherwise.

One of the most basic ways that one can study the heritability of psychiatric or medical conditions is by examining identical and fraternal twins. The difference in how often a condition co-occurs in identical versus fraternal twins represents the condition's heritable component. To date, only two twin studies have examined dissociation in general; neither examined depersonalization in particular.[11] Interestingly, these two studies reported conflicting findings, leaving us uncertain about how much of dissociation is heritable. Notably, both of these studies looked at disssociative symptoms in twins as measured by the Dissociative Experiences Scale; neither one used formal interviews to actually diagnose dissociative disorders. The Waller and Ross study found no heritable component to dissociation, whereas the Jang et al. study found about a 50% genetic component. Thus, the heritability of dissociation is still very much up in the air.

The idea that people with DPD have a predisposition toward the condition is perhaps supported by some of the personal stories they relay. Some remember fleeting moments of depersonalization from an early age, before the disorder ever set in with permanence and severity. Some may not even recall passing instances of the symptom itself, but rather a willingness or readiness to distract or detach themselves from disturbing happenings around them. With a predisposition to depersonalization, something eventually happens to trigger the actual onset of DPD. These triggers can be highly variable in different people.

Depersonalization Triggered by Drug Use

One trigger that has become readily and indisputably apparent is the use of drugs. Although not considered the most common trigger, in a sizable portion of the population, incidental or casual drug use, even one-time drug use (presumably when there's an underlying vulnerability) can on occasion throw an individual into a chronic depersonalized state. This is frequently seen in people who post their personal stories on Internet websites or participate in some of the discussion forums on these sites. These are clearly not cases of a straightforward, short-lived reaction or a high from the drug. (Bear in mind that "high" used here is a relative term that denotes a broad range of experience.) Marijuana and LSD seem to be the primary triggers, but DPD can also be precipitated by some less commonly used drugs like ketamine (special K) or the increasingly used drug ecstasy (MDMA).

How do people go into this high and never come out of it? They wake up the next morning and find themselves in a different state of mind that doesn't ease up and in which they remain stuck for months and years. One possible answer is that a very specific chemical trigger has tipped something off balance in the brain of a person who is already biologically vulnerable. This neurochemical change manifests itself in the form of depersonalization. Other explanations for drug-triggered onsets are also plausible. The actual experience of the high, especially after a bad or very disturbing trip, could be overwhelming to the self and consequently throw certain people into an altered state of selfhood.

One clinical example of this involves a patient who had an intense phobia of death. There were many instances in her life in which she behaved "counterphobically"—that is, she deliberately approached this fear by taking risks in an effort to overcome it. Her fear was probably related to a near-drowning experience she had when she was around 5 years old, from which she never fully recovered. When she used ecstasy, she encountered the idea of death psychologically and became terrified. She depersonalized and then did not come out of this state. So, it can be hard to know whether the triggering event was chemical, psychological, or both.

Depersonalization disorder is not the only psychiatric condition that can be triggered by drug use. For example, some schizophrenic patients can trace the onset of their schizophrenia to the use of marijuana or cocaine. They may become psychotic, then stop using the offending drug, but the schizophrenia continues. The drug acts as a chemical trigger that in some way throws them over the edge, presuming they were already biologically predisposed and vulnerable. Panic disorder can emerge in the same way. An initial panic attack can be triggered by marijuana, for example, but people may then develop full-blown panic disorder that continues long after they've ceased using the drug. This is not to imply that these people are in some way psychologically weaker than others, or that they couldn't handle the drugs that their friends took frequently with apparent immunity. Their biological makeup is different, just as people have different blood types, different allergies, or different genetic vulnerabilities to certain diseases.

Onset of depersonalization brought about by drugs has been well-documented and quantified by recent studies. Among the 117 Mount Sinai subjects, 13% described a clear time-linked and immediate trigger with marijuana, whereby they smoked, went into a high, and then never came out of the depersonalized state. About 6% recounted clear triggering by hallucinogens. In two cases, the drug ecstasy was the catalyst, and one case involved ketamine, the "dissociative anesthetic," which has long been known to induce dissociative states and is no longer used to induce medical anesthesia in humans.[12] Similarly, the Institute of Psychiatry reported that a notable number of chronic depersonalization cases were triggered by drugs (40 out of 164). Of these 40 individuals, 20 attributed the onset of their depersonalization to marijuana, 4 to ecstasy, 2 to LSD, and 1 to ketamine; the remaining 13 attributed the onset to drug combinations involving at least 1 of these drugs.[13]

Thus, the four implicated illicit drug classes and how often these were culprits in triggering lasting depersonalization were similar in the U.S. and British studies. These findings suggest that there is something specific to the biological action of these drugs, in how they affect particular neurochemical systems in the brain, which may give us useful clues in unraveling the biology underlying depersonalization. More about this follows in chapter 6. Interestingly, the particular types of depersonalization symptoms, as well as their severity and chronicity, do not differ depending on whether depersonalization was initially triggered by an illicit drug. Simply stated, once chronic depersonalization sets in, it looks the same no matter if it was initially triggered by drug use, by some other trigger, or by no immediately identifiable trigger at all.

Psychological Triggers

Other types of triggers, unrelated to drug experiences, are more often reported in association with the onset of chronic depersonalization. In the American sample, 25% of all people reported onset of depersonalization during a period of severe stress, 12% with panic attacks, and 9% with depression.[14] Similarly, in the British sample, 15% of people reported onset with a "psychological" trigger, while 14% reported onset with a "traumatic event."[15] It is important to remember that in all these people suffering from primary chronic depersonalization, the depersonalization clearly persisted after the initial emotional trigger, traumatic stress, panic, or depression had lifted. In other words, an extreme mental state of any sort may be capable, in vulnerable individuals, of triggering a depersonalized state that, in some, then becomes persistent and takes on a life of its own, independent of its initial trigger. Such triggering events can apparently threaten the very integrity of the sense of self and induce a profound, anguished state of "who am I?" This can, in turn, set off chronic depersonalization symptoms that over time can become autonomous from the precipitating state.

When depersonalization is initially triggered by an episode of another psychiatric disorder, like depression or panic, sufferers are particularly likely to be misdiagnosed and have their depersonalization symptoms dismissed as part and parcel of the other condition. Surprisingly, this often happens even when patients clearly describe that the symptoms of depression or panic are long gone and that they are distinctly aware of now suffering from something very different. Patients with DPD often become demoralized and hopeless about their condition when one practitioner after the other tells them that the depersonalization is just a symptom of their depression or anxiety and should be treated (typically unsuccessfully) as such. In this light, the onset of chronic depersonalization in the context of another more common and better known psychiatric condition presents a challenge to accurate dissection and diagnosis.

Severe lifetime stress is also commonly reported as a trigger of chronic depersonalization in DPD patients: 25% reported this trigger in the Mount Sinai sample.[16] Although such stressors are usually not of a magnitude meriting the characterization "traumatic" in the minds of many, these stressors can be highly traumatic for the individuals undergoing them. Lifetime traumatic stress of all sorts can thus trigger DPD. Some people describe prolonged, severe stress with poor marriages and divorces, major life transitions such as leaving home for college, or extremely demanding work conditions that lead to burnout.

Why a stressful life event may prove particularly overwhelming for certain people can often be quite mysterious and not apparent to the untrained observer. For example, one patient went into chronic depersonalization when she found out that the sister of a very close friend of hers had committed suicide. This is, of course, tragic, but most people would not become chronically depersonalized from it. Sometimes it's necessary to look closely at the personal event and the very specific symbolic meanings that it may have had for a particular individual to truly appreciate the severity of symptoms to which it led.

It is equally important to remember that early childhood adversity (which we discuss below) and later highly stressful events have very potent interactions in precipitating all kinds of psychiatric pathology. Extensive research in recent years has highlighted how potent this interaction can be in various psychiatric disorders. A person who had a traumatic childhood is undoubtedly set up to be more vulnerable to later life stress and is more likely to develop psychiatric symptoms, whether it be anxiety, depression, depersonalization, or whatever other symptoms he or she may be biologically vulnerable to, compared to someone who did not experience similar childhood adversity. And then again, it is important to remember that childhood adversity does not always lead to later pathology. Some people are unusually strong and resilient to the effects of trauma, and the factors, whether biological or psychosocial, that contribute to their resilience are as interesting as the factors associated with pathology.

Overwhelming Joy

Incredibly, sometimes transient depersonalization might be triggered by positive experiences. One example of this was Freud's visit to the Acropolis, which we touched on earlier. Another example involves a patient with chronic depersonalization who grew up in a very disturbed family. There was no blatant abuse, but the mother was highly disturbed and made life miserable for everyone, being preoccupied with her obsessions. The house was never cleaned; there were dirty plates and food rotting everywhere. In short, the patient and his needs had been completely neglected by this mother. He was so ashamed of his home and parents that he never brought over his friends and lived in social isolation because of his dysfunctional family. Paradoxically, what seemed to throw him into bouts of intensified depersonalization was the promise of something very exciting or positive about to happen in his life. When he was finally accepted to a prestigious school in a city to which he had always wanted to go and was finally able to leave his miserable home, he was thrust into a state of depersonalization. Perhaps he was so deprived that he couldn't tolerate such intense positive feeling—for him it was an overwhelming experience. Perhaps he thought that his fortune could not be "for real" and that he was bound to lose it all; perhaps he felt intolerable guilt to leave behind his troubled mother; or maybe he simply didn't know how to contain the previously unknown sense of positive excitement and integrate it with his usual perceptions of who he was. This example illustrates that what is overwhelming for one person may not be for the next, because what we experience is laden with unique personal meaning. So it seems that overwhelming experience of any kind can trigger chronic DPD in individuals who may be vulnerable to it.

The Role of Childhood Trauma

Trauma can play a part in chronic depersonalization, and this lends support to the disorder's current classification among the dissociative disorders. But most of the other dissociative disorders have been more compellingly linked to trauma than to DPD, at least until recently. For example, dissociative identity disorder has been convincingly tied to horrific, early, ongoing childhood abuse in just about every sufferer of the condition. This abuse leads to chronic dissociation, memory disturbances, and an inability to consolidate a rudimentary cohesive identity, resulting in profound fragmentation of the self and numerous self-states that come and go.

The existing literature also tells us that people who are acutely traumatized in a severe, often life-threatening fashion commonly develop at least fleeting (lasting for minutes, hours, or days) dissociative symptoms, including depersonalization. This phenomenon is known as peritraumatic dissociation (i.e., dissociation occurring around the time of a trauma). For example, depersonalization has been described, depending on the study, in up to two thirds of people involved in life-threatening car accidents, life-threatening illnesses, serious surgery, and so on. This relates to the general consensus that dissociation is a universal survival mechanism, meant to help humans get through overwhelming stress that would otherwise leave them paralyzed with fear and unable to react. Indeed, in the short term, such a process may be very adaptive, as in the case of women who have been violently raped and describe how during the event they were no longer in their bodies but had somehow managed to "escape"—floating up to the ceiling and looking down on the horrific scene. The life-preserving value of this type of experience is obvious. However, if this experience then persists over the months and years every time a raped woman has sex, for example, even with a desired partner, then a new problem has emerged.

The Mount Sinai Research Unit has conducted the only study to date looking at childhood interpersonal trauma, up to age 18, in DPD, evaluated in a group of 60 adult patients.[17] The study compared them to individuals without psychiatric problems, looking at whether they had suffered more childhood trauma, what kind of trauma, and whether that trauma could in any way predict the severity of the depersonalization. The study used a well-validated detailed childhood trauma interview, which measures six kinds of trauma:

- separations and losses
- physical neglect
- emotional abuse (verbal and nonverbal)
- physical abuse
- sexual abuse
- witnessing violence (domestic and otherwise).

Three areas of trauma—emotional abuse, physical abuse, and sexual abuse—were greater in DPD patients than in the healthy group. This statistic in itself doesn't reveal much because many psychiatric conditions are associated with more childhood trauma than exists in "normal" people. What became evident, however, after numerous statistical analyses of the findings, was that emotional abuse stood out as the one specific type of abuse that was most intimately related to DPD. Although physical and sexual abuse were elevated in DPD, these types of abuse were not not impressively high. Certainly they did not reflect the kinds of stories heard from people with more severe dissociative disorders.

The average emotional abuse scores in the Mount Sinai study reflected frightening yelling and screaming threats like "I'll kill you," or statements like "I wish I'd never had you," of high frequency and duration, day in and day out for years on end, typically involving one or both parents, and creating a very damaging emotional environment wherein children vulnerable to dissociation may start to depersonalize, feeling that nothing is real, and therefore nothing terrible is happening to them. Indeed, this study found that of all trauma scores, only emotional abuse scores statistically predicted a greater severity of depersonalization symptoms.

Furthermore, emotional neglect, which was not measured in the Mount Sinai study, has increasingly impressed the research group at Mount Sinai as another childhood maltreatment factor that often strongly figures in the past histories of DPD patients. Some of the patients in the study encountered very little positive parenting: caring, involvement, physical warmth and affection, nurturance, support, guidance, and appropriate socialization. Such emotional deprivation can also have profound consequences and can inhibit the development of a solid sense of selfhood.

The severe dissociative disorders (dissociative identity disorder and dissociative disorder not otherwise specified, a milder variant of the former) are more common in women than men, whereas DPD is equally common in both genders. This might be explained by the fact that different types of abuse happen with different frequencies in children according to their gender. Whereas emotional maltreatment is comparable among girls and boys, sexual abuse is more common among girls. Thus, differing types and degrees of childhood maltreatment are associated with different dissociative symptoms and disorders. Some of the more horrific sexual and physical experiences can lead to conditions like dissociative identity disorder and its variants. The less horrific, but still very powerful and damaging forms of chronic emotional abuse or neglect may be more likely to lead to DPD in those vulnerable to dissociation.

There are also other kinds of childhood trauma in addition to the ones described above. For example, there are children or adolescents for whom the death of a loved one may trigger chronic DPD. One patient described a very close and loving relationship with his mother. When the mother died suddenly and unexpectedly when he was 16, he became immediately depersonalized. In the beginning he didn't know what was happening and imagined that the strange feeling would go away over time. Indeed, it could initially have been part of the mourning process; however, it never dissipated, and this chronic depersonalization lasted for several more years. Another patient had suffered through the slow, painful death from brain cancer of his best friend in high school, and chronic depersonalization set in at that time. Yet another DPD patient had lost her sister, toward whom she had highly ambivalent feelings, to suicide, and went into a state of chronic depersonalization shortly after the untimely death.

Cognition in DPD

Even people with DPD who are able to hold on to demanding jobs typically report that they are not performing at their full capacity. They often judge their ability to attend to information and to remember it to be seriously impaired, and this often hinders their work. To investigate these complaints, several cognitive neuropsychological studies of DPD were conducted at Mount Sinai to objectively measure various aspects of attention and memory, with various computerized or pencil-and-paper tests.[18] The results indicated that compared to people without the condition, DPD patients showed similar general intelligence, memory, and attention, yet had distinct difficulties with certain specific aspects of attention and memory. Their attention seemed to fail when presented with tasks involving great perceptual overload. For example, one computer task known as a Continuous Performance Test involves sorting out target stimuli and pressing a button to show that the subject has seen the stimuli. When there was a lot of visual noise in the background, people with depersonalization lost sight, so to speak, of the stimulus more than the control subjects. In another kind of attention task known as the Stroop task, selective focusing of attention in DPD was found to be intact and was not interfered with by disturbing disorder-related words, a finding very different from that typically encountered in anxiety disorders like panic and posttraumatic stress disorder.

Interestingly, although people with DPD do not suffer clinically from amnesia (e.g., they do not have gaps of lost time, coming to hours later with no memory of what they had previously been doing), it's not unusual for them to complain of a hazy, fuzzy memory sometimes as far back as childhood or from the onset of the condition. These can be subtle memory difficulties that are not necessarily obvious to others in day-to-day interactions. But patients complain of memory losses because these deficits are quite real, and they can interfere both with vivid and rich recall of their pasts and with day-to-day performance. In a memory task using neutral and negative words, the Mount Sinai team found that individuals with DPD remembered more neutral words and fewer negative words than comparison "normal" subjects. In other words, there was a dissociation of negative information in DPD, which goes hand in hand with the avoidant information-processing style thought to characterize dissociative disorders, earning the connotation of dissociative disorders as disorders of "knowing and not knowing." Taking all findings together, it is not yet entirely clear if the prime cognitive difficulty in DPD is one of attention, which then leads to memory difficulties, or of a primary difficulty with memory, or both.

In contrast, there are other areas of cognition that are fully intact in DPD, such as executive functioning, which is the capacity to follow sequences, carry out sequential instructions, and execute planned steps and actions. Also, the attention and memory difficulties of DPD clearly differ from those of dissociative disorders like disssociative identity disorder and its variants. Allen et al. and Holmes et al. have suggested that memory problems in detachment versus compartmentalizing are distinctly different.[19] In detachment, the problem involves not paying attention to information in the first place, because of the dense fog that people are in, inevitably leading to problems with laying down new memories. Information that is not attended to is not encoded. In contrast, the problem with compartmentalization is that new memories are formed but are only accessible and can be retrieved in a similar self-state (i.e., they are state dependent). Thus, we have two different kinds of dissociative memory problems, at the two tail ends of information processing and memory formation: encoding problems (depersonalization) versus retrieval problems (dissociative amnesia).

Association with Other Psychiatric Disorders

When investigating people with DPD, it is important to study the other psychiatric disorders that they may suffer from as well. A wide range of depressive and anxiety disorders may exist concurrently with depersonalization. On a lifetime basis, the following other disorders were present in the Mount Sinai sample (overlapping): two thirds also suffered from clinical, "major," depression, one third from dysthymia (chronic low-grade depression), one third from social anxiety disorder, one third from panic disorder, one fifth from generalized anxiety disorder, and one eighth from obsessive-compulsive disorder.[20] For a long time, psychiatry has frequently dismissed depersonalization as a mere manifestation of underlying depressive or anxious states, so the relationship of these disorders to depersonalization deserves serious attention and thought.

When comparing the age of onset of DPD to that of any of the disorders above, none was found to start earlier than DPD—actually, on average, panic and depression started significantly later than the depersonalization. In other words, no mood or anxiety disorder was found to have a significantly earlier onset than DPD in the Mount Sinai sample of participants. This finding strongly supports the fact that depersonalization is a *primary* phenomenon, rather than one that sometimes accompanies these other disorders.

The U.K. research program found that people with stronger depression or anxiety symptoms also had more severe depersonalization symptoms. This suggests that both depression and anxiety can exacerbate depersonalization and make it more intense. Take, for example, the case of Bob. He first experienced depersonalization when he was 14, after his best friend died of a terminal illness. At 18 he left for college and first became depressed during his freshman year. Now, at age 32, he has endured two more episodes of clinical depression, as well as periods of milder depression. The depersonalization has never remitted during the nearly 2 decades since its onset. Bob, like many other patients with depersonalization, when questioned accurately, can clearly describe the relationship between his depersonalization and depression symptoms. He says that in the first few years of depersonalization he simply did not feel depressed, despite how distraught he was about his sense of detachment from life. Later on, every time he suffered from depression his depersonalization did get worse; however, his depression would eventually lift, while the depersonalization only returned to its usual baseline. He describes it in this way: "The depression makes it worse, but the depersonalization is always there: they don't just go hand in hand with each other."

Depersonalization and Posttraumatic Stress Disorder

A diagnosis of posttraumatic stress disorder (PTSD) requires the occurrence of a major traumatic event—an event that is threatening to a person's life or integrity and that a patient can describe as preceding the onset of their symptoms. By most standards these are events that are horrific and overwhelming, such as combat, rape, assault, natural disasters, terrorist attacks, and so on. These kinds of incidents are known to cause PTSD in large numbers of previously unaffected people—roughly in about 25% of those exposed to such a trauma.

Interestingly, people with DPD show a very low (5% or less) lifetime prevalence of PTSD. This appears to be a function of the different magnitude and quality of the traumas with which DPD can be associated, which are typically, although not always, less horrific or life threatening. The very low rate of PTSD in those with DPD is in sharp contrast to the more severe dissociative disorders, such as dissociative identity disorder, which are typically associated with very high rates of PTSD. Therefore, chronic depersonalization might offer a unique model for better understanding the different preexisting vulnerabilities, types of trauma, and pathogenetic pathways that lead to dissociative versus posttraumatic stress symptoms.

Relation to Personality Disorders

Personality disorders are longstanding personality styles that are extreme and dysfunctional. The Mount Sinai researchers found no single personality disorder that was uniquely or specifically associated with DPD (the U.K. study did not assess personality disorders). The whole range of personality disorders were widely represented in DPD research participants in the U.S. sample. The three most common[21] were

- *Avoidant* (23%): These are people who are overly self-conscious in social settings, frightened to make overtures to others, and tend to be shy and reclusive.
- *Borderline* (21%): These are people who exhibit instability in their mood and tend to be impulsive, often angry, and lacking a well-formed sense of identity.
- *Obsessive-compulsive* (21%): These are people who are overly perfectionistic, detail-oriented, rigid, and controlling.

All of the other personality disorders were also represented, such as paranoid, narcissistic, dependent, histrionic, schizotypal, schizoid, and antisocial personality disorders. About 40% percent of the Mount Sinai patients did *not* have a diagnosable personality disorder. Notably, none of these personality disorders was specifically associated with the severity of the depersonalization symptoms.

A Clinical Summary

In all, the U.S. and U.K. samples yielded strikingly similar findings, and thus we can now reliably characterize how this previously obscure disorder manifests itself in the Western world, with a detailed and well-established description of DPD in more than 300 sufferers. Of interest, the Mount Sinai study found that men and women with DPD were not different in any way regarding the disorder, be it onset, course, duration, severity of symptoms, or other co-occurring psychiatric disorders.[22]

Ultimately, the following can be said with conviction about the presentation of DPD, according to current research:

- The average age of onset is in adolescence.
- Men and women are equally affected.

- It causes profound distress and dysfunction in people.
- Its onset can be either acute or insidious.
- It is typically chronic, constant, and unremitting, although a smaller percentage may have it episodically.
- It frequently overlaps with the presence of mood or anxiety disorders, but none of these disorders has a unique relationship to DPD.
- Personality disorders are also common in patients with DPD, but none of these has a unique relationship to the onset or severity of the disorder.
- The most common triggers are severe stress, episodes of other mental illness, and drug use. In a sizable proportion of cases there is no obvious immediate trigger.
- Childhood trauma, in particular emotional maltreatment, has been associated with the disorder and with its severity.

Ultimately, all of these findings support the conceptualization of DPD as a discrete disorder, with its own unique characteristics.

6 The Biology of Depersonalization

Everything should be made as simple as possible, but not simpler.

—ALBERT EINSTEIN

Einstein's advice, above, is particularly relevant when it comes to discussing the human brain, the most complex structure in all creation. While more is known about the brain than ever before, mass culture has developed a tendency to liken its functions to that of a computer, or explain serious disorders in terms of simple chemical imbalances. Such generalizations just don't do the brain justice. Let's first take a scientific look at the basic anatomy and function of the brain, then move on to a closer look at those parts of the brain that may be most dysfunctional in depersonalization.

The Doors of Perception

The most recently evolved part of the human brain is the neocortex, which lies on the surface, enveloping and connecting to the deeper, older structures within. One part of the cortex is the sensory cortex, which is responsible for receiving sensory information encoded by our various sensory organs and deciphering and translating this information into known perceptual entities, "percepts," that we can make sense of. This information is transmitted and processed via a network of interacting brain cells called neurons. Neurons communicate with each other via the various substances that together are known as neurotransmitters.

When we perceive something, say, a hand being extended for a handshake, our brain makes sense of it as a known entity that belongs to the "hand" category—it is experienced as something quite familiar, with numerous perceptual associations, and it may even spark various emotional and autobiographical memories. Sensory input, such as visual (sight), auditory (hearing), olfactory (smell), or somatosensory (touch), is first processed in the simplest sensory areas of the cortex known as the primary sensory cortex. The primary cortex for visual input is situated in the occipital lobe of the brain. For sound and smell, the primary cortex is located in parts of the temporal lobe. And for somatic sensations, the primary cortex is in the parietal lobe (see figure 1). These primary cortical areas receive the sensory information and then relay it to more complex sensory cortical areas that synthesize perceptual information within each separate sensory modality. These more complex regions are known as the secondary unimodal association areas. In our example of the human hand, the visual appearance of the newly perceived object is matched against a preexisting template of a hand stored in the visual association area of the cortex. There it's perceived as something known. Similarly, other attributes of the hand are matched against other sensory templates. Any possible scent of the hand is matched against an olfactory sensory template; any sound it might make is matched against an auditory sensory template. The possible tastes associated with a hand has a gustatory template, and the feeling of holding hands, shaking hands, or being struck by a hand in anger has a somatosensory template.

Next, all these individual (unimodal) sensory aspects of the hand come together to form the complex and unique "experience" of a hand in what are known as the cross-modal or polymodal sensory association areas of the brain. These areas are crucial perceptual areas responsible for the higher-level integration of all sensory input across the various sensory modalities. One such area is known as the inferior parietal lobule, a portion of the parietal lobe consisting of the supramarginal and angular gyrus, strategically seated at the junction of the parietal lobe and the temporal and occipital lobes. This area of the brain is also critical for something else—our ability to have a well-integrated body schema, that is, an intact and unified physical sense of self. Does depersonalization come to mind here? Clearly, it does. When something is amiss in this area, something else—a person's core sense of "body self"—can be affected.

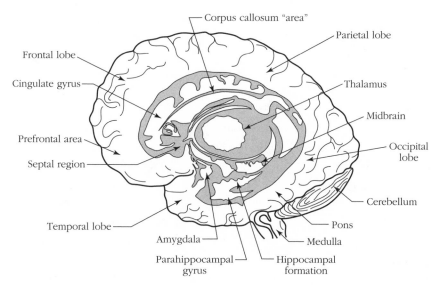

Figure 1: The brain.

Certain neurological syndromes, known as "neglect syndromes" or aso-matognosia, which result from strokes in the inferior parietal lobule, are characterized by an inability to recognize or experience parts of one's body as one's own. Instead, these body parts are treated as outside entities or as if they do not exist—the classic example being the neglect of the left side of the body with right parietal strokes. A report in the prestigious journal *Nature* in 2002 described a patient with refractory parietal lobe epilepsy who underwent a direct brain stimulation procedure to better map the damaged section of her brain.[1] Various areas of the brain were stimulated, but when the angular gyrus of the inferior parietal lobule was stimulated, the patient experienced repeated out-of-body sensations, something she had never had prior to the stimulation of that specific region.

Now back to the extended hand. Perceiving this familiar part of a person evokes not only the known percept of a hand, but possibly all kinds of associated thoughts, feelings, and memories. The sensory association areas of the cortex have connections to the prefrontal cortex, which allow us to have thoughts about the hand and to execute appropriate actions via our motor cortex in response to the handshake.

Recent neuroscience research is revealing that the initial formation of emotional memories is contingent on the activation of two tiny, almond-size bilateral brain structures known as the amygdala (from the Greek root word for almond), embedded deep in the temporal lobes. The amygdala belongs to the limbic system, an ancestral part of the brain that has not changed much over the course of evolution from reptiles to *Homo sapiens*. The amygdala plays a central role in a variety of instinctually driven emotional processes such as the conditioned fear response (e.g., when a laboratory animal responds negatively to a light or sound because it has been consistently paired to a mild electric shock in the past), the automatic reading of emotional facial expressions, and the formation of explicit emotional memories.

Much has been researched and written about the amygdala as the seat of a central animal emotion—fear. Not surprisingly, a number of anxiety disorders in humans, such as social anxiety disorder, panic disorder, specific phobias, and posttraumatic stress disorder, which are all characterized by a heightened sense of threat, appear to be correlated with an overactivation of the amygdala when a person is presented with disorder-specific frightening stimuli. Conversely, one could speculate that in dissociative states characterized by diminished emotionality and a sense of numbness, the amygdala may be underactivated when a person is emotionally stimulated.

Another important structure in the limbic system is the insula, which is responsible for registering internal bodily sensations, temperature, and pain. This is another area in which one could predict hypoactivation in dissociative states, given the sensory dullness that often accompanies dissociation.

Equally important within the limbic system is the hippocampus. The hippocampus is the seat of autobiographical memories—that is, all the memories that make up the story of our lives—stored contextually with the "stamp" of time, place, and details of what occurred. The encoding, storage, and retrieval of personal memories is a highly complex process involving the hippocampus as well as other extended cortical networks. Some neuroscientists believe that an autobiographical memory cannot be retrieved if an early "kernel" of the memory is not activated in the hippocampus, which serves as the epicenter of the distributed memory network in the brain. Of course, no autobiographical memory could be retrieved if it was not encoded in the first place. It appears that the memory difficulties experienced in the context of depersonalization are more related to failures of this initial memory encoding, making it different from other dissociative conditions like amnesia, where the problem lies more with a state-dependent compartmentalization of memory and therefore difficulty in its conscious retrieval.

Smaller hippocampi have been found in individuals suffering from a variety of psychiatric conditions associated with chronic stress and adversity, such as depression and posttraumatic stress disorder, suggesting that chronic stress is toxic to this structure. So far, no studies have examined the size or the activity of the hippocampus in dissociative disorders in the absence of posttraumatic stress disorder, so the question of its relation to depersonalization disorder (DPD) remains unanswered.

Sensation without Memory

As stated earlier, the amygdala and hippocampus are two very important subcortical structures in the brain. The amygdala is crucial to the initial processing of fear and other emotions before they're processed at a higher level by the cortex, and it is the seat of emotional memory. The amygdala is the source of the organism's immediate fight-or-flight response. The purpose of the hippocampus is consolidation of information and the retaining of autobiographical and episodic memories—personal stories of what has happened to us, with their context, their time, and so on. These two brain structures can operate quite independently of each other—which raises an interesting possibility. On one hand, a person may have little or no memory of something that happened to him, especially something very traumatic, because a clear autobiographic memory of this event may not have been registered by the hippocampus under conditions of extreme stress. But on the other hand, there may be a different kind of record of the event mediated by the amygdala—of the associated feeling that a certain kind of experience gave rise to. So, at some future time, a person could encounter something that reminds him of an old trauma and have a very intense emotional and behavioral reaction based on what the amygdala "knows" but have no concrete memory for what actually took place.

The famous neuroscientist Joseph LeDoux described the implications of this distinction between explicit and implicit memory in understanding the formation of memories in emotionally laden situations in his book *The Emotional Brain* (1996).[2] LeDoux explains that the knowledge that a particular incident was terrifying is a declarative memory about an emotional experience, mediated by the hippocampus and its connections. In contrast, the intense emotional response evoked during the event (and at times during its later recollection) activates the implicit memory system and involves the amygdala and its connections. Under sufficiently intense or prolonged stress, a stress hormone (cortisol)-mediated shutdown of the hippocampus can occur, leading to impaired explicit conscious memory functions. At the same time, stress does not interfere with, and may even enhance, amygdala functioning. According to LeDoux, "it is thus completely possible that one might have poor conscious memory of a traumatic experience, but at the same time form very powerful implicit, unconscious emotional memories."[3] This distinction is crucial to the understanding of dissociative phenomena. Stimuli may activate the amygdala without activating conscious memories, eliciting an intense emotional state that the individual has no understanding of, in which one "knows and does not know," typical of dissociation. The fact that the implicit system forgets and revises less than the explicit system over time, and also matures earlier in life, further fuels the dissociation just described, especially for early life events.

Another relevant part of the cortex is the medial prefrontal cortex, which is situated inside the frontal lobes. The medial prefrontal cortex has important connections to the limbic, or "emotional," part of the brain, playing a crucial role in modulating and dampening our emotional responses. In some psychiatric disorders characterized by high states of anxiety and arousal, it appears that this area of the prefrontal cortex is hypoactive and is not adequately inhibiting the very active amygdala and other limbic structures. Conversely, one could predict that the hypoemotionality of depersonalization disorder might involve an inverse pattern: heightened prefrontal activity with greater limbic inhibition.

It's clear now that these and other regions of the brain are ripe for exploration in the search for some specific dysfunctions that might underlie DPD. With this as a background, let's take a closer look at brain models of depersonalization and then at the neurological, neurochemical, and brain-imaging findings that are helping us to begin testing these models.

The Temporal Lobe Model of Depersonalization

The neurologist Wilder G. Penfield is well-known for his seminal work conducted in the 1940s through the 1960s at McGill University in Montreal. Penfield helped elucidate many of the structures and functions of the brain, largely through his efforts to understand, map, and surgically treat epilepsy, especially temporal lobe epilepsy. Penfield proposed what might be referred to as the "temporal lobe hypothesis" of depersonalization in 1950. Penfield and co-author Rasmussen wrote about "clear sensations of not being present or floating away . . . far off and out of this world" which were produced by stimulation of specific areas of the temporal cortex, the superior temporal gyrus and the middle temporal gyrus.[4] In trying to understand his patients' clear and vivid experiences of pure depersonalization, Penfield postulated that what was occurring was an alteration in the usual mechanisms of comparing immediate sensory perceptions with existing memory records in the brain that gave these perceptions emotional coloring and relevance. This gets to the core of the depersonalization experience because it has to do with the subjective sense of unfamiliarity. Perceptions both of the self and of the things around us that should feel familiar, and therefore real, do not feel familiar and real in depersonalization because somehow they are not appropriately emotionally tagged as "known" against preexisting memory records. Penfield's temporal lobe hypothesis is supported by additional neurological observations (summarized later in this chapter), which, for example, reference depersonalization as a frequent symptom in patients with temporal lobe epilepsy.

Not Making Connections: Cortico-limbic Dysconnectivity and Other Brain Dysconnectivities

In 1998, an interesting biological model of depersonalization by Mauricio Sierra and German Berrios, from the University of Cambridge's Department of Psychiatry, was published in the journal *Biological Psychiatry*.[5] They proposed a "cortico-limbic disconnection" model, suggesting that depersonalization involves disconnections between certain reciprocal parts of the brain that are not functioning in sync. They proposed that heightened activation (overactivation) of the prefrontal cortex, responsible for the cognitive processing and dampening of emotional experiences, may overly inhibit the limbic system, which mediates the more emotional aspects of our experiences. The hyperactivation of the prefrontal cortex and reciprocal limbic inhibition, Sierra and Berrios suggested, results in the hypoemotionality or emotional deadness that we see in depersonalization.

A more extensive dysconnectivity model for understanding the neurobiology of dissociation was proposed by John Krystal, MD, from Yale University, also in 1998.[6] Krystal's evidence is based primarily on people with posttraumatic stress disorder (PTSD), as well as healthy volunteers, but it is relevant to the mechanisms of dissociation. Krystal proposed that dissociation involves not only cortico-limbic dysconnectivity, as suggested by the Sierra and Berrios model, but also certain types of dysconnectivity between different areas of the brain's cortex, which he calls "corticocortical dysconnectivity." Furthermore, Krystal suggested that additional thalamo-cortical dysconnectivity may exist as early as in the sensory gating occurring in the thalamus. The thalamus is a part of the brain responsible for relaying and modulating incoming perceptions from the outside world via our sensory organs. For example, one part of the thalamus, the pulvinar, is involved in regulating visual input as it is relayed from the primary visual cortex to the secondary visual cortex.

Corticocortical connectivity is primarily mediated by the NMDA (N-methyl-+-aspartate) receptor, which is the receptor for the excitatory neurotransmitter glutamate. When people are given ketamine, an NMDA receptor blocker also known as the "dissociative anesthetic," or "special K," they fall into profound dissociative states. These ketamine-induced states have been extensively used as experimental models of the negative symptoms of schizophrenia, but they also clearly reflect the profound states of selflessness and deadness encountered in dissociation. Furthermore, the pathways mediating ketamine-induced psychosis versus dissociation appear to be distinct from each other, as they can be selectively blocked by different medications administered before taking the ketamine. (We've already pointed out that in some individual cases, chronic depersonalization can initially be triggered by the casual use of ketamine.)

In short, the integration and synchronized activity of the several cortical, limbic, and even thalamic areas may be necessary for a cohesive, conscious self-experience. All of these models are clearly not mutually exclusive but rather complementary, expanding on one another to offer us ways of conceptualizing the neurobiological disturbances underlying depersonalization. From an evolutionary perspective, acute transient depersonalization, typically precipitated by severe or life-threatening stress, must be viewed as adaptive in the short term, allowing the individual emotional distance and detachment from circumstances that might otherwise be overwhelming, so that steps appropriate to survival can be taken. However, depersonalization that becomes chronic and autonomous from its stressful origins is clearly maladaptive, suggesting dysregulated brain function that has failed to repair.

Any scientific model, no matter how strong it seems in theory, needs to be tested empirically. Data need to be collected in the real world. As Thomas

Kuhn has described in talking about the nature of the scientific hypotheses, the scientific data that we collect will either support or refute a hypothesis.[7] We can never prove a scientific model with certainty; better fitting or more comprehensive models could arise at any time. We can, however, disprove a scientific model by collecting empirical data in the real world that is simply not compatible with the model. What, then, is the evidence for and against these various models of depersonalization that we just described?

Neurological Studies

The neurological literature, when reviewed carefully from the viewpoint of one well-versed in psychiatric syndromes, can be very revealing. Structural abnormalities of the brain, such as those that can result from head injury, stroke, epilepsy, tumors, and many other conditions, can mimic just about any psychiatric disorder: psychosis, depression, mania, anxiety, and so on. Dissociation and depersonalization are no exception. A careful reading of the neurological literature suggests a unique role for portions of the posterior sensory cortex (temporal, parietal, and occipital), in mediating depersonalization-like experiences. Let's take a look, then, at the reports of depersonalization in the neurological literature.

Patients who have seizures, especially of the left temporal lobe, often experience depersonalization symptoms.[8] Depersonalization experiences have also been described in seizures based in the parietal lobes and can present with symptoms such as somatosensory aurae, disturbances of body image, vertiginous sensations, and visual illusions.[9] We already mentioned an epilepsy patient who, for the first time, experienced out-of-body experiences when the right angular gyrus of the inferior parietal lobe was electrically stimulated by a surgeon.[10] (Neurological problems in the parietal lobes other than strokes can also produce symptoms reminiscent of depersonalization).

In 1954, the British physician Ackner reported that tumors in the inferior parietal cortex and angular gyrus could manifest with depersonalization.[11] Strokes concentrated in the area of the right inferior parietal lobule often result in syndromes known as "neglect": ignoring one side of the body as though it does not exist; again, this is reminiscent of the somatic detachment of depersonalization.[12] Another pertinent study examined the ability to visually recognize emotions in a group of 108 patients with focal brain lesions. Once again, the results indicated that similar parietal areas (i.e., the right somatosensory cortex and supramarginal gyrus [adjacent to the angular gyrus]) were areas crucial for the accurate visual recognition of emotions.[13]

Simeon and her group were the first to propose that the unreality experiences of depersonalization may be associated with widespread dysfunction of the sensory association cortex[14]—all the neurological findings just presented are in sync with such a theory. Along similar lines, Sierra and colleagues proposed that two subcomponents of the unreality of depersonalization may be subsumed by distinct neurocircuitry.[15] One subcomponent is the "visual derealization," associated with occipito-temporal cortical dysfunction, and the other subcomponent is the "body alienation," associated with parietal cortical dysfunction. These two subcomponents have not yet been teased out in brain-imaging studies of depersonalized patients experiencing these kinds of symptoms.

Brain-Imaging Studies

Intriguing new imaging studies that either make reference to depersonalization or examine DPD specifically have also given us fresh insights into the condition. Depersonalization-type symptoms have been induced in normal people through chemical means and then visualized by brain imagery. In a PET (positron emission tomography) study by R.J. Matthew and colleagues, in which tetrahydrocannabinol (marijuana) was administered to normal individuals, the marijuana caused an increase in blood flow (and therefore presumably in brain activity) in the prefrontal cortex and in the anterior cingulate (the area that modulates attention), and this increase correlated with intense depersonalization symptoms.[16] There was also a decrease in subcortical blood flow to areas such as the amygdala and the hippocampus. This finding supports the cortico-limbic disconnection hypothesis described previously, which implicates hyperactive prefrontal and hypoactive limbic systems in depersonalization symptoms. The Matthews et al. study also provides a good model of what is going on in the brain when people go into a "high" from which they seem unable to return.

Another imaging study, by Dr. Mary Phillips at the Institute of Psychiatry in London, found changes in brain activity in normal individuals who were administered the glutamate antagonist ketamine or a placebo.[17] As expected, ketamine brought about an emotionally blunted response to viewing fearful faces. This ketamine-induced hypoemotionality, which was put forth as a model of depersonalization, was associated with reduced limbic responses to the emotionally laden faces and increased visual cortex activity in response to neutral faces.

Another set of pertinent studies in normal volunteers has attempted to look at what happens in the brain when we look at stimuli that are experienced as familiar or unfamiliar. (It is needless to say how relevant this might be to depersonalization, where the familiar is experienced as unfamiliar.) These studies of visual familiarity found that unfamiliar faces narrowly activated only unimodal visual association areas, whereas familiar (or famous) faces produced more widespread activation of transmodal association areas—specifically, the middle temporal gyrus BA21 and angular gyrus BA39.[18] These findings could imply that in depersonalization there is somehow a failure of sensory association cortex functioning, especially at the level of higher associations and connections.

Another relevant study involved PTSD but does have relevance. The well-known brain-imaging investigator, Ruth Lanius from Canada, has adopted the strategy of subdividing people with PTSD into two groups: those who when presented with traumatic reminders experience intense arousal, increased heart rate, and flashbacks, and those who when presented with traumatic reminders experience dissociative bouts with no heart rate increase.[19] Interestingly, these two subgroups look very different from each other when their brain activity is studied using functional magnetic resonance imaging (fMRI) in real time as the participants are exposed to their personalized traumatic scripts. The dissociative subgroup, in particular, showed increased brain activity in the medial prefrontal cortex and the anterior cingulate cortex (both involved in the cognitive processing and inhibition of limbic emotional responses), as well as increased brain activity in cortical sensory association areas of the temporal, parietal, and occipital lobes. These patterns of brain activity in the dissociative group are very much along the lines of what one would predict, based on the background models for dissociation that we have discussed so far, and correspond with the two imaging studies that have been done regarding DPD. Now let's look at those.

In 2001, doctors at the Department of Psychiatry, University of Cambridge, including their neuroimaging expert Dr. Mary Phillips, compared patients with DPD, patients with obsessive-compulsive disorder, and normal volunteers.[20] The researchers used the fMRI technique to detect changes in activity in different parts of the brain in real moment-to-moment sequential time frames, as people were presented with different tasks. All the subjects were shown picture sets of neutral and aversive (disgusting) objects—a cockroach was depicted in one set, for instance, as well as open wounds in another. The findings indicated that, contrary to normal and obsessive-compulsive individuals, DPD patients showed a heightened activation in their prefrontal cortex, but did not activate the insula, the limbic area responsible for experiencing the emotion of disgust, in response to the aversive pictures. When the subjects rated the pictures for emotional content, it was found that even though DPD participants knew intellectually that certain photographs were meant to be disgusting stimuli, their emotional experience was less aversive than that of the other two groups. This all goes along with the idea that depersonalized individuals hypo-activate limbic regions, the emotional regions that are important for processing emotions, and, conversely, that they hyper-activate higher cortical areas. Ultimately, this suggests a brain mechanism that may underlie the emotional inhibition, numbness, and sense of unfamiliarity experienced by chronically depersonalized people.

At the Department of Psychiatry of Mount Sinai School of Medicine, a PET imaging study comparing people with DPD with a normal group was undertaken. The participants took a standardized verbal memory test in order to control for mental activity during the uptake of the radioactive glucose by the brain, and the two groups performed equally well on this test. All the DPD patients were suffering from continuous, ongoing depersonalization, including the time when they were scanned. The results of the study, published in the *American Journal of Psychiatry,* showed no differences between DPD patients and normal individuals in the entire anterior cortex of the brain (i.e., the frontal and cingulate cortex).[21] These are the areas responsible for many higher cognitive functions such as planning and executing daily tasks, as well as the dampening of emotional responses. (Note, however, that in this study participants were not presented with emotional material.) All of the differences that were found between the two groups were localized in the posterior part of the cortex, which is made up of the temporal, parietal, and occipital lobes.

A closer look at the specific areas within these lobes, known as Brodmann areas, revealed that the two groups differed in parietal areas 7B and 39, temporal areas 22, and 21, and occipital area 19.[22] All these areas are parts of the sensory association cortex, which is responsible for processing sensory stimuli within each sensory modality, as well as for making the various associations between different sensory modalities. These include visual stimuli, which primarily involve the occipital cortex, somatosensory stimuli (sense of our own bodies) which primarily involve the parietal cortex, and auditory stimuli, which primarily involve the temporal cortex. As indicated earlier, as stimuli are received by the brain, all these areas try to make sense of them, put them together, and label them based on known and stored stimuli.

In the depersonalized group, several of the sensory association areas showed different activity from what was seen in the normal group, the Mount Sinai study found. In particular, a difference was seen in area 39 of the parietal lobe, which is called the angular gyrus, and which is an important seat of cross-modal integration among the various sensory modalities. This area also connects to the frontal lobe so that higher order processing can occur. The angular gyrus is thought to be responsible for a well-integrated body schema, so it is logical that it does indeed show altered activity in people with DPD. As noted earlier, tumors in this part of the brain can manifest with depersonalization, and people with strokes in this area of the brain often manifest what is known in neurology as "neglect syndromes": they ignore one half of their body as if it doesn't exist. There is an analogy to depersonalization here, but, of course, people with depersonalization cognitively know that their body exists, in contrast to the neurological scenario, which involves more structural damage.

To put it simply, we can think of DPD as a "softer" psychological version of the neurological neglect syndrome because, even though intellectually people with depersonalization know that their body exists, they don't feel the relation to their body in a normal way, so it's experienced as if it does not exist.

Another sensory cortex brain area showing different activity in the DPD subjects of the Mount Sinai study was parietal area 7b, which is primarily responsible for our somatosensory integration. There was a very strong relationship between higher depersonalization scores and higher activity in this area of the brain.

In summary, the limited imaging data in depersonalization have been quite consistent with theoretical models and suggest two main ideas. First, there may be a widespread dysfunction in the sensory areas of the cortex, leading to a disruption of sensory processing, which may manifest with the perceptual distortions of DPD, including derealization and somatic disturbances of one's sense of reality. Second, there may be hyperactivity of the prefrontal cortex and suppression of limbic structures, manifesting in a hypercognitive presentation wherein people know what they should feel, but because of hypoemotionality, they are not really feeling.

Neurochemistry of Depersonalization

Studies of the brain's chemical pathways tie into the theories we've looked at so far, since the function of the different brain circuits is driven by the neuro-chemicals and neurohormones that mediate them. In this section we discuss the different neurochemicals and neurohormones that have been implicated in depersonalization.

Is There a Serotonin Link?

Several experts in the field, including Eric Hollander, MD, Evan Torch, MD, and Sir Martin Roth, MD, have noted how depersonalization can sometimes look like a variant of obsessive-compulsive disorder (OCD), or that they may be related in some way. There exists, in certain patients, an obsessive-compulsive type of elaboration of the core depersonalization experience wherein they ru-minate and obsess endlessly about what it is like to be or not to be real, about life being real or a dream, and a broad range of related existential anxieties. This poses the question of whether this excessive rumination is inherent to the underlying brain dysfunction of DPD, a direct result of feeling unreal, or an elaboration that occurs only in people with DPD who are also obsessional. There is certainly a substantial subgroup of patients that engages in excessive, non-productive "thinking in circles," but it's important to remember that there are many with DPD who do not obsess. Sometimes, as we've seen, this type of thinking can occur at the earliest stages of the condition, and could even be a defensive attempt to understand and make sense of the experience of unreality, which later flattens out into emotional deadness and an accepted feeling of "no self."

An inherent obsessive-compulsive component to DPD would suggest that some kind of dysfunction of the serotonin system may play a role in, or at least contribute to, DPD symptoms. (The neurotransmitter serotonin is well known to play a role in obsessive-compulsive conditions.) However, there are very limited data to date clearly supporting this notion. There is, for example, some suggestion that DPD and migraines co-exist more often than chance would dictate, and migraines are known to have a serotonergic component. But very often the experience of migraine does not coincide with DPD or does not worsen DPD.

Another indirect source of evidence is the fact that DPD can be triggered or worsened by LSD, which is a serotonergic-acting drug (called a 5-HT2–serotonin type 2 receptor agonist). In addition, one study by Simeon et al. looked at a varied group of patients, not suffering from DPD.[23] The group was a mixture of "normals," social-phobic patients, OCD patients, and borderline personality disorder patients. The study compared responses to the inducement of depersonalization and all kinds of other transient symptoms when people were given a one-time dose of either *meta*-chlorophenylpiperazine (mCPP; a serotonin agonist used for studies such as this) or a placebo. It was found that mCPP produced a much higher rate of depersonalization in this diverse group than did the placebo, although it also induced more anxiety, more panic, and more dysphoria as well. The finding of anxiety, panic, and dysphoria is consistent with the literature that describes DPD patients for whom these symptoms are a major source of distress.

Similarly, studies in which people with PTSD were administered mCPP, done by Stephen Southwick and his colleagues at Yale, have shown that activation of serotonin induces flashbacks and dissociative symptoms in a subgroup of the PTSD patients.[24] Although these are not particularly clear-cut models for pure depersonalization, they do suggest that serotonin may play some modulating role in depersonalization symptoms.

Despite the limited evidence for a serotonin hypothesis in DPD, it has been learned through more recent studies that selective serotonin reuptake inhibitors (SSRIs; e.g., Prozac, Zoloft, and the like) are not effective in treating DPD,[25] and this would seem to negate any kind of a central role for serotonin in a hypothesis that explained depersonalization fully. The degree to which SSRIs, or other, older classes of antidepressants such as tricyclics and mono-amine oxidase inhibitors may "leach" into other pathways modulated by the serotonin pathways, or alternatively sometimes help depersonalization symptoms via a decrease in associated anxiety or depression, may account for the positive effect of these drugs

Substances That Induce Depersonalization in Normal Individuals

Several other neurotransmitter systems have been implicated in DPD, although evidence for each is somewhat scant. Four classes of chemicals have been shown to reliably induce transient depersonalized states in healthy individuals. As such, they may offer us valuable insights into the neurochemical imbalances that might underlie pathological depersonalization: NMDA antagonists, cannabinoids, hallucinogens, and opioid agonists. Let's talk about each of these.

As we already discussed, the NMDA antagonist ketamine (special K) induces a profound dissociative state in healthy subjects. In psychiatric research, the ketamine model is better known for the induction of psychotic schizophrenialike states. Yet it appears that the dissociative and the psychotomimetic effects (so named because they mimic psychosis) of ketamine are distinct. For example, the dissociative, but not the psychotomimetic, effect of ketamine can be blocked in normal subjects by pretreatment with the medication lamotrigine. Lamotrigine, also known by its brand name Lamictal, is often prescibed as an antiseizure medication and has been speculated to reduce ketamine-induced dissociation by inhibiting the release of the excitatory neurotransmitter glutamate. Glutamate is the main excitatory neurotransmitter in the brain, and it acts as an agonist on both NMDA and non-NMDA glutamate receptors. NMDA antagonists like ketamine are believed to induce dissociation by blocking glutamate transmission at NMDA receptors and consequently increasing glutamate transmission at non-NMDA glutamate receptors. Therefore, pretreatment with lamotrigine, which inhibits glutamate release, lessens ketamine-induced dissociation in healthy volunteers.[26] NMDA receptors are widely distributed in the cortex, as well as in the hippocampus and the amygdala. They are thought to mediate associative functioning and long-term potentiation of memory, facilitating new learning. So it is plausible that diminished NMDA-related neurotransmission could mediate dissociative states.

Cannabinoids, such as marijuana, have been consistently shown to induce depersonalization with a pronounced component of temporal disintegration, in both naturalistic and experimental settings in healthy subjects (the marijuana imaging study described earlier is an example). In addition to their action at cannabinoid receptors, whose natural function is largely unknown, cannabinoids have been shown to block NMDA receptors at sites distinct from other noncompetitive NMDA antagonists. Thus, the dissociative effect of cannabinoids might in fact be mediated via the NMDA receptor. There are case reports of chronic depersonalization induced by acute cannabis ingestion in some of the older literature. Such occurrences are now firmly established in the recent large studies: in the Mount Sinai series of 117 DPD participants (2003), about 13% reported the acute triggering of chronic depersonalization immediately after smoking marijuana.[27]

Depersonalized states in normal people can also be transiently induced by the use of hallucinogens, such as LSD, psilocybin, and DMT (*N,N*-dimethyl-tryptamine), in both naturalistic and experimental settings. In the Mount Sinai series of 117 DPD subjects, 6% reported the induction of chronic depersonal-ization by acute hallucinogen use.[28] As we have already discussed, these sub-stances act as agonists of the serotonin 5HT2 A and C receptors, suggesting some possible mediating role for serotonin in depersonalization.

There are three endogenous opioid systems in the brain, the mu, kappa, and delta systems. Both the mu and the kappa systems have been to some degree implicated in depersonalization. Stress-induced analgesia (the loss of sensitivity to pain) is known to be mediated by the mu endogenous opioid system (EOS). For example, in veterans suffering from combat-related PTSD, the analgesic response to combat scenes can be blocked by pretreatment with the opioid blocker naloxone. With respect to the kappa opioid system, the kappa opioid agonist enadoline has been shown to induce a "clean" deper-sonalization-like syndrome in healthy subjects when compared to placebo, with perceptual disturbances and a sense of detachment as its primary psy-chological manifestations.[29]

Along these lines, nonselective opiate antagonists, which can block all the opioid systems when used at high doses, have been reported to reduce dis-sociation in a few studies. This has been shown, for example, with high-dose naltrexone treatment in borderline personality disorder, as well as intravenous naloxone or oral naltrexone treatment in chronic depersonalization (we will be talking more about these treatments in chapter 8).[30] More selective kappa opioid antagonists that block only the kappa opioid system have been used in animal studies, but have not yet been developed and tested for human use.

The Autonomic System and Norepinephrine

The autonomic system is the part of the nervous system that regulates basic organ processes needed to maintain normal bodily functions, such as heart rate and blood pressure, and it is of particular interest in dissociation. In some psychiatric disorders associated with high levels of anxiety and arousal, such as panic disorder and PSTD, the autonomic system is hyperactive. In contrast, there is some emerging evidence that in dissociative states the autonomic system might be hypoactive. For example, decreased heart rate and galvanic skin responses have been reported in women who experienced strong dis-sociation after being raped.[31]

Specifically in DPD, there is limited but possibly compelling evidence for autonomic hyporeactivity. Mauricio Sierra and his colleagues in the UK published a study in 2002 that measured galvanic skin responses in DPD.[32] Galvanic skin responses indicate a change in the electrical properties of the skin in response to stress or anxiety and can be measured by recording the electrical resistance of the skin. Sierra et al. found that in response to emotionally unpleasant stimuli, DPD participants exhibited reduced magnitude and increased delay of skin conductance responses compared to people with anxiety disorders and healthy individuals. On one hand, the findings indicated that the DPD group was less aroused and had weaker autonomic responses to these emotional stimuli compared to the other two groups. On the other hand, the DPD group did not show diminished galvanic skin responses to non-specific stimuli, such as the sounds of a clap or a sigh, suggesting that what is occurring in DPD may be a particular selective inhibition of emotional responsiveness. As we've discussed throughout, this hypoemotionality appears to be one of the core features of the disorder.

The noradrenergic system is a stress-responsive neurochemical system that uses norepinephrine, an adrenaline-like substance, as its chemical messenger. Norepinephrine is central to facilitating alertness, orientation toward new stimuli, selective attention, and enhanced memory encoding under stressful conditions. In other words, when we are stressed either internally or by our environment, norepinephrine helps us focus our attention and remember new and emotional occurrences, ensuring better survival and adaptation to ever-changing environments. However, although bursts in norepinephrine activity under acute stress are adaptive, more chronic noradrenergic activation "for no good reason," such as that encountered in certain psychiatric conditions related to traumatic stress, is maladaptive. For example, there are a number of studies showing a heightened noradrenergic tone in people with PTSD, which goes hand in hand with the hyperarousal and intrusive symptoms.

Although norepinephrine has not been extensively studied in dissociation, there are some revealing recent studies. Dissociative patients, in a sense, present with symptoms that are opposite those in classic PTSD: instead of being hyperaroused, they're "shut down."[33] One could therefore speculate that dissociative patients exhibit a noradrenergic dysfunction of an opposite type than classic PTSD. Indeed, there are now three small studies that have found a relationship between lower norepinephrine and dissociation. Simeon's group found that in people with DPD, norepinephrine in a urine sample collected over 24 hours was strongly inversely correlated with the severity of dissociation.[34] In other words, the more severe their dissociation, the lower their nor-

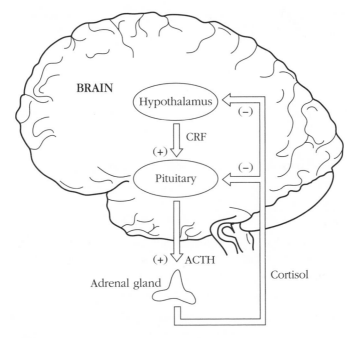

Figure 2: Hypothalamics-pituitary-adrenal axis.

epinephrine. Interestingly, Simeon's group has also found the same reverse relationship between dissociation severity and 24-hour urine norepinephrine in a group of borderline personality disorder patients with widely varying degrees of dissociation. Another researcher, Dr. D.L. Delahanty, reported that in car accident victims, 15-hour urine norepinephrine was inversely related to severity of the victims' peritraumatic dissociation (i.e., the dissociation occurring immediately after the accident).[35]

The HPA Axis

A neurohormonal system that may be involved in depersonalization is the hypothalamic-pituitary-adrenal (HPA) axis, a central system that kicks into action when we're stressed and regulates our response to stress (figure 2). When an organism is under stress, the HPA axis helps shut down several peripheral and unnecessary functions while recruiting the needed emergency responses. The circuit works as follows: The brain stem structure known as the hypothalamus is activated by stress and secretes corticotrophin-releasing hormone

(CRF). CRF, in turn, activates the brain's pituitary gland to secrete adreno-corticotropic hormone (ACTH), which in turn stimulates the adrenal glands to secrete the stress hormone cortisol. Cortisol acts widely throughout many parts of the body and the brain via the glucocorticoid receptors, mounting an immediate stress response that effectively mobilizes necessary body and brain responses while shutting down energy-wasting responses that are a luxury in the face of acute stress. Finally, the same stress hormone cortisol is also responsible for shutting down the acute stress response, by its negative feedback inhibition of the pituitary and the hypothalamus. The HPA axis then functions, in a normal individual, as a finely tuned, self-contained, and self-regulating stress-response system.

However, in some psychiatric conditions that have been linked to stress early in life or to extreme or prolonged stress, the HPA axis can go haywire, with detrimental consequences to a person's, or even an animal's, ability to mount an efficient time-limited stress response. In a series of very important studies, psychiatrist Jeremy Coplan and his collaborators showed that rhesus monkeys reared as infants under feeding conditions that were very stressful to their mothers developed an HPA axis dysregulation that persisted for years, into adolescence and well into adulthood.[36] Simply stated, this early life stress results in a permanently disrupted stress response.

Something similar appears to happen in humans exposed to severe stress. A clear dysregulation of the HPA axis has been extensively documented in individuals with PTSD.[37] Researchers at Mount Sinai speculated that dissociative disorders may in fact show a different kind of HPA axis dysregulation than that seen in PTSD. In a a study comparing baseline cortisol levels, it was reported that 24-hour urine cortisol was higher in people with DPD than in normal individuals, a finding opposite of what is seen in PTSD.[38]

This study also used a challenge test known as the "low-dose dexamethasone suppression test," which is widely used in psychiatric studies of the HPA axis. In this test, people are given a tiny dose of a medication much like the body's cortisol, which transiently suppresses the body's production of cortisol to some degree in normal individuals. But in people with various kinds of psychiatrically caused dysregulations of the HPA axis, such as depression and PTSD, one finds different degrees of dexamethasone suppression than those seen in normal individuals. The study found a significant difference in dexamethasone suppression between normal individuals and DPD patients. Those with DPD were more dexamethasone resistant, in that they suppressed their own cortisol production less in response to taking the dexamethasone.[38] This is a pattern similar to what has been consistently shown in severe depression, but in this study people currently suffering from depression were excluded. The Mount Sinai group more recently completed a much larger study comparing about 50 DPD and 50 normal participants, and replicating this same pattern of elevated resting cortisol and greater dexamethasone resistance in DPD.[39] We may, then, have one neurobiological marker that captures the stress-related chemical dysfunction of DPD.

Areas Yet to Explore

There may yet be other components of the depersonalization experience whose neurobiological underpinnings were not put forth in this chapter and that are still even less understood than the visual unreality, somatic detachment and hypoemotionality. For example, could the time distortion sometimes characteristic of depersonalization be related to dysfunction of the thalamus? What about the sensations of mind emptiness and having no self: Could it be that areas of the medial prefrontal cortex that are implicated in experiencing the sense of self are involved? In the last few years alone we've made a great start, but we still have a great deal to unravel about the complete neurobiology of depersonalization. In time, the pieces of the puzzle will likely fit together, with at least some of the mysteries solved.

In the meantime, the experience of depersonalization is nothing new, and its exploration has never been limited to the laboratory or the medical literature. In the next chapter we look at how depersonalization, or similarly mysterious experiences, have been dealt with in literature and philosophy through the centuries.

7 The Blow of the Void

Depersonalization in Literature and Philosophy

If the doors of perception were cleansed, every thing would appear to man as it is, infinite.

—WILLIAM BLAKE

The idea that reality is subjective, constructed from our own perceptions, is quite an ancient concept. "We are what we think. All that we are arises with our thoughts. With our thoughts, we make the world," said the Buddha. Depersonalization, a serious disruption in a person's thoughts or sensations about their individual self, understandably alters their entire world. A person may feel as if everything he or she has ever believed must be somehow reconstructed back to what it was, or made afresh, since little of what was once taken for granted remains solid or safe. People may find themselves in a Never Neverland with an altered sense of self, or a distinct sensation of having no self at all. Struggling with this mental change can lead down many paths, sometimes implying a spiritual awakening, while at other times the path may lead to anxiety, fruitless rumination, and, on occasion, works of art.

Alienation, isolation, and altered perceptions have for centuries served as themes for the visual arts, particularly modern art. Edvard Munch's famous painting *The Scream* depicts the essence of a private hell and detachment from all things outside of one's self. Vincent Van Gogh's vivid, frenetic interpretations of reality were long thought to be influenced by his consumption of the popular, toxic liqueur absinthe, as well as possible bipolar disorder. Some researchers now believe that he suffered from temporal lobe epilepsy, which has been definitively linked with depersonalization. This disorder, they say, may have played a role in his frenzied expressionism, highly suggestive of derealization. In the twentieth century, surrealists like René Magritte and Salvador Dali portrayed unreality in starkly realistic terms, through curious juxtapositions of recognizable objects or dreamlike landscapes.

Detachment, estrangement, as well as a heightened awareness of the infinite and the eternal, also appear in written works, from the Bible, to Shakespeare, to Dostoevsky, to modern pop lyrics. But depersonalization specifically has had its place in the arts and philosophy as well. Like the literary figure of Satan, its enigmatic face surfaces under many names, and many guises—one only need know where to look.

The essential library of depersonalization includes a surprisingly diverse group of books and stories that are all loosely interwoven by common themes. The book from which Ludovic Dugas drew the name for his subject of investigation serves as a fitting starting point. This book was Henri Frédéric Amiel's private diary, *The Journal Intime.*[1]

Amiel's *Journal* is one of literature's great curiosities. Published posthumously in 1882, it is the private diary of an obscure Swiss university professor who lived from 1821 to 1881. Day by day, over a period of more than 30 years, Amiel documented his most intimate thoughts and observations on many subjects, including European culture, politics, religion, women, and, in particular, his own identity. In all, Amiel wrote more than 17,000 journal entries.

Before his death, Amiel requested that his friends, who included several writers and literary critics, find some use for his voluminous journal. The result was a condensed two-volume work that has earned a unique place in the annals of psychology and philosophy.

Amiel's *Journal* does not reveal a solitary thinker's slow descent into madness as some had expected. It is instead the meticulous record of a man whose life never really got off the ground because he was never really grounded in this life. He was, using his terminology, from the age of 16, *depersonalized.*

Amiel was born to French parents in Geneva, Switzerland, where he lived and worked his entire life. When he was 12 years old, both of his parents died while in their 30s. Living with relatives, he was understandably forlorn and melancholy and showed a deep interest in religious ideas, particularly Calvinism, which was prevalent in Geneva. As he matured, he traveled widely and was exposed to the nineteenth century's thinkers, including Rousseau and Hegel. He completed his formal education in Heidelberg and Berlin, then returned home.

Amid the continent's social upheavals, Geneva provided a peaceful haven for someone like Amiel, who showed potential for contributing to the rapidly evolving political, philosophical, and scientific thinking of the day. He began a promising career by winning a public competition to become professor of French literature at the prestigious Academy of Geneva. Just 4 years later, at age 28, he was elevated to professor of moral philosophy. This was, at the time, the fast track to academic success. It was the perfect venue in which would-be philosophers and writers could take the time to fine-tune their thoughts and become lost in their own personal magnum opus.

For Amiel, however, the prestigious job in academia was not a fortuitous beginning but a dead end. In time, as the years passed, his friends and acquaintances began to wonder why. He was uncommonly intelligent, articulate, even sociable, yet year after year, nothing emerged from this wellspring of possibilities but dry college lectures and, periodically, literary criticism that reaffirmed his talent, followed by poetry that did not.

His closest confidant, critic M. Edmund Scherer, recalled years later: "He awakened in us but one regret; we could not understand how it was a man so richly gifted produced nothing, or only trivialities."[2]

The answer all along, unknown to his friends, was recorded in his private journal, which spawned keen interest, particularly from an unexpected quarter—the leading psychologists of the day. The journal was something yet unseen, a lifelong case history of a certain type of personality, which could be excerpted out of context to prove a point for any number of emerging psychological theories. To Dugas he was detached, *depersonalized,* to Pierre Janet he likely manifested "psychasthenia" and its characteristic *sentiment d'incompletude* (experience of incompleteness), and still others saw his life as incorporating an unlikely combination of Christian and Buddhist belief systems. But above all, his writing reflects a personal life that is symptomatic of the indecision and dysfunction so often caused by depersonalization disorder.

Amiel's depersonalization did not often manifest itself in numbness or lack of feeling. He felt things deeply. But a predominant theme permeates his journal: The world and everything in it, including his personal identity, felt unreal, unfounded, and without substance. True reality, he concluded, beyond the veil of the day-to-day world, consisted of the eternal, the infinite, God. The more the self disappeared, the closer one came to the truth and to God, he rationalized.

Theologically, these are not original thoughts and are shared by Buddhists, Hindus, and certain New Age enthusiasts of today. But Amiel's conclusions are not the result of meditation or religious training. He *feels* the absence of an individual self, and, at times, this translates into an illusive but heart-felt connection with the Infinite. While he eloquently voices the importance of this distinctly non-European point of view, one is not always sure whether he is trying to convince the reader or himself.

"Be everything while being nothing." Amiel writes, early in the journal, "effacing thyself, letting God enter into thee as the air enters an empty vessel, reducing the ego to the mere vessel which contains the divine essence."[3]

Most of his language is less preachy—less a justification of the empty feeling he is unable to shake. Reflecting on an afternoon meeting with some fellow intellectuals, Amiel makes a keen observation that is more typical of his prose: "Nothing is more hidden from us than the illusion which lives with us day by day, and our greatest illusion is to believe that we are what we think ourselves to be" (p. 84).

While many of Amiel's written observations are highly quotable and are used by writers and scholars to this day, his journal consistently and eloquently expresses the experience of chronic, lifelong depersonalization above all else. In this regard, Amiel's story is best captured by excerpts from his journal:

> I can find no words for what I feel. My consciousness is withdrawn into itself; I hear my heart beating, and my life passing. It seems to me that I have become a statue on the banks of the river of time, that I am the spectator of some mystery, and shall issue from it old, or no longer capable of age. . . . I am, a spectator, so to speak, of the molecular whirlwind which men call individual life; I am conscious of an incessant metamorphosis; an irresistible movement of existence, which is going on within me—and this phenomenology of myself serves as a window opened upon the mystery of the world. . . .
>
> What is it which has always come between real life and me? What glass screen has, as it were, interposed itself between me and the enjoyment, the possession, the contact of things, leaving me only the *role* of the looker-on? False shame, no doubt. I have been ashamed to desire. Fatal results of timidity, aggravated by intellectual delusion! Fear, too, has had a large share in it—*La peur de ce que j'aime est ma fatalite.* [The fear of what I love is my fatality] (vol. 1, p.liii, vol. 2 p. 145)

This sentiment in many ways reflects the behavior of some chronically depersonalized people, whose robotic actions stem from inhibition—a desire to act and appear normal for fear that bursts of creativity, eccentricities, or iconoclastic behavior might in fact be symptomatic of insanity or might reveal to others some kind of secret mental problem. As a result, many depersonalized people live more conservatively than they would otherwise. For Amiel, robotlike behavior is a matter of going through the motions of his job and private literary exercises that never blossom into a literary statement beyond the confines of his journal.

In the 1880s Amiel began to express frustration at the lack of achievement that resulted from his obsessive self-examination.

> I am afraid of greatness. All my published literary essays, therefore, are little else than studies, games, exercises, for the purpose of testing myself. I play scales, as it were: I run up and down my instrument, I train my hand, and make sure of its capacity and skill. But the work itself remains unachieved. My effort expires, and, satisfied with the power to act, I never arrive at the will to act, I am always preparing and never accomplishing and my energy is swallowed up in a kind of barren curiosity. . . I understand myself, but I do not approve myself. (vol. 1, p. 90)

Unfortunately for this gentle, sensitive man, instead of being instilled by his intelligence and insight with a sense of confidence and faith, his chronic introspection brought only loneliness, regret, and self-contradiction. He fills the journal with some entries that praise the value of ego-death, while other entries decry his lack of ambition and motivation and the mediocrity of his accomplishments in the academic and literary world. This dichotomy between earthly ambition and selfless, eternal unification with God, locked him in a kind of "analysis paralysis" his entire life.

Amiel became a fussy perfectionist, and because he couldn't write the perfect novel, he didn't write one at all. Because he couldn't find the perfect wife, he never married. And through it all, he obsessed about existence itself, convinced of how little his life in the world mattered because he never really felt himself to be part of it.

Mrs. Humphrey Ward, a noted literati of the time, and the translator of Amiel's work, says in her 1906 introduction:

> There were certain characteristics in Amiel which made it [success] impossible—which neutralized his powers, his knowledge, his

intelligence, and condemned him, so far as his public performance was concerned, to barrenness and failure. . . . All of the pleasant paths which traverse the kingdom of Knowledge, in which so many of us find shelter and life-long means of happiness, led Amiel straight into the wilderness of abstract speculation.[4]

Perhaps. But his writing also revealed an exceptional degree of self-awareness and truth. In May 1880, Amiel wrote:

Inadaptability, due either to mysticism or stiffness, delicacy or disdain, is the misfortune . . . the characteristic of my life. I have not been able to fit myself to anything, to content myself with anything. I have never had the quantum of illusion necessary for risking the irreparable. I have made use of the ideal itself to keep me from any kind of bondage. It was thus with marriage; only perfection would have satisfied me; and, on the other hand, I was not worthy of perfection. . . . So that, finding no satisfaction in things, I tried to extirpate desire, by which things enslave us. Independence has been my refuge; detachment my stronghold. I have lived the impersonal life—in the world, yet not in it, thinking much, desiring nothing. It is a state of mind which corresponds with what in women is called a broken heart; and it is in fact like it, since the characteristic common to both is despair. When one knows that one will never possess what one could have loved, and that one can be content with nothing less, one has, so to speak, left the world, one has cut the golden hair, parted with all that makes human life—that is to say, illusion—the incessant effort towards an apparently attainable end. (vol. 2, p. 288)

Amiel is virtually incapable of the self-deceptions that "normal" people utilize for survival or in striving toward worldly goals set by their individual egos. It has been impossible for him to play act in a day-to-day world that seems pointless and unreal.

Near the end of some 30 years of philosophical comments, in his 50s, Amiel provides the reader with some important insight into the origins of his lifelong state of mind:

Since the age of 16 onwards I have been able to look at things with the eyes of a blind man recently operated upon. That is to say, I have been able to suppress in myself the results of the long education of sight, and to abolish distances; and now I find myself regarding existence as though from beyond the tomb, from another world; all is strange to me; I am, as it were, outside my own body and individuality; I am *depersonalized*, detached, cut adrift. Is this madness? No. Madness means the impossibility of recovering one's normal balance after the mind has thus played truant among alien forms of being, and followed Dante to invisible worlds. Madness means incapacity for self-judgement and self-control. Whereas it seems to me that my mental transformations are but philosophical experiences. (vol 2, p. 304; emphasis in original)

In this paragraph, Amiel unintentionally gives birth to the term that is the subject of this book, while exhibiting the "reality testing" that additionally marks the condition. Ludovic Dugas, and others, picking up on the term, which fit so well with their Amiel-like patients, took all that he wrote quite literally. As J.C. Nemiah, MD, said,

What is of particular interest in the journal entry quoted [above] is Amiel's awareness that his capacity for insight into his condition was maintained throughout all the alterations of his perceptions of himself and the world. He also recognized that no matter how bizarre his experiences were, the preservation of insight kept them clearly out of the realm of madness. . . . Amiel's perceptive introspection revealed to him a clinical truth about depersonalization that remains a central element of the modern concept of the disorder: Patients have a keen and unfailing awareness of the disturbances in their sense of reality. . . .There appears in depersonalization to be a heightening of the psychic energy invested in the self-observing ego, the mental function on which rests the capacity for insight.[5]

Some contemporary psychiatrists have suggested that Dugas and others took Amiel too literally. The *Journal Intime* is more philosophic than symptomatic of a syndrome, they contend. But patients who have been exposed to the whole life-changing aspects of the condition would strongly disagree.

Elena Bezubbova is a psychiatrist who has studied depersonalization in Russia, treating more than 100 patients. She has also become an authority on many of the underlying themes of depression and detachment in Russian literature. As she points out,

Amiel exhibits the things that are psycho-pathologically primordial about depersonalization—the existential essence of the experience. Depersonalization is one of the very few, if not the only state, which discloses the basic, elementary fabric of being, the feeling of this fabric, the experience of this fabric. The tragedy is that depersonalization discloses itself in a "negative form," as absence, such as inner pain after an amputation, which still tells us about something we once had, but lost. With depersonalization the individual does not know exactly what he had, but still experiences something that is "lost." That is why depersonalization can be so painfully hopeless, groundless. That is why there are no words to express because literally, there *are* no words in language to express it.

Still, Amiel, and others that followed, came as close as language permits, and often, what seems like ethereal prose or languid self-pity to some people is in fact poignant, insightful, and a great comfort to others striving to put their own confounding sensations into words.

Ironically, through his private diary, Amiel accomplished some of the recognition that eluded him all his life. Today he is well known in Europe, and he even has a street named after him in France. More important, his themes of depersonalization and an inexplicable, egoless unification with the infinite, pleasant or not, were destined to repeat themselves in other, far different written works of the century to come. The significance of the dissipation of the self would gain more interest for mass audiences in the twentieth century, when it would be opened to numerous new voices.

Existentialism and Pure Reality

Amiel's lifelong depersonalization illustrates the frustration and sorrow that can result from living with one foot in this world and one foot in some other. His doors of perception were apparently cleansed, at times, with the infinite becoming overly apparent, yet the revelation was, in his eyes, fruitless. Others would express their encounters with complete depersonalization, and what has been called *le coup de vide* (the blow of the void) through different eyes. For Amiel, it was a quiet, all-encompassing shift in perception occurring at around age 16, according to his account. Sometimes, however, this shift can be ferocious and near debilitating. Nowhere is this more accurately depicted than in the novel *Nausea*, by the French writer and philosopher Jean Paul Sartre.[6]

Sartre's name invariably comes up in any discussion of the philosophy of existentialism. The term "existential angst" is something of a cliché to modern culture, more suggestive of Woody Allen movies than a serious topic of discussion. But despite its connotation of nervousness and negativity, existentialism is a philosophy with a positive message of ultimate responsibility for one's own actions. This message emerges from certain realizations about being that are expectedly frightening, and which unfortunately associate the term with a meaninglessness existence, atheism, and the like. Depersonalized people don't have to study philosophy to know about existential angst, they *feel* it, in a way not imaginable to most intellectuals.

Existentialism is seen by its proponents as a way to react *against* depersonalization, as caused by the modern world's dehumanization of the individual. Interestingly, however, several of the best known existentialist writers depict depersonalization in their fictional characters so poignantly and realistically that one wonders if they suffered from the disorder themselves. One could speculate that if they did, a disorder gave birth, at least in part, to an entire philosophy.

While his intentions were philosophical, Sartre portrayed the misery of head-on encounters with pure depersonalization in his first, and arguably best, novel, *Nausea*. Nothing in literature or in case histories quite equals this novel because, unlike Amiel's *Journal Intime*, it is not a written recording of feelings and thoughts, but thoughts as they happen. It is not a clinical review, but the voice of depersonalization unfolding second by second in an individual's consciousness.

Nausea is the story of a French history student and writer, Antoine Roquentin, who is inexplicably horrified at his own existence. Told in an impressionistic style, using the device of a diary that has been unearthed, the story is within Roquentin, who interprets even mundane daily life in the provincial town of Bouville (Mudville) as unreal, or *too* real, and consequently, nauseating. He even names the sickening sensations that build to a terrifying crescendo in his consciousness—"the filth."

"Things are bad!" the character Roquentin writes at one juncture. "Things are very bad: I have it, the filth, the Nausea. And this time it is new: it caught me in a café. Until now, cafés were my only refuge because they were full of people and well lighted: now there won't even be that anymore" (p. 18).

Written in 1935, *Nausea* occurs in a far removed time and place, but
Roquentin's overconsciousness and overanalysis will be immediately familiar
to depersonalized individuals today, as exemplified by this chilling excerpt:

> I buy a newspaper along my way. Sensational news. Little Luc-
> ienne's body has been found. Smell of ink, the paper crumples
> between my fingers. The criminal has fled. The child was raped.
> They found her body, the fingers clawing at the mud. I roll the
> paper into a ball, my fingers clutching at the paper; smell of ink;
> my God how strongly things exist today. Little Lucienne was raped.
> Strangled. Her body still exists, her flesh bleeding. She no longer
> exists. Her hands. She no longer exists. The houses. I walk be-
> tween the houses, I am between the houses, on the pavement; the
> pavement under my feet exists, the houses close around me, as the
> water closes over me, on the paper the shape of a swan. I am. I
> am. I exist, I think, therefore I am; I am because I think, why do I
> think? I don't want to think any more, I am because I think that I
> don't want to be, I think that I. . . . because. . . . ugh! I flee. (p. 100)

Precious little occurs in *Nausea* in terms of plot. Roquentin's mind *is* the
plot, which reaches an important denouement late in the book. Wandering
near a town beach, the protagonist sees *through* those things being enjoyed
by everyone else. It fills him with cynicism and disgust:

> I turn back, lean both hands on the balustrade. The true sea is
> cold and black, full of animals; it crawls under this thin green film
> made to deceive human beings. The sylphs all round me have let
> themselves be taken in; they only see the thin film, which proves
> the existence of God. I see beneath it! The veneer melts, the shin-
> ing velvety scales, the scales of God's catch explode everywhere
> at my look, they split and gape. Here is the Saint-Elemir tramway,
> I turn round and the objects turn with me, pale and green as oys-
> ters. (p. 124)

He boards the tram aimlessly and continues:

> I lean my hand on the seat and pull it back hurriedly: it exists.
> This thing I'm sitting on, leaning my hand on is called a seat.
> They made it purposefully for people to sit on. . . . I murmur: "It's

a seat," a little like an exorcism. But the words stay on my lips: it refuses to go and put itself on the thing. . . . It could just as well be a dead donkey . . . and I could be sitting on the donkey's belly, my feet dangling in the clear water. Things are divorced from their names. They are there, grotesque, headstrong, gigantic and it seems ridiculous to call them seats or say anything at all about them: I am in the midst of things, nameless things. Alone, without words, defenseless, they surround me, are beneath me, behind me, above me. They demand nothing, they don't impose themselves: they are there. (p. 125)

Roquentin's heady overconsciousness and hyperawareness of objects and the names assigned to them builds into claustrophobic urgency until he plows past the conductor and jumps off the tram before it has time to stop. He finds himself in a park, where his phenomenological quest climaxes, in view of a massive chestnut tree. An all-important change finally occurs:

I drop onto a bench between great black tree trunks, between the black, knotty hands reaching towards the sky. A tree scrapes at the earth under my feet with a black nail. I would so like to let myself go, forget myself, sleep. But I can't, I'm suffocating: existence penetrates me everywhere, through the eyes, the nose, the mouth. . . .

And suddenly, suddenly, the view is torn away, I have understood, I have *seen*. (p. 126)

Later, he analyzes what has happened:

I can't say I feel relieved or satisfied; just the opposite, I am crushed. Only my goal is reached: I know what I wanted to know; I have understood all that has happened to me since January. The Nausea has not left me and I don't believe it will leave me soon; but I no longer have to bear it, it is no longer an illness or a passing fit: it is I. . . .

. . . in the park just now. The roots of the chestnut tree were sunk in the ground just under my bench. I couldn't remember it was a root any more. The words had vanished, and with them the significance of things . . . I was sitting, stooping forward, head bowed, alone in front of this black, knotty mass, entirely beastly, which frightened me. Then I had this vision.

It left me breathless. Never, until these last few days, had I
understood the meaning of "existence . . ." (pp. 126, 127)

Roquentin spends several pages formulating a theory about what has
been revealed to him and consequently liberated him: the realization that
existence is only in the moment, that everything else past or present or connected to a name is an illusion. Things and names are "in the way."

For both Amiel and Roquentin, feeling unreal has become a glimpse into
a different, and in their eyes, a *true* reality—timeless and free of our subjec-
tivity—seen with the filter of the ego removed. Amiel's perception includes
infinite love and a Deity, Roquentin's does not. But unlike Amiel, Roquentin
refuses to let this glimpse behind the façade of life lock him in limbo, stuck
between two worlds. Instead, he sees complete freedom and a call to action.
By the end of *Nausea,* his manner of action becomes clear. He decides to
devote his life to writing. Clearly, Sartre himself followed that path, not by
creating an introspective diary, but rather by giving voice to a philosophy.

Basing his conception of self-consciousness loosely on philosopher Martin Heidegger's thoughts on being, Sartre proceeds to sharply delineate between conscious actions ("for themselves") and unconscious ("in themselves").
It is a conscious choice, he claims, to live one's life "authentically" and in a
unified fashion, or not—this is the fundamental freedom of our lives.

Sartre's language, in French or an English translation, can be dense and
overbearing to the average reader. A simpler expression of existentialism, and
another manifestation of depersonalization, gained notoriety not too long
after *Nausea,* and through it, nearly every high school student has been exposed to depersonalization unawares. Published in 1942, Albert Camus's *The
Stranger* portrays the deadness of an unfeeling, robotlike existence. On first
reading, students are often struck by the indifferent and blasé attitude of the
character Mearsault, apparent in the very first lines of the novel: "Mother died
today. Or, maybe, yesterday; I can't be sure. The telegram from the home says:
YOUR MOTHER PASSED AWAY, FUNERAL TOMORROW, DEEP SYMPATHY.
Which leaves the matter doubtful; it could have been yesterday."[7]

While in *Nausea,* the reader sees Roquentin throughout the process of
receiving complete, ego-diminishing depersonalization, the protagonist of
The Stranger is already existing within it. He is far beyond the anxiety and
ruminating preceding oneness or nothingness. There is no reality testing, nor
any mystical unification with an infinite being.

Dugas, in his study of depersonalization, described a patient much like

Mearsault, who "experienced a strong feeling of 'apathy' to the point that, according to him, had anything bad happened to his loved ones, he would only have felt unhappy in retrospect. Apathy can be so marked that patients will not struggle against any experience, however disturbing."[8] To a large degree, this defines Mearsault. Yet there is a philosophy behind his indifference. He lives in the moment, but without anxiety, without worry, only a knowledge that human life is absurd and meaningless, except for the present moment in which to live.

Again, describing a comparable patient, Dugas writes, "he lives in the present. He is thus able to adapt to new situations and to feel at ease anywhere; his ongoing perceptions fully occupy his attention and he is not obsessed by memories or ruminations about the past."[9]

Written during World War II and the German occupation of France, Camus's message was not intended to illustrate any kind of disorder. It was, rather, a message of resistance to the realistic tension of the German occupation, and beyond that, a world that is meaningless, absurd, and indifferent. The only answer for the individual is to rebel against the absurdity felt by the mind. Accordingly, Mearsault is not passively indifferent but rather actively avoidant of events, actions, and feelings.

In *The Stranger*, set in Algiers, Mearsault kills an Arab in a spontaneous reaction to the environment—the heat and glare of the sun. In the ensuing investigation, he is convicted mainly for his failure to show "proper feelings" for his deceased mother, rather than for the crime of murder. Aghast at his apparent lack of love, the jury condemns him to death. As a literary work, the novel develops the concept of the absurd and the belief that a person can still be happy in the face of the absurd. For Mearsault, the apathy and numbness of depersonalization are reactions to life itself. Life's absurdity is driven home by the way in which he is tried and convicted. Happiness remains only in the moment, in the ways in which he adapts to his prison cell, through a beam of sunshine coming into it, or from his ultimate "moral" victory over the blind mob awaiting his execution.

Although today, the "absurdity" of life may seem more like an observation of a jaded cynic or maladjusted teenager, it is also something that is often felt by depersonalized people. When looked at objectively, without emotion or full participation, most human activities, from going to work, to religious ceremonies, to daily bodily functions, do seem strange, if not absurd. Whatever his rationale, Camus chillingly depicted the apathy with which the depersonalized person can perceive the world.

Being in Nothingness

Other interpretations of *le coup de vide*, followed by or accompanying the sense of no-self, also emerged in the 1990s, concurrent with the increased popularity of New Age "theosophy," the attempt to bring together the traditions of eastern and western mystical traditions—something Amiel felt, but never formulated into doctrine. These included a flurry of books in the "Christian contemplative" tradition, as well as more secular works, which, lacking any specific genre, happened to fall under the New Age umbrella.

Contrary to popular assumptions, the Christian tradition goes beyond phenomena like St. Paul's being "blinded by the light." It also includes centuries-old mystical experiences involving the elimination of the individual self. This is somewhat different from the personal, conversant relationship with Christ that fundamentalists espouse today. In the 1860s, the writings of an obscure Jesuit priest, Jean-Pierre de Caussade, were published, more than a century after they were written. (He would certainly have been tried for heresy during his lifetime.) Commenting on the no-self experience, he wrote in 1731: "Often indeed God places certain souls in this state, which is called emptiness of the spirit or of the intelligence; it is also called: being in nothingness (*être dans le rien*). This annihilation of our own spirit disposes wonderfully to receive that of Jesus Christ. This mystical death of the operations of our own activity renders our soul apt for the reception of divine operations"[10]

More recently, Bernadette Roberts's *The Experience of No-Self* reflects this type of being, and hearkens to Amiel's desire to be an "empty vessel" filled with the presence of God. Roberts's writing describes her personal struggle with mysterious moments of deep, silent "stillness" that from early childhood she interpreted as the presence of God. To explore the source of this stillness, she entered a convent. But whenever she meditated in an effort to recapture it, she felt herself losing her identity, and suffered intense fear because of it.

"It was a fear of being engulfed forever, of being lost, annihilated, or blacking out and possibly never returning. In such moments, to ward off the fear, I would make some movement of abandoning my fate to God—a gesture of the will, a thought, some type of projection. And everytime I did this I would gradually return to my usual self—and security. Then, one day, this was not to be the case."[11]

Roberts writes of the no-self experience as a voyage, a "passageway" wherein panic reactions, emptiness, and depression are merely part of the trip to the final unity with God at the other end of a metaphoric tunnel. She was not unfamiliar with the psychological theories behind her strange feelings of emptiness, however, and recalled a book in which a psychologist described psychological "dissociation without compensation."

> At the time I could not imagine what he was talking about, but felt sure it was something terrible and was glad I had never known any condition as dire as this sounded. But here, during the Passage, I recalled the statement because it seemed to epitomize my present situation. . . . I took it for my own condition of being completely cut off (dissociated) from the known, the self, without any compensating factor to take the place of the void so encountered. It meant a state of no feelings, no energies, no movements, no insights, no seeing, no relationships with anything, nothing but absolute emptiness everywhere you turn. (p. 66)

After 9 years, she left the convent, married, and raised four children. The pervasive, periodic inner silences came and went, until, while visiting a monastery near her home, she experienced the stillness again and awaited "the onset of fear to break it up." But "instead of the usual unlocalized center of myself, there was nothing there, it was empty; and at that moment of seeing this there was a flood of quiet joy, and I knew, finally I knew what was missing—it was my *self*" (p. 23, emphasis in original).

Roberts's "passage" ultimately led her to a complete perceptual shift.

"When I visually focused in on a flower, an animal, another person, or any particular object, slowly the particularity would recede into a nebulous Oneness, so that the object's distinctness was lost to my mind. . . . it became impossible for the mind to perceive or retain any individuality when all visual objects either faded from the mind, gave way to something else, or were 'seen *through*'" (p. 36).

Strikingly similar to Roquentin's awakening by the chestnut tree, this type of changed perception is hard to manage. For Roberts, terror returned intermittently, but with a vengeance: "The silence within was not seen as freedom from self, rather, it was seen as an imprisoned self, a frozen, immovable self that was all part of the scene, part of the insidious nothingness choking the life out of everything. Even now it had frozen my body on the spot. How could I survive another moment?" (p. 48).

Then, while on a retreat, she made an effort to face it once and for all. Seeking to eliminate this demon through her usual meditative practices, the final experience is described much like an exorcism, or an orgasm.

My head grew hot, and all I could see were stars. My feet began to freeze. Finally I fell back against the hill in a convulsive condition with my heart beating wildly. . . . It took me a while to realize my body was lying still on the hill, because initially, I seemed not to have one. I knew a great change had taken place. . . .

God is neither the see-*er* or the seen, but the "seeing." . . . After a long passage, the mind had finally come to rest, and rejoice in its own understanding. . . . Now it was ready to take its rightful place in the immediacy and practicality of the now-moment.
(p. 92)

The View from the East

Ultimately, the stage was set for Roberts's depersonalization by a specific religious upbringing, intentional meditative practices, and reinforcement from clerics who were familiar with the traditions of Christian mysticism. This raises the issue of whether the depersonalization experience can be influenced by existing cultural biases. What happens when an atheist or non-Christian experiences essentially the same thing? Roquentin's encounter with the chestnut tree provides one answer. Suzanne Segal's *Collision with the Infinite* provides another.[12]

For many DPD sufferers, Segal's experiences hit closer to home than Roberts's perplexing spirituality. Segal's book centers on an event that occurred while boarding a bus in Paris in 1982. She was 27 years old and pregnant. As a young woman Segal had been involved with the transcendental meditation movement, which was trendy in the 1970s. After several years, however, she became disillusioned and left the organization entirely.

She then studied at the University of California-Berkeley, where after 2 years she gained a degree in English literature. She moved to Paris where she married and gave birth to a daughter. As she waited in line to get on the Paris bus, a life-altering event occurred. Suddenly she felt her ears pop, and was at once "enclosed in a kind of bubble" which cut her off from the rest of the scene, and left her acting and moving in the most mechanical way. In *Collision*, she describes that moment in detail:

I lifted my right foot to step up into the bus and collided head-on with an invisible force that entered my awareness like a silently

exploding stick of dynamite, blowing the door of my usual consciousness open and off its hinges, splitting me in two. In the
gaping space that appeared, what I had previously called "me" was
forcefully pushed out of its usual location inside me into a new
location that was approximately a foot behind and to the left of
my head. "I" was now behind my body looking out at the world
without using the body's eyes. (p. 49)

Walking home from that bus ride, she felt like a "cloud of awareness" was
following her body. The cloud was a "witness" located behind her and completely separate from body, mind, and emotions. The witness was constant
and so was fear, the fear of complete physical dissolution. The next morning,
when nothing had changed, she wondered if she was going insane, and if she
would ever be herself again.

What Segal then refers to as the "witnessing" continued for months, and
her only relief came in sleep, into which she "plunged for as long and as often
as possible." She explains, "In sleep, the mind finally stopped pumping out its
unceasing litany of terror, and the witness was left to witness an unconscious
mind" (p. 53).

Recalling her earlier experiences with transcendental meditation, it occurred to her that this might be some kind of "cosmic consciousness," something her guru had described to her as the first stage of "awakened awareness." But it seemed impossible to her that this hellish realm could have
anything to do with an enlightened state.

After months of the presence of this mystifying witness, it disappeared,
Segal writes, leaving her in a new state that was far more baffling, and consequently more terrifying, than the experience of the preceding months. "The
disappearance of the witness meant the disappearance of the last vestiges of
the experience of personal identity. The witness had at least held a location
for a 'me,' albeit a distant one. In the dissolution of the witness, there was literally no more experience of a 'me' at all. The experience of personal identity
switched off and was never to appear again" (p.54).

Although internally Segal knew that she had changed radically, no one
else noticed. She functioned as smoothly as ever, "as if there were an unseen
doer who acted perfectly" (p. 65). She even managed to earn a doctorate in
psychology in the years to follow. And yet, she writes, "The oddest moments
occurred when any reference was made to my name. If I had to write it on a
check or sign it on a letter, I would stare at the letters on the paper and the

mind would drown in perplexity. The name referred to no one. There was no Suzanne Segal anymore; perhaps there never had been" (p. 55).

She consulted psychiatrists in an attempt to understand what had happened to her. Some diagnosed her with depersonalization disorder. Others had no clear explanation. As she lived in this mysterious state day after day, she became increasingly filled with fear. "Everything seemed to be dissolving right in front of my eyes, constantly. Emptiness was everywhere, seeping through the pores of every face I gazed upon, flowing through the crevices of seemingly solid objects. The body, mind, speech, thoughts, and emotions were all empty; they had no ownership, no person behind them. I was utterly bereft of all my previous notions of reality" (p. 63).

She later reasoned that the fear that pervaded her life forever after the "bus hit" came from the mind's attempts to make sense of what had happened to her. She reasoned that the mind created fear because it had lost control of the illusion of the person Suzanne Segal.

In time, a further shift occurred. Driving though a wintry landscape, she observed, "everything seemed more fluid. The mountains, trees, rocks, birds, sky, were all losing their differences. As I gazed about, what I saw first was how they were one; then, as a second wave of perception, I saw the distinctions. From that day forth I have had the constant experience of both moving through and being made of the 'substance' of everything" (p. 130).

She got in touch with spiritual teachers within the California Buddhist community and gained additional reassurance, which helped ease the non-stop fear she had previously endured. They also provided explanations in the form of Buddhist teachings regarding *anatta* (no-self) and *shunyata* (emptiness). Her kind of no-self experience was not only understood, something like it was actually being cultivated, through daily regimens of rituals and meditations by those wanting to follow certain spiritual paths.

Buddhism, she felt, provided a plausible explanation for it all. In simplistic terms, the Buddhist interpretation states that "personality functions" remain even when one's self has disappeared. These are known as *skandhas* or "aggregates," and include form, feelings, perceptions, thoughts, and consciousness. Their interaction creates the *illusion* of self. They do not actually make up the self. There is no self, Buddhism claims. When the truth of the *skandhas* is revealed, as suddenly happened to Segal at the bus stop, it is seen that there is no self, only the *skandhas* still functioning as they function; the truth is that they are empty, they don't constitute a self, but their interaction creates the illusion of self. In Tibetan Buddhism this is known as "realization of emptiness," in Zen Buddhism it is known as realizing "no mind." (There have been Western explanations through the years, notably the philosopher Alan Watts's *Wisdom of Insecurity* and *The Book*, in which he explains ancient Vedantic traditions of "oneness" and no-self through metaphors and in simple English.)

Buddhism stresses that changes of consciousness be met in stages: devotion (*saddha*), discipline (*sila*), detachment (*caga*), and depersonalization (*panna*). The rituals and self-preparation are essential lifelong processes, with depersonalization as the final goal. Understandably, an unplanned, unexpected fast-track to *panna* could be quite terrifying, even with some knowledge of Buddhism.

When Segal's "collision with the infinite" became widely known, she received numerous "congratulations" from spiritual teachers, both East and West. From India, the well-known guru Poonjaji wrote, "In between the arrival of the bus and your waiting to board, there was the Void where there was no past or future. This Void revealed itself *to* itself. This is a wonderful experience. It has to stay eternally with you. This is perfect freedom. You have become *(moksha)* of the realized sages" (p. 122).

Closer to home, one of Poonjaji's American-born disciples (who took the name Gangaji) reassured her: "This realization of the inherent emptiness— which is pure consciousness—of all phenomena is true fulfillment. In the face of conditioned existence, much fear can be initially felt. Ultimately, the fear is also revealed to be only that same empty consciousness" (p. 122).

Unfortunately for Segal, the fear which had disappeared eventually returned with renewed intensity. (Recall that this happened to Bernadette Roberts as well.) She stopped all public appearances and withdrew into virtual seclusion. She continued meeting with fellow therapists and, in time, revealed that she had suffered a long history of migraine headaches, and, to the surprise of many, she began to recover memories of abuse during her childhood. She died in 1997 of a brain tumor.

Through a Glass, Darkly

Suzanne Segal's recovered memories of childhood abuse, as well as her migraines and brain tumor, raise the question of whether she was in fact on the path to enlightenment or suffering a classic dissociative response to early trauma or disorders of her brain. Does this make her experience less valid?

Would her spiritual leaders take back their congratulatory comments as a result? Should they be congratulating all DPD patients? Unfortunately, Segal passed away before the things she revealed so late in her life could be explored further. But her revelations do raise the question of whether changes in brain chemistry are the *cause* of unusual events, visions, or no-self experiences like Segal's, or merely the physiological phenomena corresponding to such things, irrelevant to their validity.

One well-known twentieth century writer, Aldous Huxley, was intrigued by changes in brain chemistry, as reflected in his novels *Brave New World* and *Island*. Fascinated by both natural and synthesized psychedelic drugs as tools for intentionally changing perception, Huxley's most famous work on the subject was *The Doors of Perception*, published with a second lengthy essay, *Heaven and Hell* in 1954.[13] Although his writings do not involve depersonalization as a disorder, *The Doors of Perception* does describe the unreality and loss of the individual self, not spontaneously, but through the use of psychedelics, specifically the cactus-derived substance mescaline.

Huxley rekindles a theory that the functions of the brain, nervous system, and sense organs are primarily eliminative, rather than productive. In other words, instead of absorbing all information like a sponge, they are designed to keep information that is not of practical use *out*, for the sake of survival.

> Each person is at each moment capable of remembering all that
> has ever happened to him and of perceiving everything that is
> happening everywhere in the universe. The function of the brain
> and nervous system is to protect us from being overwhelmed and
> confused by this mass of largely useless and irrelevant knowledge.
> . . . According to such a theory, each one of us is potentially Mind
> at Large.[14]

However, to make biological survival possible, "mind at large" has to be funneled through the reducing valve of the brain and nervous system. "What comes out the other end is a measly trickle of the kind of consciousness which will help us to stay alive on the surface of this particular planet" (p. 23).

This kind of speculation can be compelling to depersonalized people trying to make sense of their feelings of "mind emptiness" and hollowness. With such disturbing and unrelenting feelings, it's natural to wonder if somehow the reducing valves have broken open in preparation for something special to enter in. Unfortunately, however, that feeling of hollowness in the head is a thing unto itself, a preparation for something that never comes.

Huxley continues his reductive theory by saying that man, in order to express his highly reduced awareness, "has invented and endlessly elaborated those symbol systems and implicit philosophies we call languages" (p. 23). Each individual benefits, but also pays heavily for this linguistic tradition, the argument goes. We benefit because language gives us access to the records of other peoples' experiences; we suffer because it makes us believe that our "reduced awareness" is the *only* awareness. These linguistic limitations, as we've seen, clearly apply to attempts to describe the otherworldly aspects of depersonalization, which must ultimately rely on comparisons and metaphors.

Certain drugs can open the doors of the mind so this different awareness can take hold, Huxley felt. Cultures around the world used mescaline, peyote, or hashish for this very purpose in their religious rites. But, in addition, these doors seem to swing open for the special genius of certain artists or visionaries.

Huxley was not as interested in losing his self in the Buddhist sense as he was in transcending his own limited consciousness to visit the less ordinary worlds of visionaries and creative geniuses like William Blake or Johann Sebastian Bach. In the presence of an investigator/companion and a tape recorder, he ingested mescaline and waited to record its effects, which were ultimately recounted in *The Doors of Perception.*

The onset of a new, different perception began with a simple vase in the room, which contained a rose, a carnation, and an iris. He had noticed the colorful flowers earlier in the day, but now, under the influence of mescaline, he writes, he was not just looking at an unusual flower arrangement.

> *I was seeing what Adam had seen on the morning of his creation—*
> *the miracle, moment by moment of naked existence.* . . . I continued
> to look at the flowers, and in their living light I seemed to detect
> the qualitative equivalent of breathing—but of a breathing without
> returns to a starting point, with no recurrent ebbs but only a re-
> peated flow from beauty to heightened beauty, from deeper to ever
> deeper meaning. (p. 17)

All the words Huxley had known from Buddhism—Mind, Suchness, the Void, the Godhead—now seemed completely understandable, he says, as reality was being experienced moment to moment by a "blessed 'not-I'" (p. 19).

Spatial relationships meant nothing while under mescaline. The mind was primarily concerned not with measures and locations, but with being and meaning. And along with indifference to space there went an even more complete indifference to time.

Visually, what Huxley experienced was not an hallucination, but a look at existing things that took on a Van Gogh-like intensity when perceived through different eyes. Secrets that were hidden, seen only as if "through a glass, but darkly," to use the biblical phrase, with the help of mescaline seemed not only clear and bright, but intensely detailed, as if the glass had become an electron microscope.

Whether this is the same "pure reality" initially perceived with terror by Sartre's Roquentin, or by Roberts, Segal, and many people today living with intense derealization, or whether it constitutes some form of higher knowledge will no doubt be a long-running topic of philosophical debate.

One 43-year-old writer who has experienced depersonalization chronically for more than 20 years has created his own metaphor to describe his feelings about higher consciousness: "To me depersonalization seems to have been my mind tapping at the door of some mystical experience, or even some kind of higher knowledge. But it never got in because it didn't know the password. So it walked away and decided it was just sick. The mind never knew what amazing things lay on the other side of that door, nor how to access them."

While Huxley could indeed articulate the ecstatic nature of his own experiences in compelling language, he was not so naïve to think that there could not also be a dark side to opening the doors of perception. In *Heaven and Hell*, he brings up the point that visionary experience is not always pleasant. Hellish images and feelings can come from within or without as easily as sacred ones.

"Sanity is a matter of degree," Huxley writes, "and for some, the universe can be transfigured—but for the worse. Everything in it, from the stars in the sky to the dust under their feet, is unspeakably sinister or disgusting; every event is charged with a hateful significance; every object manifests the presence of an In-swelling Horror, infinite, all-powerful, eternal."[15]

While this negatively transfigured world has from time to time found its way into literature and the arts, such as in Kafka's stories and in the "writhing" within Van Gogh's later landscapes, Huxley adds, it is also accompanied by bodily sensations. Blissful visions usually involve a pleasant sense of separation from the body, a "feeling of deindividualization" that is not disturbing, while in negative visionary experiences the body becomes more and more dense, more tightly packed.[16] (This seems to parallel Bernadette Roberts's alternating experiences of "freedom from self" and "imprisoned self.")

Unfortunately, "deindividualization" manifests itself as unpleasant more often than not. People subjected to it are not looking for a visionary experience nor an opportunity to detach from their previous selves. The result is much more hellish than heavenly, as evidenced by so many of today's personal accounts.

The Alice in Wonderland Syndrome

Huxley's novels and essays are important because they sparked in popular culture an intellectual and literary inquiry into territories previously reserved for scientists, shamans, and anthropologists. While his novels were universally applauded as prophetic and visionary, his essays, by today's standards, may seem more in the realm of pseudoscience. But they did lay the groundwork for further explorations of the mind and the self through psychedelic drugs in the years to come.

In the early 1950s, before writing *The Doors of Perception*, Huxley was trying his hand at screenwriting and living in the Santa Monica Canyon west of Los Angeles. This area was part of the literary L.A. scene at the time and hosted such full or part-time residents as Huxley and his wife Laura, novelists Christopher Isherwood, Charles Bukowski, and periodically, Henry Miller, Anaïs Nin, and the Beat poet Allen Ginsberg. Also living in the neighborhood was Ginsberg's cousin, a psychiatrist named Oscar Janiger.

Janiger's primary interests as a doctor and scientist were the study of consciousness, the origins of creativity, and the mysterious nature of something he had experienced himself as a teenager in upstate New York—depersonalization.

It was inevitable that Janiger and Huxley would become acquainted before long, and they quickly learned that in addition to the obvious, they shared an interest in something else—a derivative from ergot, which, discovered by Albert Hofmann while working for the Swiss firm Sandoz Laboratories, came to be known as LSD-25.

More than a decade before the drug would make its way into popular culture amidst Timothy Leary's mantra of "turn on, tune in, drop out," LSD was seen as possibly being a viable key to help unlock the doors of schizophrenia and other mental illnesses. Many people were interested in exploring its potential. But in 1954, Janiger began the first and largest comprehensive study of LSD, involving more than 950 volunteer men and women from all walks of life, ranging in age from 18 to 81.[17] Like Huxley, Janiger was interested in tapping into those areas of the mind that might harbor untapped creative potential or provide glimpses into a broader reality than perceived in normal day-to-day life.

Each of the subjects was carefully screened for preexisting psychological problems and general health. The setting for their LSD session was not clinical, but rather in the ambient surroundings of a rented house and its small patio and garden. Objects in the room were limited to a few paintings, record albums, and assorted bric-a-brac. Another room was set up with art supplies for the purpose of a substudy involving artists. For the hundred or so people who used this room, a colorful deer kachina doll served as a solitary model.

Each subject was asked to write his or her impressions on small note cards and then give a full report of their experience later. Janiger stayed nearby to monitor the experience but did not interfere with it. The artists were asked for two renderings of the kachina doll, one before LSD, one during. After the last of the sessions was completed, some 8 years later, piles and piles of neatly stacked note cards, tapes, and all data pertinent to the study remained in Janiger's files for nearly 40 years. A few minor scholarly papers reviewed some of the study's findings, but it wasn't long before LSD was a pariah, unobtainable legally, and a major drug of abuse within the 1960s counterculture and beyond.

In the 1990s, however, new and unbiased interest in the positive uses of LSD began to enjoy a renaissance. Janiger passed away in 2001, but the complete record of his LSD experiments was published posthumously in 2003 in a book co-written with medical anthropologist Marlene Dobkin de Rios.[18] The published results of the study, which give detailed accounts of a broad spectrum of LSD-induced phenomenon, have relevance to the study of depersonalization today:

> Of all the big changes you notice, the change in self-concept and body image is most immense. You feel at first no definite sharp location of yourself. This you, which stands outside yourself, shows no rigid shape. You feel dissociated and removed. Things, yourself, feel strange. You may have a strange reaction to the mirror, as if seeing a stranger. You feel able to step out of the rented costume of the self you held rigidly within narrow bounds.[19]

The subjects' recorded notes about their LSD experiences involved things that were novel then, but more widely familiar today, such as visual disturbances, vibrant colors, intensity of music, sense of "oneness" with the universe, and sensations of detachment and depersonalization.

Condensed comments regarding depersonalization included: "I'm inside of me and outside of me at the same time . . . My self boundaries seemed to expand until other people or objects were included within myself . . . I seem to be able to watch myself like an observer . . . My voice has a detached quality . . . Funny things happen to your sense of ego. A sort of double personality permits me to be and at the same time to observe from the outside."[20]

Interestingly, of the hundreds of volunteers, some of whom suffered anxiety, terror, and the fearful hallucinations that can accompany a "bad trip," none felt that the dissociative or depersonalization aspects of the trip were difficult or unpleasant. One subject, in fact, wanted to be under LSD's influence while having a tooth pulled because of its intense dissociative effects.

Also, no cases of chronic depersonalization were reported after the fact, even though there have been claims by some patients in recent years of LSD having served as a trigger for the condition. Factors affecting this outcome may include the dosage and purity of the drug used in the study, the setting, and the fact that all participants were carefully screened. This may also support the argument that victims of DPD harbor a preexisting tendency toward the condition. For them, LSD can serve as a trigger; for people in this study who had no such predisposition, the depersonalization was transient, expected, and even pleasant.

Perhaps the most interesting findings of the study involved artists' portrayals of the kachina doll. Most often, the pre-LSD renderings were realistic, predictable, and drawn to scale. They also often reflected an artist's known style. The LSD-inspired paintings and drawings were abstract, brighter, more emotionally compelling, and nonrepresentational.

Many theories were and can be evolved from these findings. But to the artists, it was as if for the first time, they were free of their individual selves, with all the learned behavior, repetitive ruts, and "baggage" to which they had become accustomed in daily life. It was as if for the first time they were able to fuse their self with the object being perceived. They no longer experienced time or space, but became, with the kachina doll, a new, pure reality. For the first time they understood what Picasso meant when he said, "When you paint an apple, you should *be* an apple."[21] Obviously, this type of phenomenon appears not to be the negative depersonalization from which so many suffer, but rather a positive manifestation of the detached, no-self experience.

Janiger and de Rios provide one explanation: "People suffering from depersonalization have a permeable membrane between their consciousness and their unconscious. They are not 'crazy', but the world often looks very different to them than to other people. Such individuals do have a curtain between these layers, but at times the boundary is quite permeable and frightening, while at other times its permeability is quite gratifying."[22]

These rarer, gratifying times, the authors suggest, are when the depersonalization experience can be used by artists or writers for whom the terms genius or visionary are reserved—people like William Blake, James Joyce, Franz Kafka, Van Gogh, and hundreds of other writers, artists, and musicians throughout history. The idea that you must lose the individual self first and foremost, then emerge anew like the phoenix, may apply not only to climbing the ladder of spiritual enlightenment, but to the steps toward unique artistic vision as well. Despite the common notion of success going hand-in-hand with a strong ego, complete depersonalization, even in its negative form, may be a prelude to something far beyond conventional success. Ironically, the thinking goes, artists who may somehow have shed their individual selves may ultimately produce great works of individuality. This is not an unfounded nor unexplored notion. The concept, in part, was examined in the mid-1950s by the young British writer Colin Wilson in a book called *The Outsider.*[23]

As an unusual blend of literary criticism and fresh take on existential philosophy, *The Outsider* examined the lives and work of certain people who made a lasting impact on their respective creative fields. It also peered into the psyches of the fictional characters created by these people. From Dostoevsky to Camus to Tolstoy to Nietzsche to the Russian dancer Nijinsky, the subjects of *The Outsider* all share an inherent detachment from day-to-day reality.

"What can be said to characterize the outsider is a sense of strangeness, or unreality. Even Keats could write, in a letter to Brown just before he died: 'I feel as if I had died already, and am now living a posthumous existence.' This is the sense of unreality, that can strike out of perfectly clear sky . . . And once a man has seen it, the world can never afterwards be quite the same straightforward place."[24]

"The Outsider is not sure who he is," Wilson states. "He has found an 'I' but it is not his true 'I.' His main business is to find his way back to himself" (p. 159).

This, in fact, is one of the dilemmas philosophically facing all depersonalized individuals: If I feel as if I have lost my old self and am filled with fear because the world seems strange, where is my new self? What do I do with this new way in which I'm seeing things?

Apparently, some rare individuals are able to float in and out of these no-self states, use them, or live with them to find some level of peace or satisfaction, even if the world at large calls them crazy or "outsiders" during their lifetimes. These unique and creative people are what Amiel could have been, but never became, for reasons he himself came to realize. And, unfortunately, for most people, depersonalization does indeed appear as "the blow," a sucker punch that catches you unaware and keeps you down on the mat, never letting you up enough to see the new and better reality that just might be there before you.

Back from the Looking Glass

The broad variety of manifestations of depersonalization we've seen allow us, for the moment, to arrive at some logical conclusions. Detachment, depersonalization, and derealization within the context of an anticipated and induced hallucinogenic experience, or within the framework of long-term intentional meditative experience, generally are not perceived as horrific, but rather as eye opening and often liberating. But when it comes on unexpectedly and disrupts one's life, such experiences are almost invariably horrifying and decidedly unwanted.

All of the parties we've quoted regarding psychedelic experience ultimately agreed that psychedelics are not a *preferred* way to find a higher consciousness, or to uncap hidden creative energies on one's own. Nor should they ever be used alone, or recreationally. Oscar Janiger discreetly harbored the results of his research for many years when the drug became an object of abuse; Aldous Huxley stated that civilization could not exist if people used mescaline regularly, and Alan Watts, who knew both of these mind explorers personally, put it this way:

> Psychedelic experience is only a glimpse of genuine mystical insight, but a glimpse which can be matured and deepened by the various ways of meditation in which drugs are no longer necessary or useful. If you get the message, hang up the phone. For psychedelic drugs are simply instruments, like microscopes, telescopes, and

telephones. The biologist does not sit with eye permanently glued to the microscope, he goes away and works on what he has seen."[25]

The psychedelic experiences we've examined do not clinically fall into the category of depersonalization disorder. *The Diagnostic and Statistical Manual of Mental Disorders*, 4th edition (*DSM-IV*) makes a point of this in its diagnostic criteria: "Depersonalization that is caused by the direct physiological effects of a substance is distinguished from Depersonalization Disorder by the fact that a substance (e.g., a drug of abuse, or a medication) is judged to be etiologically related to the depersonalization."[26]

It's safe to say that the majority of people seeking help when they experience depersonalization simply want to resume life as they once knew it, or live the kind of well-adjusted, balanced, or "normal" life they instinctively know exists. This doesn't mean they have to ignore or deny the deeper meanings depersonalization may potentially hold.

Said one recovered depersonalized individual, a mother in her 40s, "depersonalization changed my perspective forever, in an existential way. But when I first experienced it, all I wanted was a way out. It took me a long time to realize that I wasn't going insane. I'll always envy people who just live within the framework of normalcy. Yet sometimes, I feel a little sorry for them, especially when they're overly self-confident. They think they know who they really are."

Instances in which depersonalization can be channeled into creative or visionary outlets remain quite rare—so is true enlightenment, despite the fact that there are millions of practicing Buddhists. Fear, as Amiel noted, is certainly an inhibiting factor. And depersonalization is intensely isolating and fear provoking by its nature. Without the assistance of a knowledgeable "guru" to serve as a guide, a person must make their way through these fearful waters without a clue as to where they may be headed or when they may sink.

With this in mind, is depersonalization akin to some kind spiritual enlightenment? Are mystical experiences, meditation, and depersonalization the same? Recently, compelling data has begun to emerge, providing these issues with more material for discussion.

In 2001 Andrew Newburg of the Department of Radiology at the University of Pennsylvania Medical Center published two single photon emission computerized tomography studies, one looking at Franciscan nuns and the other at Tibetan Buddhist meditators. In both groups, intense meditation was associated with increased brain activity in the prefrontal cortex, dorsolateral and medial orbitofrontal, and the cingulate gyrus—areas involved in cognitive control and focused concentration on the self. Also of interest in both studies, the activity in the prefrontal cortex was inversely related to activity in the superior parietal lobe, possibly reflecting the altered sense of body and space experienced during meditation. As discussed in chapter 6, these are the areas involved in the experience of depersonalization.

Does this new data tell us that spirituality, or depersonalization, is completely in the brain, or is the brain letting in something else from outside? There's no clear answer on this. As Newburg has pointed out,

> If we take a brain image of a person when she is looking at a picture, we will see various parts of the brain being activated, such as the visual cortex. But the brain image cannot tell us whether or not there actually is a picture "out there" or whether the person is creating the picture in her own mind. To a certain degree, we all create our own sense of reality. Getting at what is really real is the tricky part.[27]

As such studies continue, certainly more will be learned. But changes in brain activity that come about as the result of deliberate meditative practice seem to be experienced far differently from those that are neither desired nor voluntary. Once again, from a medical perspective, the *DSM-IV* makes its position clear here as well: "Voluntarily induced experiences of depersonalization or derealization form part of the meditative and trance practices that are prevalent in many religions and cultures and should not be confused with Depersonalization Disorder."[28]

Much has been learned about the negative aspects of depersonalization, and, in time, more is likely to be learned about any positive attributes as well. Certainly, no matter how much they ruminate, suffer, or seek help, most depersonalized people are likely to learn firsthand what Frederic Amiel observed at the outset—we simply are not what we think ourselves to be.

Everything and Nothing

Perhaps the best way to leave this topic is with one of the greatest and most mysterious figures of the arts, William Shakespeare. What went through the mind of the man who wrote "to be or not to be?" Why does Richard III say that inside himself he plays the part of many, and what prompts Iago to curiously utter "I am not what I am"? The Argentine writer Jorge Luis Borges, whose poetry and prose is rich with esoteric meaning and intuitive perspectives on the nature of existence and nonexistence, a *real* self versus *no self*, provides his own speculation as to the mystery of Shakespeare, with thought-provoking relevance to the subject at hand.

In the short story, *Everything and Nothing*, which we excerpt here, Borges tells of a man who played many parts as an actor and assumed many roles primarily because he cannot realize his own identity.

> There was no one inside him…behind his face . . . there was no more than a slight chill, a dream someone had failed to dream. . . .
>
> At first he thought that everyone was like him, but the surprise and bewilderment of an acquaintance to whom he began to describe that hollowness showed him his error, and also let him know, forever after, that an individual ought not to differ from its species. . . .
>
> At twenty-something he went off to London. Instinctively, he had already trained himself to the habit of feigning that he was somebody, so that his "nobodiness" might not be discovered. In London he found the calling he had been predestined to; he became an actor, that person who stands upon a stage and plays at being another person, for an audience of people who play at taking him for that person.

Borges explains how this man found happiness for a time in playing others on stage, but inevitably "when the last line was delivered and the last dead man applauded off the stage, the hated taste of unreality would assail him. He would cease being Ferrex or Tamerlane and return to being nobody."

For 20 years, Borges adds, the actor created characters to play onstage, and once in a while, hinted at his own particular selflessness through the words of one of his creations. But in time, the actor is overwhelmed by being so many different people on stage, while never really being himself. He stops writing and assumes the life of an English bourgeois, concerned only with money and daily maintenance of his affluent lifestyle. Even his last written item, his will, is commonplace, showing no sign of the literary genius that once flourished under its author's pen.

In the end, Borges provides an answer to this life of being no one, in a manner that reflects the enigmatic wonder of depersonalization itself:

History adds that before or after he died, he discovered himself standing before God, and said to Him: *I, who have been so many men in vain, wish to be one, to be myself.*

God's voice answered him out of a whirlwind: *I, too, am not I; I dreamed the world as you, Shakespeare, dreamed your own work, and among the forms of my dreams are you, who like me are many, yet no one.*

8 Medication Treatment

What we feel and think and are is to a great extent determined by the state of our ductless glands and viscera.

—ALDOUS HUXLEY

As shown in the last chapter, the world of depersonalization, like the ocean, is vast, mysterious, and deep. But someone who is drowning couldn't care less about that. He wants to be safely back in the boat or on shore. Only from that perspective, when his immediate fears have subsided, can he begin to explore the wonder of what nearly killed him.

People suffering from depersonalization disorder (DPD) don't appear at a doctor's or psychiatrist's office to explore mysticism, philosophy, or the deep blue sea. They make the appointment because they are in pain. Some want and expect relief from that pain just as if it were the result of a broken limb or an infection. Others are more content to find hope, a piece of buoyant debris to cling to while awaiting rescue. Unfortunately, they often visit doctor after doctor, finding neither. Even when they are lucky enough to locate a psychiatrist who is familiar with DPD, there is no simple treatment, no magic bullet to make that pain go away quickly, no quick and miraculous rescue. But relief can be provided as one embarks on the journey toward complete recovery. Physicians have at their disposal a huge arsenal of pharmaceutical treatments with which to combat mental illness. Not all medicines affect everyone the same way, but the medicines in use today are quite sophisticated and present a promising rainbow of possibilities. As is true with a number of mental disorders, trial and error is sometimes the only route toward finding the most efficacious treatment of DPD.

To date, there are no specific pharmacological treatment guidelines for depersonalization, though both pharmacological and psychotherapeutic efforts have been shown to be effective. Historically, DPD has been notoriously resistant to treatment. That's the bad news. The good news is that the individual ways in which DPD manifests itself can often be treated effectively, if those manifestations include anxiety, obsessiveness, or depression, or if a patient suffers concurrently from these more widely recognized and treatable conditions.

Clinical research as to what works best for depersonalization has been limited, although there have been numerous anecdotal reports implicating the possible success of several medicines and forms of treatment, often in combination.

The history of the medicines used, and often cited as being effective for treating depersonalization, is as old as the study of the disorder itself. In 1939, Paul Schilder reported favorable results in nine severely depersonalized patients using the respiratory stimulant metrazol (pentamethylenetetrazol).[1] Others reported success with intravenous methamphetamine (used only with electroconvulsive therapy [ECT]), pentathol, +-amphetamine, amobarbitol, and intramuscular thipentone.[2] These drugs are rarely used today because of their significant side effects and the availability of safer alternatives. ECT, recommended in some of the earliest papers discussing treatment, was ultimately found to be more effective for depression alone. In a study of 15 patients with severe depression and depersonalization, depression improved following ECT, but depersonalization was unaffected.[3] At the Mount Sinai program, no DPD participants who had ever undergone ECT treatment reported benefit.

In Europe and in the United States during the 1950s and 1960s, the tricyclic antidepressants (TCAs) became popular, followed by the monoamine oxidase inhibitors (MAOIs), because of their proven effectiveness in fighting depression and panic disorder. Although occasional reports appeared over the years about isolated individuals with DPD who had benefited from these medications, the overall impression remained that for most with depersonalization they did little.

In more recent years, different clinicians throughout the world experienced in treating patients with depersonalization have developed their own pharmaceutical treatments for the condition, which they apparently find to be more effective than no medication, at least in some patients. Having dealt with more than 100 depersonalized patients in the former Soviet Union, Dr. Elena Bezzubova, now at the University of California, Irvine, has observed that some people with chronic and unremitting depersonalization need some stimulant, some "waking up" in a sense, as opposed to being "put more to sleep" by tranquilizers that are often prescribed to quell their anxiety. Dr. Evan Torch, whose treatment methods are predominantly psychotherapeutic and rooted in treating the obsessive aspects of DPD, often prescribes a selective serotonin reuptake inhibitor (SSRI) or other antidepressants coupled with modafanil (provigil), a nonamphetamine stimulant. Torch calls this combination of an SSRI and a stimulant "the hidden pearl that can really help DPD."

Beyond the anecdotal, then, what harder evidence do we have as to whether any medications can successfully treat depersonalization? We present below all the systematic studies done to date looking at this question.

Clinical Research on Drug Treatments

Retrospective Treatment Reports from 117 Patients

In a study of 117 patients with DPD carried out by Daphne Simeon at Mount Sinai and published in 2003 in the *Journal of Clinical Psychiatry*, participants were asked to describe, in retrospect, all the treatments that they had previously received.[4] If a trial of medication appeared reasonable enough in dose and in duration to count as an adequate treatment trial, it was tallied into the results. This retrospective record revealed that there was very little success with a variety of different medications in treating DPD. Participants were asked whether each particular drug had left their depersonalization the same, worse, slightly better, or definitely better. Two considerations are important to bear in mind in interpreting this information. First, the data are based on participants' best memory, often from a long time ago, and therefore they cannot be considered as accurate as conducting a treatment trial in the present, where investigators strictly record the numbers of weeks of treatment, the maximum dose reached, and patients' compliance with taking the medication. Second, DPD sufferers who had already experienced a good medication response would probably be less likely to enroll in the research program in the first place. Therefore, the collected treatment information from the 117 subjects must be taken with a grain of salt, but it still does not paint an optimistic picture in terms of the effectiveness of most traditional psychiatric medications in DPD.

The study reported essentially no effectiveness for the traditional tricyclic antidepressants. Out of 31 treatment trials, only 2 led to slight improvement and 1 to definite improvement. The tricyclic antidepressants (TCAs), an older class of drugs that includes nortriptyline (Pamelor), imipramine (Tofranil), desipramine (Norpramin), and amitriptyline (Elavil), are effective and inexpensive antidepressants but often have more side effects than newer antidepressants. In depressed individuals, TCAs typically bring about an elevation in mood, improved appetite, better sleep, and reduced morbid preoccupations.

Similar to tricyclics, the old monoamine oxidase inhibitors (MAOIs) appeared equally ineffective. Of 16 reported trials, only 2 had resulted in slight improvement. MAOIs are generally prescribed to treat depression that hasn't responded to other therapies. Monoamine oxidase is an enzyme that oxidizes (inactivates) certain amines in the brain. By inhibiting monoamine oxidase, these drugs extend the life of these amines. The MAOIs have a broad scope of action, affecting the levels of serotonin, noreprinephrine, and dopamine in the brain. Taking high doses of MAOIs can sometimes be helpful in stimulating more alertness, as amphetamines used to supplement other drugs might. The MAOIs include phenelzine (Nardil), tranylcypromine (Parnate), and isocarboxazid (Marplan). Although these drugs have proven very effective for depression, doctors don't prescribe them frequently because they can have serious interactions with certain foods and medications. Eating foods that contain tyramine, such as aged cheeses, wine, or pickled or aged products, can cause a severe rise in blood pressure in some people.

Another newer antidepressant, buproprion (Welbutrin, Zyban), known to work for depression as well as for smoking cessation, was similarly ineffective in DPD. Of 11 individuals who had tried it, only one reported having experienced definite improvement. Similarly, the newer antidepressant venlafaxine (Effexor) appeared ineffective; of 7 trials none had resulted in improvement. Venlafaxine belongs to the SNRI class of antidepressants (serotonin and norepinephrine reuptake inhibitors), which effectively lead to an increase of both serotonin and norephinephrine activity in the brain.

The 117 participants reported a total of 60 SSRI trials. SSRIs are commonly prescribed. These are relatively new designer drugs in that they were specifically designed to act on the serotonin system, unlike many older drugs that affect numerous neurotransmitter systems at once. SSRIs affect how much serotonin is available in the brain by blocking its reabsorption during transmission from one nerve cell in the brain to another. It is this blocking action that causes an increased amount of serotonin to become available at the next nerve cell. Serotonin is known to be involved in depression, anxiety, and obsessive-compulsive conditions. Because varying degrees of obsessiveness can occur in depersonalization, it was initially thought that SSRIs may be helpful in DPD. The SSRIs include fluoxetine (Prozac), sertraline (Zoloft), paroxetine (Paxil), fluvoxamine (Luvox), citalopram (Celexa), and escitalopram (Lexapro).

Of the 60 SSRI trials reported, 14 had led to slight improvement and 9 to definite improvement of depersonalization, according to the participants. This 38% effectiveness appeared somewhat promising in this retrospective report, certainly better than that of other antidepressants. We'll examine more rigorous research of the SSRIs in treating DPD shortly.

First, let's look at medications used to treat anxiety. Benzodiazepines are central nervous system depressants (medicines that slow down the nervous system) and include alprazolam (Xanax) , clonazepam (Klonopin), lorazepam (Ativan), and many others. They can be used to treat a variety of anxiety disorders such as generalized anxiety, social anxiety, and panic attacks. Dependence and tolerance to these medications can develop after taking them on a regular basis for several weeks, so they can be addictive if not used judiciously. The benzodiazepines enhance the action of the neurotransmitter GABA (gamma amino butyric acid). Once released, neurotransmitters signal inhibition or excitation of neighboring brain cells. GABA is the major inhibitory neurotransmitter in our brain. The function of GABA is to slow or calm things down. Benzodiazepines increase the action of GABA, thus causing greater inhibition or calming.

In the retrospective report of the 117 subjects, 35 benzodiazepine trials were reported. Of these, 8 (23%) led to slight improvement and 10 (29%) led to definite improvement. Again, this appears to be quite a promising response for a condition that is so hard to treat. Yet, there still are no clinical trials that have examined the effectiveness of benzodiazepines in DPD. Benzodiazepines seem to work at least partly for some patients, usually the highly anxious ones. It appears that by significantly diminishing anxiety, they can result in some improvement of depersonalization.

Another antianxiety medication, with entirely different action from the benzodiazepines, is buspirone (Buspar), which acts as an antagonist of a particular serotonin receptor, the 5HT 1A receptor. Of the 15 trials of buspirone reported in the 117 participants, none had any effectiveness.

Of the 117 participants, 9 reported trials of stimulants, medications that typically act to enhance the dopamine system in the brain, and are used for conditions such as attention deficit disorder because they improve attention and focusing. Two of these trials led to slight improvement.

Of the remaining classes of medications reported in the study, all were virtually ineffective. These included mood-stabilizing medications, such as lithium (none of 9 trials worked) and anticonvulsants (valproic acid and other newer anticonvulsants), in which only 1 of 12 trials led to slight improvement.

Notably, antipsychotic medications, used to treat psychotic disorders such as schizophrenia, appeared to do nothing for depersonalization, even though these were commonly prescribed for depersonalization in the past and still appear to be used in general practice to treat the condition. None of 13 trials of traditional antipsychotics, and none of 7 trials of the newer antipsychotics known as atypicals, exhibited any effectiveness in treating depersonalization.

Do SSRIs Work in Depersonalization?

In the past 10 years, a small open series (a study using few cases and no placebo) and two single case reports suggested that SSRIs alone may be effective in treating primary DPD.[5] It was thought that SSRIs might work because of the efficacy in treating obsessive-compulsive spectrum disorders, and obsessive thinking often manifests itself within the overall symptoms of DPD. In 2004, however, a definitive study published in the *British Journal of Psychiatry* failed to show benefit with fluoxetine (Prozac).[6]

In this study, 25 individuals with DPD were randomly assigned to fluoxetine treatment and 25 to placebo treatment. The patients were not allowed to take any other medication. The treatment lasted 10 weeks, and participants built up to a rather high dose of fluoxetine, almost 50 milligrams per day. The study found that the people taking fluoxetine showed statistically significant overall improvement in their depersonalization, as opposed to those taking placebo. However, when this improvement was "corrected" for changes in anxiety and depression, fluoxetine no longer appeared better than placebo. Furthermore, the overall improvement of depersonalization on fluoxetine was on average rated as "minimal," indicating that the effect was not potent enough to be considered clinically worthwhile by usual research standards for treatment symptom response. Finally, the actual depersonalization symptoms of participants in the two groups were rated both by a clinician-administered and by a self-report scale, and neither scale showed any differences between fluoxetine and placebo. This numeric finding closely reflected the typical descriptive reports of participants who had received fluoxetine, who stated that their depersonalization symptoms had not changed, but rather they felt somewhat better and were less bothered by them. The only clue pointing at which DPD sufferers might derive some degree of benefit from fluoxetine was the finding that within the fluoxetine-treated group, the DPD participants who experienced some benefit were more likely to have also shown improvement in concurrent anxiety disorder, in addition to their DPD. Thus, it seems plausible that those with major anxiety which responds to fluoxetine can also show some degree of improvement in their particular depersonalization experiences.

Clomipramine

Clomipramine (Anafranil) is a tricyclic agent that is helpful with both depression and obsessional disorders. Like other tricyclics, clomipramine inhibits norepinephrine and serotonin reuptake into central nerve terminals, thereby increasing their concentration at receptor sites. In contrast to most tricyclics, it is a very potent serotonin reuptake inhibitor, like the SSRIs. It is this ability to alter serotonin activity that makes clomipramine effective in treating obsessive-compulsive disorders as the SSRIs do, but unlike the other tricyclics. Clomipramine also has a mild sedative effect, due to its anticholinergic properties, which may be helpful in alleviating anxiety.

Several years ago, Simeon and colleagues conducted a small study evaluating clomipramine versus desipramine treatment of DPD (desipramine is another tricyclic antidepressant that does not have strong seroternergic properties like clomipramine).[7] The small number of subjects in the study did not allow statistical comparison of the two medications, but the study did find that of the four subjects treated with clomopramine, two showed significant improvement of DPD. One of these two patients showed almost complete remission for years afterward while still taking clomipramine, yet suffered setbacks whenever she attempted to discontinue clomipramine or switch over to other medications like SSRIs. This older drug may still merit attention for treatment of DPD.

Lamotrigine

In recent years there has been a flurry of interest in treatment of DPD with lamotrigine. As we discussed in chapter 6, this evolved because of the finding that although N-methyl-+-aspartate (NMDA) antagonists like ketamine induce potent dissociation by increasing glutamate transmission at non-NMDA glutamate receptors, pretreatment with lamotrigine, which inhibits glutamate release, lessened ketamine-induced dissociation in healthy volunteers.[8] This finding gave hope that treatment with lamotrigine might be helpful in dissociative conditions in general.

Along these lines, there was a promising preliminary report of lamotrigine treatment in chronic depersonalization which described improvement in five patients with the disorder.[9] These patients were not taking lamotrigine alone, but were also on other medications, mostly SSRIs, and they were not participants in an organized treatment study, but rather they were individuals who responded to lamotrigine in routine treatment.

Subsequently, the same research group followed nine patients treated in a systematic study of lamotrigine in DPD. They conducted what is known as a "crossover" trial, a design in which all participants received both lamotrigine and placebo, in random order. Disappointingly, the results were completely negative: none of the subjects showed any notable improvement while taking lamotrigine.[10]

Opioid Antagonists

Opioid antagonists have also been of some recent interest in the treatment of dissociation more generally, and depersonalization in particular. Naltrexone is a nonspecific opioid antagonist, which at low doses blocks the mu opioid receptors (the receptors involved in mediating analgesia, or an increased pain threshold, under stress, see chapter 6). At much higher doses, naltrexone can also block other opioid receptors; blockade of the kappa opioid receptors might be of particular interest here, as the kappa opioid agonist enadoline has been found to induce a "pure" depersonalization syndrome in healthy volunteers.

Naltrexone at a high dose of 200 milligrams per day was reported to decrease general dissociative symptoms in borderline personality disorder over a 2-week period of treatment.[11] Nalmefene, a medication similar to naltrexone not yet marketed in the United States, was reported to decrease emotional numbing in eight veterans with posttraumatic stress disorder.[12]

What about depersonalization specifically? Nuller and colleagues reported results from an intravenous naloxone trial in 11 patients with chronic DPD.[13] Naloxone is a medication very similar to naltrexone but much shorter acting, and thus it can be administered only intravenously. Of the 11 patients, 3 experienced complete remission, and 7 had marked improvement of depersonalization symptoms with the treatment. However, this study reported only immediate treatment results, leaving unclear what might happen later on, without continued treatment of naloxone.

Simeon and her colleagues at Mount Sinai in New York recently completed a preliminary naltrexone study in 14 individuals with DPD.[14] Participants were treated with naltrexone for 6–10 weeks, at a fairly high average dose of 120 milligrams per day. The general clinical impression was that three individuals were found to be very much improved by the end of the treatment, and another one was much improved. The three dissociation scales that were specifically used to measure depersonalization symptoms in the study revealed, on average, across the three scales, a 30% decrease in depersonalization symptoms with treatment. Although these results may appear somewhat modest, especially since there was no placebo treatment in this study, they may still hold some promise regarding the effectiveness of opioid antagonists in DPD, but it is too soon to tell. This class of medications therefore deserves some more study in the treatment of depersonalization.

Other Medication Options, Present and Future, and Clinical Practice

There may be some additional medication options for people with depersonalization disorder. Some individuals report that they benefit from benzodiazepine treatment (e.g., clonazepam), as discussed earlier. It is our impression, although no studies have been done, that this may be particularly true in those who also experience strong anxiety or panic, which typically exacerbate their depersonalization symptoms.[15] However, we have encountered other individuals with DPD who report that, although benzodiazapines may have lessened their anxiety, these drugs did not affect the symptoms of dissociation at all.

As mentioned earlier, some DPD patients report improvement, at least in attentional and focusing difficulties, and may feel a little "clearer" and less "foggy" with various stimulant medications.[16] Although our impression is that this improvement is slight overall, it can still make a difference for some patients. There is also some theoretical rationale for using medications that enhance dopamine in depersonalization. Dopamine DA1 receptors enhance sensory input to the amygdala, one of the emotional centers of the brain. Another group of domamine receptors called the DA2 receptors decrease the inhibition of the amygdala by the prefrontal cortex. Therefore, increased activity at either of these two dopamine receptors would be expected to enhance emotional activation in the brain, and this is relevant because, as we discussed in chapter 6, one neurobiological model of depersonalization proposes diminished activity of the limbic system. A variety of medications have stimulant properties and might be used to treat depersonalization, such as dextroamphetamine (Dexadrine), methylphenidate (Ritalin), and buproprion (Welbutrin).

Another class of medications that could be of interest in treating DPD, which has not been systematically studied, are medications that enhance noradrenergic transmission. Norepinephrine (noradrenaline) is one of the neurotransmitters in the brain that plays a crucial role in sharpening attentional processes, alertness functions, and encoding of emotional information. Norepinephrine has been widely implicated in stress-related disorders. There are various medications that act on this chemical process, including yohimbine (Yohimbex), which is a noradrenergic agonist, or atomoxetine (Strattera), which is a noradrenergic reuptake inhibitor. Each drug in its own fashion enhances noradrenergic transmission, and, as we discussed earlier, there is growing evidence for lowered autonomic and noradrenergic activity in DPD.

NMDA agonists are another class of medications that, at least on theoretical grounds, might be expected to be helpful in depersonalization. Because NMDA antagonists, such as ketamine, induce potent dissociative states, conversely, NMDA agonists could be expected to lessen dissociation. To our knowledge, the only trial of this sort to date has been conducted by the Mount Sinai group (unpublished data), examining the effect of +-cycloserine, one NMDA agonist, in DPD, but this small trial did not have positive results. However, NMDA agonists with more refined properties developed in years to come might still hold some promise.

Another class of medications that could be of interest in DPD is the serotonin 5HT 2A and 2C antagonists (remember that agonists of these serotonin receptor subtypes such as the hallucinogens can trigger depersonalization symptoms). One such antagonist, however, known as cyproheptadine, was not found to be effective in treating DPD in a small trial recently done at Mount Sinai (unpublished data).

New classes of medications currently under development may also hold some promise, in the near future, for DPD. CRF (corticotropin-releasing factor) antagonists (not yet marketed) and glucocorticoid receptor antagonists (such as mifepristone) are thought to hold promise for depression, and they may also help depersonalization to the extent that the hypothalamus-pituitary-adrenal axis abnormalities in depersonalization might resemble those of depression.

Neuropeptide Y is a neurochemical that was found in some interesting recent studies to be inversely related to dissociation severity: the higher the neuropeptide Y, the lower the dissociation.[17] These studies were conducted in "super-normal" Special Forces personnel subjected to extremely stressful simulated intensive military training. Thus, neuropeptide Y analogue substances, not yet available to the market, could be of some interest in the treatment of dissociation.

Anticannabinoids could be yet another promising treatment for DPD. Given that marijuana and other cannabinoid agonists are one of the most predictable inducers of acute and chronic depersonalization, drugs that act as antagonists of the cannabinoid receptor in the brain could conceivably have antidepersonalization effects. Although such drugs are not yet marketed, it is expected that the first such drug might soon be marketed in the United States for the treatment of obesity.

Altogether, then, it does not appear that any of the currently available medicines have a potent antidepersonalization effect. Still, several medications can be used to combat DPD's gamut of symptoms, from high anxiety to panic to depression to difficulties with attention, absence of mood, mind-emptiness, or overconsciousness, to the unremitting and unstoppable obsessiveness about reality and existence. Some of these manifestations appear inherent to depersonalization itself in various individuals, while others may be attributable to co-existing conditions such as clinical depression or anxiety disorders. Medications that target these kinds of symptoms typically do not lift the depersonalization itself, but can result in partial relief for some patients. Some medications act directly on specific brain systems, while others have more of a shotgun approach, penetrating a variety of neurochemical systems at once.

Working with Psychiatrists

Unfortunately, the pharmacological treatment of DPD remains a trial-and-error approach, and therefore the judicious and well-supervised use of various medications that make clinical sense is the current state of the art. Clearly, treating depersonalization pharmaceutically may seem as much like alchemy as science. Had DPD been given the attention that other disorders have received through the years, this might not be the case. Hopefully, the future will hold the promise of more thorough research and testing, and the necessary acknowledgment of the condition as well as the funding to do the research.

Will a Prescription Be Enough?

Can medicines, however effective, do the job alone? Most experts believe not. Dr. Bezzubova points out that in Russia, in both the pre- and post-Soviet era, psychotherapy was given as part of the "prescription" that had to be taken in treatment of DPD. Dr. Torch states that his current treatment plan involves about 20% medication and 80% psychotherapy. And both the research units at Mount Sinai and in the U.K. build in therapy as part of the overall treatment plan while using a variety of medications in tandem. Still, people who can trace their onset to a specific incident such as the use of drugs, or who see the condition as purely physiologically based and having occurred for no apparent reason, are likely to resist such thinking. "I know what happened, and all the talk in the world isn't going to make it better," is the typical conclusion. And, for the person who once had a strong, independent self, the stigma of mental illness and blind long-term reliance on a therapist can be quite a deterrent. Yet the notion of what psychotherapy actually entails has changed greatly in recent years. Even doctors with strong biological biases concede that in the case of DPD, an effective combination of medicine and therapy is a wise course of treatment. "People who have suffered with DPD for years, and have tried everything are anxious to take that chance," Torch says. One patient who had found relief through a variety of medications, expressed his ongoing dissatisfaction in this way: "Medications have helped my depersonalization a lot, but they've been like showing a cross to a vampire. The cross keeps him at bay, but I'm still looking for that spike in the heart that will finish him off." In the next chapter, we'll look at some of the psychotherapeutic techniques that, with or without medication, attempt to deal a mortal blow to this treatment-resistant disorder.

9 Psychotherapy Treatment of Depersonalization

If the patient can tolerate the experience of unrealness for a time, he can make for himself a new reality which is more solidly grounded for his own needs and perceptions, and in a sense more "real" than his old compromises were, however comfortable and familiar they might have felt.

—J. S. LEVY AND P. L. WACHTEL

Can depersonalization be successfully treated with psychotherapy? Although traditionally the psychotherapy literature has been rather pessimistic on this issue, more recent advances in psychotherapy technique aimed specifically at treating this condition leave us with more reason to be optimistic. To say that psychotherapy works, or always works fully, may be misleading or overly optimistic. But to say that it cannot work, at least for some, and cannot lead to important symptom improvement and better life adaptation would be overly pessimistic and incorrect. Logically, therapeutic approaches can sometimes seem as diverse as the manifestations of depersonalization disorder (DPD) itself, but this isn't tantamount to a hit-or-miss philosophy. Evidence of success stories that have emerged through therapy tailored to the psychological makeup and specific symptoms of patients, has, over time, accumulated into a body of suggested approaches that are now worth considering. In this chapter, we first examine the more traditional approaches, some of which are outdated, while others remain relevant and useful. Later, we'll look at the state-of-the-art therapies that have proven to be most effective thus far.

Psychoanalytic Approaches

We have come a long way from the traditional psychoanalytic literature of half a century ago. However, even that literature expressed some cautious optimism, at least by those who had studied DPD closely and had put much thought into how to best treat it. For example, in 1935, Bergler and Eidelberg wrote:

> We think that this absolute pessimism is not justified; however, it is a prerequisite for the therapy that one knows the mechanisms and starts on the right point. Furthermore, a very long time is necessary. While the analysis of a more severe case of obsession neurosis takes at least two to two and a half years, the double space of time is a requirement for the treatment of depersonalization.[1]

Schilder expressed more optimism in treating the condition, whether by individual or group psychotherapy. He emphasized the essence of the depersonalized condition as "a state of the personality in which the individual feels changed in comparison to his former state."[2] He saw two components to this change: first, the altered awareness of the self and the world around, and second, the inability of depersonalized individuals to acknowledge themselves as personalities. One present-day patient aptly captured this drastic change as her "old self" and her "new self," clearly implying how unrelated the two states felt. Yet, she, of course, was still the same person, so that the first stages of therapy centered on this shift in self-perception. Unacknowledged yet unbearable anxieties and conflicts had been present and active in the idealized old self and had triggered and become perpetuated in the new self, which was seemingly even less accessible now, masked by the dense distraction and angst of the depersonalized state of mind.

Some other prominent professionals who tackled the psychotherapeutic treatment of depersonalization in past years emphasized some additional important points. Cattell and Cattell felt that traditional psychoanalysis, which involves use of the couch and no eye contact between patient and therapist, was not indicated in depersonalization because it could enhance the experience of disconnection and unreality.[3] Writing for the *British Journal of Guidance and Counselling* in the mid-1980s, Fewtrell noted the powerful relief that patients can experience when they are encouraged to verbalize to their doctors or therapists, often for the very first time, their subjective sensations of depersonalization.[4] Levy and Wachtel suggested that it can be useful for patients to temporarily learn to accept and tolerate their depersonalization and to reframe it as a new reality rather than an unreality, reflecting underlying needs and meanings.[5]

Before examining the psychology behind an altered self, it makes sense to first look at the normal self. How does an individual, over time, create a predictable, cohesive sense of self? As part of their investigation into depersonalization, Frances, Sacks, and Aronoff considered this question as a point of departure in a 1977 article.[6] The first self is a "body self," they wrote. Subsequently, the realm of self-representations expands beyond this simple core body self to include an amalgam of various ongoing self-experiences with transformations (internalizations) of important object (other) representations, eventually to form an integrated structure. One of the early developmental tasks is to gradually establish differentiated self and object representations. Only later, and again gradually, is there progression to more integrated development that results in a stable and unchanging sense of one's self and of others, referred to as "self and object constancy." This process eventually leads to the creation of an average, expectable self which is felt to be "me."

Any challenge to self-constancy could result in depersonalization in a person who is vulnerable to it. The depersonalization implies that self-constancy has been somehow disrupted; the result is a disparity between the new sense of the actual (depersonalized) self and a previously held "average, expectable self." There are various components of the average, expectable self, such as the body-self, the thinking-self, the feeling-self, the action-self, the gender-self, the other-relating self, and so on. A challenge to any of these self-components can disrupt the self-structure and manifest with depersonalization symptoms. In this sense, depersonalization or heightening depersonalization is a signal denoting a disruption of self-constancy. Frances and colleagues speculated that depersonalization is experienced more strongly in one or another of these spheres by different people, according to which part of their self-structure is most vulnerable. Thus, some patients feel most alienated from the body, whereas others feel most alienated from their thoughts, feelings, or actions.

Frances and colleagues suggest that it is useful in treating patients with depersonalization to determine whether the difficulty with constancy lies in one of three areas: differentiating self from others, self-constancy, or other-constancy. A person with a personality structure bordering on psychotic has difficulties in all three areas. A person with a borderline personality structure can differentiate self from others but has trouble with constancy to the self and of others. A person with a narcissistic personality structure has achieved a tenuous self-constancy that requires the stable input and presence of others to maintain it. Finally, a person with a neurotic personality does not have particular difficulties in any of these areas, but rather may experience depersonalization when challenged by overwhelming internal conflict. These basic personality structures are widely accepted in psychodynamic models of the mind, and correspond to some degree, but not strictly so, to the more traditional psychiatric personality disorders in the *Diagnostic and Statistical Manual of Mental Disorders*, 4th edition (*DSM-IV*), discussed in the descriptive studies of chapter 4.

Let's look at some brief vignettes of patients with depersonalization representing these four levels of personality organization to help bring them to life. Lisa was a 35-year-old woman with schizoid personality. She had experienced a striking absence of physical and emotional warmth throughout her childhood and felt profoundly threatened by the slightest attempts of others to be intimate with her. Any social contact exacerbated her depersonalization, with the exception of her husband, with whom she felt very comforted and safe. When relating to others she almost felt as if she were losing herself, as if an invisible protective envelope surrounding her started to melt. Lisa's personality was organized at a near-psychotic level, and she had difficulties with self-other differentiation. Therefore, the first phase of Lisa's treatment focused on helping her appreciate how her depersonalization symptoms heightened whenever her sense of "separateness" from others was threatened.

Danielle, on the other hand, was organized at a borderline personality level. She came from a background of intense and prolonged physical abuse and some sexual abuse, and as a 25-year-old adult she experienced large fluctuations in self and other constancy accompanied by feelings of depersonalization. She became a prostitute and when engaged in sex she felt out-of-body, examining from a distance the men whom she despised. When she spent time with her 2-year-old son, she often felt like a detached automaton going through the motions of the caring and affection expected of her. During times when she was able to acknowledge and reflect on these states, she felt more connected and real. The early part of Danielle's psychotherapy concentrated on tracking her depersonalization symptoms as these related to her shifting sense of who she "was" in her different states of being.

Owen was a handsome young man whose childhood was memorable for the constant admiration of parents and peers for his early modeling and athletic accomplishments. As an adult his aspirations and career goals had changed; yet, whenever he did not feel noticed and the center of attention, he depersonalized into feeling almost invisible and inanimate, robotic and dead. Owen had narcissistic personality difficulties and required reflection from others to feel cohesive. The early stages of Owen's psychotherapy thus centered on how he depersonalized more when he felt fake or disgenuine.

Finally, Michael was a middle-aged man with strong traditional values who believed in family and in making his marriage work. He had two young children, and after several years of intense doubt and torment about his deteriorating relationship with his needy wife, he decided to leave her. Depersonalization set in during this phase and lasted for about a year. It was triggered by neurotic dynamics having to do with his feelings of guilt over betraying his wife, reactivating a nascent conflict over his intense frustration and pain growing up with a helpless, dependent mother. Therefore, Michael's therapy grappled with his feelings of betrayal and guilt toward women.

Rationale for Cognitive-Behavioral Approaches

Cognitive-behavioral psychotherapies seek to identify and correct thinking patterns and to change maladaptive behavioral patterns as the main means of achieving symptom change, as opposed to psychodynamic approaches, which concentrate on emotional states underlying the symptoms.

Although a number of authors had noted cognitive characteristics of chronic depersonalization such as catastrophic fears about the illness, obsessive ruminations, and hypochondriasis, a comprehensive cognitive-behavioral model for chronic depersonalization had not been put forth until recently. In 2003, Elaine C. M. Hunter and colleagues at the Institute of Psychiatry in London proposed that transient depersonalization is a common occurrence and that a cognitive-behavioral model of the chronic symptom needs to therefore account for the mechanisms by which the symptom becomes perpetuated in some individuals but not in others.[7]

Hunter and colleagues worked from the premise that there is evidence linking DPD with the anxiety disorders, particularly panic disorder. As we indicated in chapter 1, the *International Classification of Mental and Behavioural Disorders*, 10th revision (*ICD-10*) places DPD within the category of "neuroses: other," as opposed to the *DSM-IV* classification, used in the United States, which lists DPD among the dissociative disorders. These differences in classification set the stage for Hunter et al.'s rationale for cognitive-behavioral therapy modeled primarily after that used with the anxiety disorders. "Although DPD is classified as a dissociative disorder in DSM-IV, it is also strongly associated with the anxiety disorders, particularly panic; although DPD may be conceptualized from either perspective, an anxiety disorder framework facilitates a cognitive-behavioral model of DPD," the authors state.[8]

Clearly, someone who feels detached from his former sense of self, or his surroundings, is experiencing dissociation. And the arguments establishing DPD as a dissociative disorder are valid and strongly supported. But while Hunter and colleagues acknowledge that subjective detachment from the external world and from their own mental processes places DPD patients in the realm of dissociation, they also stress that several of the primary characteristics of the other dissociative disorders, such as amnesia, fugue, and identity alterations, do not occur. DPD sufferers do not experience significant periods of memory loss or identity shifts. Although there may be a sense of detachment from the external world, there is no loss of conscious awareness of the self or of the external environment in DPD. Also, unlike other dissociative disorders where there is typically a pattern of alternating between nondissociative and dissociative states, depersonalization, as a full-blown disorder rather than a transient symptom, is most often unremitting, with little fluctuation in severity. Finally, while recent research has found childhood emotional abuse to be a predictor of DPD, it is usually not of the extreme degree and type of abuse evidenced in cases of dissociative identity disorder.[9]

Following these observations, Hunter and colleagues conceptualize DPD as an anxiety-related disorder treatable through cognitive-behavioral therapy (CBT). Cognitive symptoms experienced by DPD sufferers are typically those of increased arousal, such as having "racing thoughts" or "mind emptiness," with subjective deficits in concentration and attention. They point out, as we explained in chapter 5, the high incidence of depersonalization/derealization symptoms that co-occur with anxiety disorders, such as panic, generalized anxiety disorder, posttraumatic stress disorder, obsessive-compulsive disorder, and hypochondriasis.

Of course, in the final analysis, it hardly matters to a suffering patient which classification his or her disorder should rightfully be in. Since symptoms of dissociation, anxiety, mind emptiness, and feeling unreal are all likely to appear during its course, DPD, like the head of Medusa, is a thing unto itself that can bite you any number of ways without the slightest concern about the genus to which it belongs. But a rationale must back up any therapy plan, and the Hunter and colleagues' reasoning is worth mentioning in this context.

How Cognitive Behavioral Therapy Is Used

With these conceptualizations proposed, Hunter and colleagues suggest that some individuals who experience temporary depersonalization may attribute it to a variety of stressful situations (stress, depression, anxiety, panic, drugs) and pay little attention to it, thus leading to the timely decrease in symptoms as the situational factors are alleviated.[10] Other individuals, however, may catastrophically misinterpret the transient symptoms of depersonalization, taking them to mean that they are going crazy, about to lose control, becoming invisible, or have an irreversible brain disease. These kinds of thinking can understandably lead to an increase in anxiety, which in turn fuels the continuation and even worsening of depersonalization symptoms, in effect locking in a vicious cycle of fear of the symptoms, leading to worsened symptoms. Furthermore, these individuals can develop a range of cognitive biases and behaviors that further serve to maintain the depersonalization symptoms. Situations that exacerbate the symptoms—for example, social situations or crowded, overstimulating settings—start to be avoided. The sense of detachment can also lead to a demotivation and a difficulty in enjoying previously pleasurable activities, resulting in low mood, frustration, and decreased engagement in life. Sufferers also adopt so-called safety behaviors—behaviors believed to help prevent feared outcomes. Patients can try hard to act normal and appear engaged, only leading to an increase of their sense of unreality and their symptoms. Individuals also develop cognitive and attentional biases, so that an increase in monitoring and focusing on the symptom leads to increased awareness of it and an increased likelihood of perceiving threatening situations that might trigger the symptom. And patients can develop a tendency to heightened introspection and overintellectualization of their experience, which only serves to accentuate their emotional detachment.

Based on this model, five interventions were proposed by Hunter's group, and there is now some evidence that these interventions can help decrease depersonalization symptoms.[11] A study describing the effectiveness of these techniques was published in 2005, in which 21 patients with DPD were treated with CBT for an average of 13 individual sessions. The treatment resulted in significant improvements in depersonalization, depression, anxiety, and general functioning, and at the end of the therapy about 30% of the participants no longer met the diagnostic criteria for DPD. The five components of the CBT are listed below.

1. *Psychoeducation and normalizing* focuses on the naming and appreciation of the symptoms for what they are, their frequent occurrence in the general population, and the protective function that they serve by emotional distancing from overwhelming feelings.

2. *Diary keeping* can help patients become more aware of fluctuations in their symptoms, as well as become more aware of thoughts and behaviors that affect their symptoms.

3. *Reducing avoidance* involves what is known as *graded exposure*, which is gradually increasing exposure to situations that exacerbate the symptoms and are therefore habitually avoided. Role-playing and techniques are also taught to counter safety behaviors and help people interact in a more genuine and meaningful way.

4. *Reducing self-focused attention* is achieved through a variety of refocusing and grounding techniques that help individuals break the cycle of self-focused attention on their symptoms by specific techniques that either ground them more comfortably in their immediate reality or enhance the willful control of attention, moving attention away from symptoms and toward specific tasks.

5. *Challenging catastrophic assumptions* involves the gradual deconstruction of the various catastrophic ideas about depersonalization, through education, experimentation, and evidence-gathering of outcomes.

Reports from the Trenches:
Other Thoughts on Psychotherapy

A number of therapists and psychiatrists in private practice have developed their own psychotherapeutic techniques based on symptoms they have witnessed most often, their ongoing education, and the successes and failures they've known in treating DPD. While invariably their approaches are based on needs of the individuals they treat, some have distinct views about the nature of the disorder which may or may not always be consistent with the clinical research or textbook definitions.

Atlanta-based Evan Torch, M.D., who has written on the obsessional aspects of DPD, believes that psychotherapy is essential in achieving wellness. "You're never going to cure a DPD patient with medicine alone," he states. "Someone entrenched in the pure disorder will need psychotherapy. People with DPD live with a sense not only of constant depersonalization but an obsession about it," he adds. Torch agrees with the assessment of Hunter and co-workers that there is usually a strong anxiety component as well as a hypocondriacal focus within the disorder:

> Chronically depersonalized people are often very competitive
> and somewhat anxiety-laden people who are not only battling
> with depersonalization, but often battling the world at large. The
> DPD emerges as if the brain is setting up a shield for them. There
> should be some secondary gains from this—the brain now has this
> to focus on rather than the other things. But the brain doesn't seem
> to realize that doing this is more painful than the original problem.

Torch's treatment involves a combination of medicines plus psychotherapy aimed at getting at the engine that fuels the obsessive focusing on the self that often marks DPD. The condition, in part, in Torch's assessment, is a problem of initial low self-esteem marked by the patient's obsessive-compulsive sense of disappointment in themselves, usually because of some family or caregiver situation. When these perfectionistic people realize that everything cannot be controlled, nor be perfect, their recovery process begins.

Torch says that his success rate has been high because patients realize that they weren't "just fine" until they got DPD. The disorder is the result of the problem that was already happening, not the cause of it, he claims. For people who have already been to dozens of doctors and suffered with DPD for years, the time frame of psychotherapeutic treatment, even if several years, is something they are rarely reluctant to undertake.

In Laguna Beach, California, Elena Bezzubova, M.D., Ph.D., who practiced psychiatry in Russia, now devotes much of her full-time work as a psychotherapist treating DPD. Bezzubova believes that there is simply a certain type of person who is predisposed to DPD. For them, the condition is permanent and chronic, like arthritis, which may permit the patient to dance on one day, but cause them to lie in bed in pain on another. And while DPD may present itself in many ways, all depersonalized people have common traits as defined by the condition itself.

> In Russia we didn't have the language of dissociation, but the symptoms, in the way they exhibit themselves, are the same world-wide. The paradox in depersonalization is that it is the very feeling that you lost yourself that enables you ultimately to find yourself. Healthy people do not know that they have their selves. They just have feelings. They may reflect once in a while, but they are not focused on their thoughts, their mind, and their body like deper-sonalized people who often can think of nothing else. You need a depersonalization to really realize that you have a persona. In this sense, depersonalized people can find it helpful to have creative therapy. Writing, painting, art therapy, drama are all great venues for depersonalization.

Bezzubova also believes in the contemporary conception of the therapist as a "coach" who helps one proceed through life with a condition, providing and listening to individualized insights.

Patients often don't like the idea of therapy from the moment they dis-cover they have depersonalization, Bezzubova says. This is normal. In time, however, they often come to it, willingly, like a horse drawn to water. And that is the way it should be done.

"Psychotherapy is something very personal—it is something 'I make the decision to do,' not 'something that is done to me.' It is something that I do willingly. This will of a self taking the effort to understand and remake itself begins a healthy process of change and adaptation."

Depersonalization that has its roots in the structure of society and the demands it may make on an individual can also be treated effectively through psychotherapy, according to psychologist Orna Guralnik, Psy.D. Guralnik, who took part in many of the clinical studies conducted at Mount Sinai in past years, now treats depersonalization in private practice in New York's Soho. Her approach to depersonalization stems from the view that depersonalized people are often those for whom an aspect of their selfhood is not recognized by their environment. They are, in a way, persecuted by their environment, whether within the home or in society at large. Their "exit strategy" to avoid submitting to those powers is to depersonalize. "It's their maneuver to try to save something in themselves," she says.

Guralnik's interest is in the societal factors that can cause depersonalization, and her current areas of exploration, in many ways hearken back to observations about social factors made by Cattell and Cattell in the 1970s (see chapter 3). Guralnik feels that a combination of one's makeup, family dynamics, social environment, and friends all contribute to the ability to withstand the forces coming from outside the self. One develops a strategy for dealing with this, and it is not always an exit strategy. But looking for an exit strategy becomes part of some people's character structure. In dealing with internal conflicts, some people exit through depersonalization.

The language, traditions, legal, and other systems of society all work to create and dictate the ways in which we understand ourselves. When that becomes too offensive to certain parts of one's personhood, it can create problems for that individual. "You may try to continue to make your way, you may submit, or you may have some sort of existential crisis," Guralnik says.

An example is being gay in a society that denies that one can be gay or that maintains that being homosexual is a sin, or the most shameful thing one can be. The result is an existential crisis for the person, and a very good exit strategy is to become depersonalized.

Guralnik encountered two case histories in which the societal climate, coupled with childhood family dynamics, created individuals who had no choice internally but to seek a psychological exit of some sort. For them this exit strategy turned out to be depersonalization.

In one instance, a black woman was raised in a household that never acknowledged its ethnicity. The woman went to white-dominated schools, the family's friends were white, and they all lived in a white neighborhood. The issue of being black racially never came up in the household at all. But intense, unexplored feelings about being so different continued through her young life. She started to feel depersonalized in adolescence, when identity issues usually become most pressing. But it got worse and worse because she continued to function in a predominantly white environment. This was complicated by other family dynamics that went unnamed. There were "unthought knowns"—things that she was forbidden to ever think about, or give voice to, and the entire family functioned this way. There were many "self" facts that were not discussed. Internally, she never developed a language for processing within herself, or with other people, very important chunks of her experience. In an attempt to fit in, around her white friends she thought and acted "white," but when around black people she adopted a different persona inwardly and outwardly.

Still an astute and intelligent woman, she became depressed in time, then did some research and concluded that she was suffering from depersonalization. Treatment with medication helped, but a year of intense psychodynamic therapy—geared largely toward giving expression to her unformulated experiences—brought about resolution and relief. It is important, Guralnik says, that the woman was intent on getting through depersonalization and getting well.

In another instance where societal taboos played a role, a gay man was brought up in an intensely Catholic family; sexuality of any kind was never discussed. On top of this struggle with sexuality in general, he was, in his youth, also becoming aware that he was attracted to men, and this was not acceptable in his own mind. The only option was to be a nonsexual person. Aware that something was going on within him, he gave it no name. Internally he felt he was constantly trying to undo something that was wrong, and sometimes when it became too intense he would try to put himself into self-hypnosis to try to trance out. Actually wanting to depersonalize in some way, the feeling grew too big and blossomed into an unpleasant, constant state of feeling hollow. All the dissociative aspects of DPD were then present.

Some doctors diagnosed him as having generalized anxiety. Then he learned about depersonalization and recognized the symptoms in himself. He wasn't depressed, so medication probably would not have helped in his case, Guralnik says. With therapy, however, the condition improved dramatically. Through having an "authentic" experience with the therapist, the unseen parts of the person's self were seen, recognized, named, and understood by another person for the first time. Parts of his experience that he did not see as even being human became recognizable. Guralnik adds.

> The therapy was not just about cognition—it had to be intense experientially. Having a strong experience with another person in which he felt recognized completely was crucial. Within that context, he was able to name what was going on within him, and give it reality, and also recognize the forces that were operating against him—the family, the church—all working to disavow his experience.

The important part of therapy in each of these cases was to give these patients a "language" that recognized them and made them part of the human discourse, Guralnik explains. This enabled them to expand what they included as their "selfhood." They were no longer "outsiders."

Mount Sinai's Brief Psychotherapy Treatment Study

Drawing from worldwide sources and years of in-house research, the doctors at Mount Sinai in New York have put together a multistep program that has been effective for certain individuals suffering from DPD. The following case history describes how this program is implemented.

John was a 27-year-old man with chronic depersonalization, who first was seen in Mount Sinai's research program for a general evaluation. He was Australian and was living temporarily in New York working as a visual artist. His girlfriend was American and in the process of completing her business degree at a local university, with 2 more years to go. He described that his depersonalization had begun about 3 years earlier, when he visited New York City, met and fell in love with his current girlfriend, Martha, and then had to return to Sydney, Australia, to continue his work as a graphics consultant to a large business. Although he felt very conflicted about leaving his first true love to pursue his career path, he felt this was the right thing to do. He also knew that his parents, who were greatly concerned about his future as well as that of his younger brother, would be gravely disappointed if he sacrificed such a promising position without good reason.

Shortly after returning to Sydney, John began to feel more and more asleep, dreamlike, spaced out, and confused in time and memories. He was not clinically depressed; he was eating and sleeping normally and going about his daily business with his usual energy. Yet he felt very detached from his emotions, almost in a trance, seeing everything around him as if through a heat wave, fuzzy and far away. He was quite insightful, and explained this state as a "protective reaction to a period of severe stress." After 10 long months of this mental torment, John decided to give up his job in Sydney and return to New York City to rejoin Martha, with whom he'd kept close phone and e-mail contact. He moved in with her and started working as a freelance graphics consultant, barely making ends meet.

Despite his happiness at being reunited with Martha, his depersonalization failed to clear, actually becoming denser over the next couple years before visiting the Depersonalization Research Unit at Mount Sinai. Prior to this episode, John had never experienced actual depersonalization or derealization symptoms. However, he did describe, with some sense of conviction about its relevance, that he had always been "detached" in some way since he'd been a young child. He valued his privacy and had liked to spend many hours alone, reading existential philosophy and pondering the meanings of existence, an undertaking that had only intensified his sense of detachment from the real world around him. At present he described his depersonalization as quite constant, hardly fluctuating in intensity. He believed that the symptoms greatly interfered with his capacity to feel close to other people, as well as with his attention and memory and, therefore, his work performance. He denied any other important concurrent psychiatric conditions, such as depression or anxiety, beyond his worry and demoralization over his persisting depersonalization. John described that he had grown up in a happy and well-off family, and his parents were still together and lived in Sydney. He had never received any kind of psychiatric treatment, talk therapy, or medication.

At Mount Sinai, John was treated in the course of a brief 10-session weekly psychotherapy. The therapy was "eclectic," a mixture of various techniques. These included psychoeducation; symptom monitoring with diary keeping; identification and working through core dynamics associated with the depersonalization; cognitive-behavioral interventions including cognitive corrections, distraction task training, thought blocking, grounding techniques, and positive reinforcement; and exercises modulating arousal level. All sessions were fairly structured, beginning with a review and elaboration of the interceding week in terms of symptoms, diary keeping, personal observations, and effectiveness of the various assigned techniques. Each session built on the one before it, introducing finer nuances, elaborations, and modifications to previous understandings and techniques to be used and elaborated by John over the next week. Below we describe, session by session, John's course in treatment.

In the first session, the background history was reviewed, and the therapist and John arrived at a mutual understanding of his depersonalization symptoms as a reaction gone haywire, triggered by a period of severe stress in his life, which John did not yet fully understand. After all, although he had been through a difficult time, nothing catastrophic or extremely traumatic had happened to him. This clearly had two implications. First, John might have some innate vulnerability toward depersonalization, a hypothesis supported by his childhood experiences of retreat and nonbothersome detached reverie. Second, a relationship conflict that for many might have been quite painful but not lead to pathological symptoms, for John had in some fundamental sense been intolerable—or how else could one make sense of the profound symptoms that it triggered? John's "homework" assignment for the first week was to keep a daily diary of his depersonalization symptoms, which he completed right before going to bed every night. In it he would have to chart on the same 0 to 10 scale, week after week, the intensity of his depersonalization symptoms as three daily estimates. The scale represented at its extremes 0 as no depersonalization at all and 10 as the worse the depersonalization had ever been in his life. John had to record an average intensity of symptoms for each day, a low, and a high; decimal points could not be used, as some people can get too preoccupied with numbers and miss the essence of the exercise. For each day's low and high point, John needed to briefly write down the circumstances and state related to it: what he was doing and feeling when it happened. The goal of the sessions would be, over time, to make sense of the patterns of what triggered and alleviated John's depersonalization and of how he could come to recognize that all symptoms, even the most constant, do have variations that a person can gradually gain more control over.

In the second session, John and the therapist reviewed his first diary and noted that over the past week his depersonalization had peaked as high as a 7 and had been as low as a 2. Given this considerable variation in the intensity of the symptoms, they began to explore the various emotional states and thought patterns that were associated with these fluctuations. John realized that several of the situations that had triggered his depersonalization over the past week shared something in common, times when he had felt powerless and helpless when faced with a choice or a confrontation. Whenever conflicting interests and needs had to be reconciled, John felt stuck and "frozen." With his therapist, he developed a corrective thought to reframe these states when they'd occur: "I really do have choice and agency." John also began to develop grounding tasks, aimed at reconnecting him with himself whenever he felt more depersonalized. These tasks were gradually modified and improved over the course of the sessions to best fit his needs and to maximize their effectiveness. Initially John chose the task of focusing his visual awareness on one object in his surroundings, until this became mentally clear and the dreamlike surroundings began to fade.

In the third session, John revealed that his depersonalization had peaked during an incident when he went out to dinner with two business partners. The two men began to heatedly argue over dinner about how to handle a recent financial crisis in the company, and John felt more and more dissociated to the point where the restaurant looked like dreamland, and he felt sure the others could sense his detached state. He found the arguing intolerable and felt compelled to mediate and solve it, but his mind was blank and he could think of nothing to say. He was increasingly aware of how uncomfortable it was for him to be surrounded by any conflict.

In his fourth session, John was getting much better at identifying conflictual situations that worsened his depersonalization, and in his diary he summarized five trigger states for his depersonalization: feeling that he let others down; feeling stuck in the middle in conflicts between two sides; feeling powerless to make his own choices so that choices were made for him; feeling he hurt others by asserting his own views; and feeling guilty for doing what he wanted instead of what others expected of him. In other words, a central theme was emerging to John's depersonalization, having to do with asserting his own beliefs or needs rather than placating others and avoiding conflict. Now one might ask, why experience depersonalization as a result of this seemingly rather common predicament? Why not experience panic or depression? Presumably, all of us carry our own unique vulnerabilities, predisposing us to experience the impact of stress with a particular set of symptoms. Additionally, in this session John brought up the fact that intense aerobic exercise often helped to alleviate his symptoms, and a half hour of such exercise daily was added to his daily routine.

In session 5, John reported that his grounding exercise was minimally effective; he often would get lost in a state of absorption on a single focal object, rather than achieve greater clarity. A modified exercise was developed, in which John would willfully shift his gaze among various focal points in his environment while compellingly telling himself "I'm here, I'm real, I'm alive." In this session, John also reflected on the onset of his depersonalization, describing how overwhelmingly distraught he had felt at the time, not being able to reconcile his girlfriend's wish to be with him with the successful career path that was so important to his parents.

John also described a breakthrough incident during the prior week which would previously have left him very dissociated, but on this occasion did not. At a recent meeting, his two colleagues with whom he had gone out to dinner were disagreeing again about an aspect of strategic planning for the company, each using some of John's ideas as an argument for why his own agenda made more sense. Rather than feeling frozen and blank, John was able to clarify what he personally thought should be done, and how his position was both similar and different to what each side was proposing. He felt grounded and articulate, and was visibly pleased with his accomplishment.

In session 6, John reported that his new grounding technique was proving much more successful, giving him a sense of willful control and self-affirmation. He had been able to take mental breaks throughout his day whenever he began to feel more depersonalized, taking in the reality of his being and his surroundings and bringing himself back to reality. He had also been able to do more aerobic exercise on a treadmill, and found that this made him feel more "alive," though the feeling was only temporary. He also reported, of his own accord, a dream in which his two parents were fighting about a recent career decision that his father had made, as John stood in a corner helplessly listening in. He was awakened by the bad dream, and was struck by his feeling of devastation and by the intensely depersonalized state in which the dream had left him.

John continued to experience gains in his treatment. He stood up to a very difficult customer at work who was challenging his position with only a slight intensification of his symptoms. He also had a fight with his girlfriend about their future plans as a couple, again with only a mild worsening of his depersonalization.

By session 8 John reported that he had had some very good days, feeling quite connected after exercising, asserting his mind, and not giving in to mental retreat. He described another breakthrough, commenting how he had been able to let his boss know that he needed to visit his sick grandfather on short notice, overwhelmed by the feeling of letting others down, while at the same time struggling to correct his thinking about needs and priorities. The mere description of the incident led him to strongly depersonalize in session to a peak of 8. The therapist noticed the spacey look in his eyes, and the accompanying breakdown in the richness of his narrative, then commented on these observations. John unexpectedly began to cry, sharing with great difficulty how uncomfortable it felt for him to have his feelings revealed. He felt "found out," and related this intolerable feeling to growing up in a family where conflictual and disturbing feelings always needed to be buried.

John's subsequent homework placed even greater emphasis on the awareness of unacceptable feelings triggered by numerous situations and his interpretations of them. By session 9, he reported that grounding techniques remained helpful on a daily basis. He had even been able to get teary in a recent argument with his girlfriend and remain engaged, rather than detaching. He stated that he had really tried to stay in touch with his feelings all week, and expressed succinctly the inner devastation of feeling guilty in betraying conflicting loyalties. He further described what an unsolvable conflict this had been in his childhood, with his two parents often at conflict yet pretending to hide it in a semblance of normality, only expecting the same of John. For the following week, the emphasis continued on the awareness of intolerable feelings that John still needed to avoid at all cost by detaching.

In the tenth and last session, John reported that he was now able to feel mounting anxiety first, in his chest and stomach, before becoming detached, and that he would then try to soothe himself, with varying degrees of success, by telling himself, "there is no devastating conflict here, everything is OK." In other words, he had now gotten better at detecting the early signals of the emotional states that were capable of activating his dissociative tendencies, and by doing so to lessen their impact. He could now recognize the pervasive theme that guilt over letting others down had played and was continuing to play in his life.

At the end of 10 sessions, John was not free of his depersonalization symptoms, but he definitely felt better. He felt that the most useful components of his treatment had been learning to identify the causes and triggers of his depersonalization, experiencing it as more episodic and being more tuned in to its fluctuations; having some capacity to ground himself; knowing how to keep a diary to help him look back on each day and identify what went on; using stimulation exercises (aerobics) to get transient relief; and being more able to identify feelings, conflicts, and dynamics activated by different situations. He felt that his depersonalization was much better overall, improved by about 40% from the beginning of treatment. Interestingly, his feelings of anxiety and depression, although mild overall, were not better. If anything, he was now more aware of such symptoms as preludes to increasing dissociation. He said, "Definitely my symptoms have changed since the start. They seemed constant then, now I'm more aware of their fluctuations. I understand them better. I see it as episodes now rather than a constant daze; that helps me to control it. Overall I'm more active, more alert, less fatigued. I'm feeling more. I'm less detached."

Summary of Principles in Treating Chronic Depersonalization

In this section we summarize the basic principles in the psychotherapeutic treatment of depersonalization disorder. It is based on a variety of sources, including:

- detailed historical writings on the condition and its treatment,
- Mount Sinai Center's efforts toward developing a systematic treatment approach for the condition,

- work of other leading centers,
- general principles of psychotherapy,
- extensive experience with patients suffering from depersonalization.

Psychoeducation: Know What Depersonalization Is and Isn't

It is extremely helpful for patients to understand what it is that they are suffering from, in particular when it is the kind of experience that others have in different ways dismissed in the past or have simply been unable to comprehend. Most sufferers from depersonalization have never encountered another person suffering from their condition, although the development of Internet communication has substantially decreased this isolation in recent years. Giving the syndrome a name and describing to patients how it typically presents itself, what brings it on, and what can be expected in the future can be tremendously reassuring. Equally relieving can be the reassurance that depersonalization, no matter how severe, never evolves into something worse or different: people never actually become crazy, psychotic, or schizophrenic as a result of it. There is also no evidence of irreversible brain damage with DPD, at least not by brain imaging and activity assessments available to us at the current time. It also helps patients to know that the course of DPD, although sometimes chronic, can be quite unpredictable. For some, episodes can last for weeks, months, or even years, and then gradually fade. Often, each person's unique history is the best predictor of future course.

Sometimes people are also caught up in the guilt or self-blame of what it was that they initially might have done, or failed to do, that triggered the illness, whether it was smoking marijuana or allowing themselves to be subjected to severe, prolonged stress. It can be very therapeutic to overcome the exaggerated sense of responsibility and blame associated with these thoughts. Ultimately, people do all kinds of things for all kinds of reasons, and these may or may not result in lasting symptoms. What happens is in one sense fortuitous, and often beyond our control or our best predictions. Many people are subjected to similar scenarios and might develop other types of symptoms or no symptoms at all. Patients might also be encouraged, when appropriate, to share some of their depersonalization experiences with others, overcoming the barrier of a secret illness that cannot be understood by others or may be misconstrued as madness. Although this may not bring about immediate improvement, it may help restore some basic sense of sharing and connected-ness that is important to everyone's well-being.

Interpreting the "Physicality" of the Depersonalization Experience

The physicality of the symptoms need have nothing to do with a physical or irreversible nature of its cause. Yet many patients with depersonalization feel this way. They extrapolate that if symptoms set in suddenly, for no apparent reason, or feel like their mind is empty, or are associated with a fullness in the head or a tingling in the scalp or a visual fog, this must somehow mean that the depersonalization is indicative of brain damage and, even worse, irrevers-ible brain damage. Proof of how powerful this conviction can be is the large number of depersonalization sufferers who have consulted numerous other medical professionals before becoming convinced, or despairing enough, to finally see a psychiatrist. Ophthalmologists, neurologists, ear-nose-and-throat doctors, endocrinologists, and chronic fatigue specialists have frequently been consulted. These professionals will typically run a battery of tests pertinent to their expertise which in the vast majority of cases yields no pathological findings. Finally, they will try to convince the patient that what he or she is experiencing is "just stress," or maybe anxiety or depression, leaving them as bewildered as they originally were and often minimally reassured.

Yet, physical manifestations of psychological states, as we well know, cannot be simply linked to irreversible physical causes. For example, patients with clinical depression who can't eat do not have a physical derangement of their appetite system; patients with panic attacks who suffer from shortness of breath do not have irreversible physical damage of their lungs and respi-ratory system, and so on. Psychoeducation aimed at separating the seeming physicality or permanence of the symptoms from any inferences about their cause or reversibility is a key component of the treatment of depersonalized patients.

Who Controls Whom? The Person Controls the Symptoms, Not Vice Versa

Not unlike patients with other kinds of psychological symptoms, patients with depersonalization can often feel that the symptoms, be it one, several, or several that alternate, are running and ruining their lives. This may be true to some extent, but typically not to the extent subjectively perceived. Therefore, it is important in the early stages of treatment to demonstrate to patients suffering from depersonalization that they do and can have some, even if limited, control over their symptoms. This is often hampered by the perception of the symptoms as constant and unfluctuating, independent of any psychological determinants that have meaning, driven mainly by physical environmental factors such as sleep, lighting, level of environmental stimulation, and so on. There are different ways of helping patients, even those who perceive their symptoms as most unwavering, to start to notice that indeed they vary, and that they can make sense out of these variations. One way to help patients become more aware of fluctuations is to have them keep a written or mental diary of their depersonalization and to note even minimal fluctuations in its intensity, attempting to relate them to changes in internal emotional state. Patients can be helped over time to put more sophisticated labels on their experience, from the simple stressed or depersonalized, to saddened, angered, overwhelmed, anxious, frightened, and so on. Patients can also start to use various cognitive-behavioral techniques to help modulate the intensity of their symptoms. If these techniques meet with any initial degree of success, even transient or partial, patients may come to appreciate that their symptoms do not completely have a life of their own, but can be controlled. More about these approaches follows.

Diary Keeping

As described by Hunter and colleagues from the Institute of Psychiatry in London, diary keeping can be an invaluable technique, especially in the early stages of treatment, in tackling depersonalization.[12] In Mount Sinai's program, participants are given a daily calendar, and in it they chart at the end of each day the intensity of their depersonalization for that day on a 0 to 10 scale, 0 being none and 10 being the worst ever for them. The average, maximum, and minimum for each day is charted. For the maximum and minimum, patients also chart the context and their subjective emotional state at the time. The therapist and patient then review the diary together at their next session, and almost unfailingly, patterns begin to reveal themselves. The external conditions and internal states associated with the fluctuations, even tiny ones, in depersonalization, start to become increasingly apparent. Increasing awareness of the associations of these fluctuations can be put to many uses. First, they show patients that the symptom is not simply flat and unvarying in intensity.

Second, they give patients an emergent sense of control over the symptoms: if they can get worse, they can also get better. Third, conditions that can lessen the symptoms can be understood, pursued, and reinforced, whereas conditions that worsen the symptoms can be understood, avoided, and substituted with more adaptive reactions.

Obsessions and Compulsions Surrounding Depersonalization: Is It Still There?

Not all patients with depersonalization obsess about their symptoms, but many do. For some, this can even be one of the more extreme and damaging manifestations of the condition. For example, they might spend countless hours ruminating about the nature of human existence and its illusionary qualities; they may repeatedly check hundreds of times in a day their perceptions and how real or unreal they feel at any moment; they may obsess about the cause of their condition, endlessly wondering if they had not smoked marijuana or had not broken up with a partner if any of this would have happened; they may keep looking at their hands to determine if they look any more or less real than they did an hour ago; or they may check their vision incessantly to determine if it's getting more foggy.

Like other types of obsessions, those about depersonalization serve no useful purpose. They are a way to unwittingly channel anxiety about the symptoms, try to undo or prevent them, and engage in magical thinking along the lines that if one worries and checks enough, somehow a solution will be found. In reality, obsessing only exacerbates all symptoms, including those of depersonalization. It is much like playing with a sore tooth with your tongue. It's difficult to avoid doing it, even when you know you may be doing further harm. It is therefore very important in any treatment of DPD to assess closely if obsessions or compulsions are present, in any form. Sometimes patients will not readily reveal this or even be fully aware of it. Detailed questioning of moment-to-moment interactions in the therapy might be necessary and quite helpful. For example, one patient in therapy would pause in her recounting of recent events and associations and appear increasingly distracted. This quickly became apparent to be a habitual pattern. Questioned as to what was going on in the moment, she eventually revealed that, as she related stories in her usual detached fashion in sessions, she would gradually feel more and more depersonalized. This led her to become increasingly preoccupied with her detachment and increasingly engaged in checking and grounding techniques in an attempt to contain the symptoms, while simultaneously trying to go on with the manifest stories so that her internal state would not be revealed to others. Such processes need to be identified for what they are and dealt with.

Thought blocking, response prevention, and cognitive correction techniques can be helpful along these lines. Patients can learn to substitute their obsessing, as soon as they become aware of it, with alternative behaviors such as engaging in any distracting daily life tasks, or even in ritualistic behaviors such as counting. Or, they can engage in cognitive corrections of the distorted thinking that underlies the obsessing. For example, "no one has solved the existential mystery and neither can I," or "I am as real as I am, no matter what my checking tells me," can serve as appropriate cognitive corrections for "is existence real or is it a dream" or "my hand looks a little more plastic now than it did this morning."

Grounding

Most patients with depersonalization, by nature of the symptoms, will in one way or another describe that they do not feel grounded within their real self. Those who are able to even transiently feel a little more grounded, either by their willful control or spontaneously, can readily relate to the term "grounded" and to the importance of learning how to feel that way. The goal of feeling more grounded in internal and external reality is not limited to depersonalization but extends to all dissociative states. Some patients are initially unable to describe any procedures that can help them feel more grounded, while others have on their own developed complex repertoires that help them attain a more grounded state before ever consulting a professional. It is important for the therapist, then, to assess a patient's sense of what grounding means for them, of what circumstances naturally help them fit the term's definition, and of any techniques that they willfully employ to achieve some sense of grounding. Subsequently, in a collaborative approach with the patient, the therapist can help, session to session, develop more effective grounding techniques, assessing their effectiveness on an ongoing basis.

We previously described John's attempts at this. There are some common techniques that can be useful for different patients. Whereas focused, selective attention to a single stimulus can often have a hypnotic trancelike effect (indeed the "dot paradigm," staring at a dot incessantly for minutes, is an experimental technique used to induce dissociation even in those who do not have it), the controlled and willful shifting of attention from one to another reference point within or external to the self, while attempting to actively take in perceptions rather than give in to the state of nonbeing, can have a grounding effect. Sometimes looking in the mirror and intently identifying the reality of the reflected self can help, usually in conjunction with a self-affirming recitation along the lines of "this is me." (Ironically, staring too intently at one's self in the mirror can also have the opposite effect, even in "normals," fostering a fleeting sensation that the reflection is strange or belongs to someone else.)

Use of nonvisual modalities can also help with grounding: closing the eyes and intently listening to a compelling piece of music, smelling a favorite aroma, or tasting a special treat, works better for some than the visual modality. Willful immersion in the senses can be grounding for many. Willfully touching different parts of the body can also help, like squeezing an earlobe, the palm of the hand, or stroking the arms—every patient can discover their own physical manipulation that can help ground them. Physical sensation bordering on pain can also be helpful to some. One patient who had been depersonalized for many years described in his initial evaluation that he had felt alive only twice in recent memory, once when he experienced intense romantic love, and once when he was accidentally smashed against a wall and felt intense pain. The rubberband and similar techniques can also be helpful in grounding: snapping a rubberband hard, but not too hard, against one's wrist can engender a sense of being alive, and it is certainly a more adaptive solution than more extreme and destructive means of alleviating deadness such as self-cutting and burning.

The Vicious Cycle of Fear and Anxiety

Depersonalization is a quintessential stress-induced symptom, and as such it only makes sense that the perpetuation of fear and anxiety about it can be very damaging, maybe more damaging than desperation over other kinds of psychological symptoms. Fear of the symptoms appears to accentuate them and lead to more stress and fear as fuel for a vicious cycle of an ever-worsening psychological state. Giving in to this cycle can be tremendously frightening and demoralizing. Conversely, making a dent in it can be uniquely empowering. Hunter and colleagues, for example, have proposed that the initial triggering of such a vicious cycle may be the central process that differentiates those individuals who in response to an initial stressor develop transient depersonalization from those who get caught up in an ever-worsening early course of depersonalization.[13] While the stories of some patients who do not recall early angst about their symptoms do not readily support this notion, others clearly do. Some describe that they were unable to ignore or calmly attend to initial feelings of unreality and normalize them by attributing them to intense circumstances or internal states; their terror over the initial unreality and their conviction that something irreparable had occurred only served to intensify and prolong the early course of the disorder.

Helping patients conceptualize depersonalization as a stress-response symptom can help them understand why the symptom naturally worsens whenever stressing about it intensifies. Undoubtedly, from what we know so far, highly stressful internal mental states, such as anxiety or depression, can trigger depersonalization. In a similar vein, internal angst over early depersonalization symptoms and their implications can act as a severe internal stressor that precipitates a worse course.

Understanding the Meanings of the Symptoms

Nothing can be more helpful and empowering than making sense of something that makes no apparent sense. This is true of most things for sentient humans, and it is no different for depersonalization. As we've already noted, sometimes the physicality of the symptom, its out-of-the-blue onset, or its unvarying course regardless of how else one is feeling might give the impression that the symptoms have little to do with meaning. We are convinced that this is not so. Actually, Simeon, in her experience with a large number of patients suffering from depersonalization, has been struck by the often complex and deep meanings that can be attributed to these symptoms. She has also found that working through these meanings can have therapeutic impact, at least for some people.

Patients may come to their initial evaluation completely unaware of any emotional triggers. It might seem that their depersonalization just set in one day, an ordinary day no different from any other. Yet careful exploration can often reveal, even in one meeting, that the ordinary was not so ordinary. Although a major traumatic event, along the lines of what we think about in posttraumatic stress disorder or in the more extreme dissociative disorders probably did not occur, equally compelling precipitants often become apparent. Actually, the detached, disconnected nature of the depersonalization experience per se inherently disrupts the capacity to make meaningful links to such precipitants; simply put, one is too cut-off to make connections. A depersonalized individual can feel so disconnected that, automatically, almost as if on purpose, symptoms disrupt the links to relevant meanings.

Take, for example, Sam, who first experienced depersonalization when he was 18. On the surface it occurred on an ordinary day, like any other. But at the same time, on more detailed questioning, it turned out that this was a day soon before Sam was about to leave home and live on campus for the first time ever, a couple of months into the start of the first semester. Furthermore, Sam felt confused about his sexual orientation, liking both boys and girls while considering the latter to be more acceptable. Yet he was about to move in to an off-campus apartment with three male roommates, two of whom were gay.

Twenty-two-year old Ben, on the other hand, could appreciate a more direct connection between the onset of his symptoms and precipitating events. When he was 17, his mother, whom he dearly loved, had unexpectedly died of a heart attack at age 58; he had had no opportunity to say good-bye. Ben could not deny the temporal relationship between the onset of depersonalization and his mother's death, but still he could make no meaningful connection between the two. Anyone deeply hurt, even devastated, should still be able to eventually recover, he felt. What was it, then, that led Ben to become chronically depersonalized after his mother's death, where others might not have become so symptomatic? It turned out that Ben's mother had been very loving and involved with him, but deeply unsatisfied in her personal life, something painfully evident to Ben as far back as he could remember. She had lost her own parents at a young age and was married to an uninvolved and self-absorbed man who had little to offer her emotionally. Ultimately, Ben had always felt, without much awareness, the ultimate responsibility for his mother's happiness. Only he could "bring her to life," so that Ben ultimately failed her when she died. His psychic reality was too painfully overwhelming to bear, and left Ben feeling unreal for a long time.

George had felt depersonalized for about 3 years, in the face of mounting stress in his life, not of an extraordinary sort. In just a few years, he had finished graduate school while simultaneously working numerous increasingly demanding jobs, relocating to several homes, marrying, caring for his ailing parents, and preparing to have a family of his own. Yet he was barely able to acknowledge all the pressures and expectations that he put on himself by focusing only on his drive to achieve and move forward. He initially had described his childhood as a happy, "regular" one, and only later in treatment revealed how he had often felt caught up in conflict between his two parents. His mother was a very successful professional who looked down on his stay-at-home father and inevitably chastised George that he would amount to nothing better than his father. When he was accepted to a good college, she was reluctant to financially support him despite her means, unabashedly stating that her investment was likely to go to waste, and forcing George to take out large amounts of unnecessary financial aid. So, for George to become established and successful was not a mere ambition; it was a life-and-death matter of self-definition and self-worth, and he succumbed to the internal pressures by eventually dissociating.

Melissa was 34, and she grew up in a home where much of the time her two parents were yelling or screaming at each other. Since she was little, Melissa wondered why they stayed together. The parents' constant arguing scared her and distracted her, and as she grew older, she also saw it as being disrespectful of her need for peace and privacy in her own home. Despite her pleas, her parents did not appear interested or capable of controlling their behavior when she was around. Melissa vividly recalls the first time when she consciously tried to tune them out, becoming very absorbed, almost hypnotized, by a painting on her bedroom wall. After that incident and over the years, Melissa became increasingly depersonalized. Now as an adult, she found it very hard to focus even on interesting tasks, and she described how she often became distracted by conversations in the background in which she had no interest, yet could not quite block out. Eventually a connection was made in treatment: Over the years, Melissa had become expert at dividing her attention between tasks on which she wanted to focus and irrelevant surrounding information that she wished she could screen out more effectively. Yet at the same time, she probably felt compelled to monitor it all since it was threatening and relevant to her well-being. So she became proficient at being distracted and attending to different aspects of her environment, to the detriment of her ability to effectively focus on one thing when she needed to.

Modulating Arousal

The question of whether individuals with chronic depersonalization are overaroused or underaroused is a challenging and unresolved one, and we touched on it from a biological standpoint elsewhere. It's relevant here because it can have therapy implications. In the mid-1980s, Fewtrell insight-fully raised the issue of arousal in treating chronic depersonalization.[14] He noted that in 40 anxious patients with progressive relaxation, 7 had become distressed by the technique and experienced "relaxation-induced anxiety." Retrospectively, these 7 turned out to be individuals who were suffering from concomitant depersonalization. In 1946, Shorvon made the observation that depersonalization often sets in with the relaxation that follows intense and prolonged stimulation or stress.[15] At Mount Sinai, Simeon and colleagues' clini-cal experience concurs with Shorvon's observation in at least a proportion of patients, while in other patients depersonalization can be triggered as their stress and anxiety reaches a peak. The triggering of depersonalization may therefore have more to do with abrupt or large shifts in arousal than with a high or low arousal state per se; it may also have to do with a mismatch be-tween subjectively perceived stress and physiologic arousal. Regardless, the phenomenon prompted Fewtrell to recommend that "attempts to alleviate the condition should not conform to an arousal or arousal-reduction model, nor should therapeutic procedures assume that depersonalization is an anxiety state." He went on to say that "distress does not always mean excitation, physi-cally or otherwise, and the depersonalized state does not generally require relaxation as the therapeutic goal."[16]

When considering the appropriate treatment of a depersonalized patient, it can be helpful to think of the patient as being in either a "high-arousal" or a "low-arousal" states, which reflect the opposite ends of the spectrum of symp-toms DPD can present. The "high-arousal" patients are often very anxious and can derive considerable benefits from interventions such as meditation and yoga, which can help induce a more relaxed state. The "low-arousal" patients, in contrast, experience more numbing and stupor than they do anxiety. These patients can feel worse with meditation and yoga and seem to benefit from stimulating interventions such as aerobic exercise and other activities that can heighten physical or emotional excitement.

The Heritability Fear: Will I Pass This On?

Both men and women who suffer from depersonalization sometimes express worry about whether their children are likely to develop the condition. Al-though the definitive answer to this question is not out, overall, clinicians can reassure patients that, from what we do know, the likelihood of this occurring is quite low. For one, although there have been no formal family studies that interviewed the relatives of those with depersonalization, the reports of depersonalized patients rarely reveal parents or siblings who experience the symptom. Also, as we've described earlier, there have been only two twin studies examining the heritability of dissociation, although not depersonalization in particular, which had conflicting results. Finally, there appears to be a strong environmental stress-related component to the genesis of the disorder. So, although no one can reassure a person with depersonalization that their children will not manifest the disorder, one can say that, thus far, it appears less likely than it does for numerous other psychiatric conditions, and rather unlikely.

General Behavioral Measures

Although these sets of preventive measures are essentially common sense, and many patients are well aware that altering certain habits could be helpful to their symptoms, they do not necessarily follow through consistently with these changes. Changes need to be tailored to each individual, after a thorough assessment of all the factors that exacerbate their depersonalization. Some of the more common and easy-to-change habits are sleep hygiene (too much or too little sleep can worsen depersonalization); reducing environmental overstimulation wherever and whenever possible; and substituting fluorescent lights with more natural lighting.

Are these techniques the answer for all people? Perhaps not. As we've seen in earlier chapters, depersonalization often manifests itself in ways that are nothing less than bizarre, sometimes so odd and seemingly abnormal that a patient may be reluctant to describe them to a doctor or therapist for fear of being put in a psychiatric ward. But it's important to remember that DPD in all of its manifestations is still part of the same syndrome. Parts of it can be helped with psychotherapy, while other symptoms might be helped pharmacologically. It is completely within the realm of human experience, a part of life, however one may interpret it.

Ultimately, knowing what DPD is, educating oneself about its manifestations, and dealing with it head-on may prove to be the key aspect of improvement through therapy. The quote from psychiatrists Levy and Wachtel which began this chapter has come to confirm what many experts and patients have since come to believe as well. Depersonalization is, in the final analysis, a life-changing experience. If a person can deal with and overcome its most horrific symptoms, through today's advanced medications and tested therapies, the end result may be a new, and perhaps better self than the one that had existed previously. For the patient, this "new self" may indeed be "more real" than his old compromises were, however comfortable and familiar those might have felt.

Epilogue

Living Unreal

To be nobody but yourself in a world which is doing its best night and day to make you like everybody else means to fight the hardest battle any human being can fight and never stop fighting.

—E.E. CUMMINGS

Depersonalization disorder (DPD) is a thing unto itself. It is a condition that is inherently deceptive and contradictory, and yet, the common threads of a sense of unreality and the loss of the independent, individual self usually persist throughout its duration. Its symptoms are finite, clearly defined, and delineated after a century of study. But it remains highly misdiagnosed, misunderstood, or even ruled out completely as a disorder. Like the devil himself, it seems to draw its greatest strength from people who simply deny its existence.

We have, within these pages, condensed what is known to date, and perhaps swayed any skeptics who, if even aware of the condition, have acted on the assumption that DPD is always a part of something else. For those who experience it, no argument is necessary. For those who deny its existence in light of the research, no evidence will ever be enough. We've looked at pharmacological and psychotherapeutic ways of dealing with the condition. Now let's examine some final considerations.

DPD and the Family

How do you live with someone suffering from DPD? Obvious answers to this question, such as "be supportive" or "be patient" amount to little more than clichés that can apply to depression or most other mental problems.

Said one patient's father: "I keep wanting her to wake up and become the person she was. I want to help, and I've spent a fortune on psychiatrists with very little results. The worst thing is, I don't have a clue as to what she is going through. It's impossible for my wife and me to relate to it."

Doubly mystifying is the fact that this patient is able to hold a job and lead a "normal" life as far as her co-workers and friends are concerned. Only the closeness of her relationship with her parents prompted her to reveal the actual pain in which she lived every day.

Despite this father's difficulty in relating to the condition, a large portion of the population has experienced at least fleeting depersonalization at some point, and this may help people understand at least some of what their family member is enduring around the clock. Since depersonalized individuals are neither delusional nor crazy, open and truthful discussions are possible and helpful. Being able to discuss their thoughts, however bizarre, and their feelings, or lack of feelings, can obviously have some therapeutic effect. As we have said, the knowledge that the condition is real, and access to others with it or at least informed about it, may provide a tremendous sense of relief. Herein we have tried to arm doctors, patients, and family members with the pertinent data.

As we've seen, depersonalized people are often caught up in existential thinking, ruminating about the nature of existence and the validity of everything in which they have been indoctrinated since childhood. Many long-held beliefs or conventions often seem strange to the individual with DPD, as if they had just arrived from Mars. But they haven't. DPD is a human disorder that falls within the realm of human experience. Both patients and loved ones should reinforce the fact that DPD presents itself in "as if" experiences. Individuals with DPD have not lost their self; it only feels as if they have. So avoid getting into lengthy philosophical arguments if possible; the powers of pure reason are strained when battling sensations that defy conventional logic.

Encourage Life

Depersonalized people often exist on shaky ground because the one thing most people feel secure about and rarely think about—their own existence and sanity—has fallen into question, and often obsessive questioning. "I can't trust my thoughts, or my feelings. I'm afraid of what I might do," are common remarks. In time, some people, like the writer Frédéric Amiel, find they have spent their whole lives in a kind of dress rehearsal, readying for the moment of real life that never actually comes.

But others combat their depersonalization with the resolve often achieved by the characters in existential literature—a defiant attitude toward the condition, with the conscious decision to go on with their lives despite it, as long as the urgency of panic or periods of anxiety are kept in check or endured in the knowledge that they lead to no catastrophe. "Think of it this way," reads one website post. "DPD is a way for our minds to allow us to separate from ourselves or the outside world to protect us from a perceived threat. Think of it this way and deal with it accordingly as opposed to worrying about it and endlessly analyzing it."

The Wisdom of Insecurity

Despite its unsettling aspects, people with DPD take comfort that they have not fallen into unheard-of or insane trains of thought. Many are simply hyper-aware of the obvious realities and abstract concepts that most people either don't think about or respond to with long-held coping mechanisms that keep such states at bay. Infinity, eternity, and the fluid nature of consciousness, the view that nothing exists but the now-moment, even the fragility of the human body itself, are just accepted by most people or put on the back burner until a time of crisis or tragedy. Dwelling on such things surely leads to madness, they feel. Depersonalized people, however, often seem forced to face these realities head-on at the most inopportune times—somewhat like reluctant prophets who receive a calling but would much prefer to remain in the familiar meadow tending their sheep. But if philosophers, gurus, and gifted writers of every culture have chosen to make these realities the focus of their own lives and work, perhaps there is something to be said for being thrown into it willy nilly.

Says one long-term depersonalized person,

I don't consider myself "enlightened," but I have to say that in the last analysis, I'm glad I haven't seen things through what seems like a pretty narrow perspective—the things I've been taught since childhood. I don't know why this happened to me, but there must be some reason. In a way, I've feel like I've become no one, but at the same time, everyone. There's no fear of death, no thought of an end. I'm beyond that now. I feel more like I'm just a part of what has always existed and what always will exist.

While the clinical data cannot verify it, most observers regard people with DPD as highly intelligent and introspective. Beneath the fog of the feeling of no self may in fact lay a fiercely individualistic personality that has been held in check by fear. That self has not disappeared; it just feels as if it has. If you're battling DPD, remember that the ultimate goal is not to be like everybody else, but rather to emerge with a new, better sense of self from which your true individuality will ultimately find expression. To deal with the pain and seek effective treatment for DPD is justified and well advised. Then the philosophical aspects of depersonalization are always ready to be explored, or left alone.

We still may not have treatments, therapy or medication, that are powerfully effective in treating depersonalization. Still, within only a decade we have come a long way. The disorder is now on the map, well documented in its characteristics and course, and coming to light in its neurobiological and neurocognitive underpinnings. Treatments have begun to be tried and tested in the serious methodical fashion used in other mainstream disorders. Neuroscience and mental health treatments are unfolding at an accelerating pace. We can only be hopeful that continued research and perserverance will soon uncover effective interventions, maybe even a cure, for this previously obscure condition that afflicts so many people.

As Milton observed, the mind is indeed its own place that can make a hell of heaven and a heaven of hell. Depersonalized people, as we have seen, experience a region of the mind into which most only get a fleeting glimpse. For most it is indeed a place in hell where the confidence of personal identity is shattered; for others it's a strange, sometimes heavenly place where the need for that identity is dissolved. It becomes a place of safety and stoicism that seems somehow more in tune with the true nature of existence than the material world will ever be. Its horrors can be conquered, and for some, as illustrated by the poem below, it ultimately can be a source of liberation.

Wind within itself, self-involved dancer
you are in this hall—an empty cage.
How long will you question without answer,
contain the creeping silence and hollow rage?
People have long since gone away
curtains closed, lights blackened, stage swept;
still center front, abandoned you stay
and dance the old routines to promises kept.
Speak to the night; it hears you no more
than your own ears, bored with the known—
deaf to music pouring through an open door.
You wonder at how distant from life you've grown.
Dance, till no form remains
and the strength that binds you undoes your chains.[1]

Frequently Asked Questions

Why do some people who experience depersonalization describe it as weird, but not especially uncomfortable, while other people find it horrific and unbearable?

This seeming contradiction applies not only to depersonalization, but other psychiatric syndromes as well. Some people who experience chronic depersonalization may describe it as almost comforting in ways, placing them in a state of a kind of apathy, stoic resignation, or awareness of the "larger picture" of life. It prevents them from being able to feel many painful things that they could feel before. It protects them from overwhelming social anxiety, since social interactions feel so distant and unreal. Or it makes very painful memories seem distant and removed, as if they belong to someone else. It can sometimes make them feel as if no adversity can befall them that could be worse than the one they are already experiencing. But these people are a minority.

The large majority of depersonalized people find it profoundly disquieting, in a variety of ways, whether it be the disconnection from others, the inability to focus and be productive at work, the ultimate sense that their existence is unreal and devoid of meaning, or simply the torment of experiencing an altered state of being, as if they were losing their minds. Believing that they can no longer trust their own minds, they live in insecurity and fear. Often they will guard their depersonalization as an unbearable secret that they have never shared with others.

We do not know why some people are less tormented than others. Every individual is unique, and the way each experiences depersonalization is probably as variable as the innumerable ways that human beings experience any sort of adversity. For some it may be that they have experienced the symptom for so long, maybe even since early childhood, that it has become all they know and are paradoxically familiar with. Other people may have a personality style that helps them put this kind of mental adversity aside more easily, and go on with their lives. Still others may have sources of meaning in their lives, whether it be the importance of others, dedication to a career or a cause, or religious faith that helps them to keep going and disregard the symptoms as best as they can. Still others try to find existential meaning in the depersonalized state, attempting to come to some acceptance of the altered state of consciousness that has befallen them. Different philosophies may reinforce the idea that they are living in the only true reality, the "now" moment, the reality of only the present, and they try to adapt accordingly.

What are the ways people with depersonalization recover without medication?

This is not a question that has been systematically explored in research; yet it is clear that some people do recover without medication. In some, the depersonalization may be transient, lasting for weeks, months, or even a few years, and may gradually abate as the circumstances that initially triggered it recede into the past. For example, getting through the mourning of the death of a loved one, getting out of a profoundly stressful and seemingly endless situation, or even abstaining from a drug that initially triggered the state can sometimes lead to recovery. Others, whether through their own determination not to get caught up in a cycle of fear, stress, and worsening depersonalization, or through talk therapy to work through what troubles them early on in the manifestation of DPD, get better. It seems that a sense of control over the symptom early in its course can be very helpful in facilitating more successful recovery. For other people, possibly those who are more inherently vulnerable to depersonalization, or those who become caught up in the cycle of fear and worry typical of the condition, resolution of the initial stressor may not lead to recovery—it is as if the depersonalized state takes on a life of its own.

Do people become depersonalized from drug abuse?

This is a tricky question, since a trigger is not the same as a cause. We now know enough to say that, without doubt, use of particular drugs triggers the onset of DPD in a substantial portion of people. We also know that typically only certain drugs can do this—marijuana, hallucinogens, ecstasy, and ketamine being the main culprits. We also know, of course, that the large majority of people who use these drugs do not ever become depersonalized, even if they have "bad trips" and experience great fear and anxiety during the intoxication. So, for some people with depersonalization, drug use seems to be a necessary, but not sufficient, factor for its onset. Two more caveats come to mind regarding both the "necessary," and the not-sufficient. Although a drug may have been the necessary ingredient for the onset of a particular depersonalization episode, this does not mean that the same person may not have become depersonalized later on in their lives, without using drugs, for some other reason. This is a possibility for which a person may never know the answer, yet it is an important one to keep in mind because some people with drug-induced depersonalization have great trouble overcoming the guilt and regret over their drug use and the sense that they brought on their own misfortune in a way that could have been easily avoided. Yet, we have seen some people with depersonalization, especially those who get it in serial episodes and in between are free of it, who can have one episode triggered by a drug and another episode triggered by something totally different, like severe stress. This takes us to the next point, which is that any trigger is not "sufficient" for developing the disorder. People who develop depersonalization, just like other people who develop anxiety or depression or schizophrenia over the course of their lives, have a vulnerability or propensity to the particular disorder which can express itself at some point in their lives, and which other people do not have. This vulnerability may be in part genetic or in part driven by early developmental psychological and physiological processes. We do not yet know what the particular vulnerabilities are for depersonalization because the necessary research has not been done. We hope that in the near future studies examining genes possibly relevant to depersonalization and their variants in those afflicted with it will teach us more.

Does depersonalization have something to do with sleep patterns?

This is a very interesting question and one that has not been studied. Certainly for some people there seems to be a relationship to sleep, and for others not. For some, depersonalization is at its worst in the first hours of the day after they wake up and still feel sleepy, and it lessens as they feel more alert over the course of the day. For others it gets worse later in the day, as they feel more tired. Others report that their depersonalization is particularly sensitive to lighting or changes in lighting during the day. For example, it may be worse on a bright, sunny day, or worse when light gets dimmer or at dusk. Also, people with depersonalization often liken it to bad jetlag and feel much worse when they travel across time zones. Therefore, it makes sense to think that circadian rhythms and their disruption can affect depersonalization and its intensity, but not trigger it in the first place, perhaps by affecting wakefulness and arousal. Again, there is hardly any research in this area in depersonalization, but the question is worth looking at. We do know, for example, from a couple of biological studies that more severe dissociation and depersonalization symptoms are associated with lower norepinephrine levels in the urine, and norepinephrine is one of the neurotransmitters in the brain that modulates arousal and alertness. Clearly, a state that is so often described as "dreamlike" warrants further research into its relationship to sleep, dreaming, and wakefulness.

What is it about adolescence that often triggers depersonalization?

The average age of onset of depersonalization is around adolescence, age 16 in the large U.S. research series and age 22 in the large U.K. series. Depersonalization disorder is not alone in this. Many other psychiatric disorders, such as schizophrenia and bipolar disorder, tend to start around adolescence as well. Part of the explanation may be biological. The brain undergoes its last phase of rigorous development and rewiring in adolescence, during which old connections are pruned away while other new ones form and solidify. In this way the adolescent brain is particularly vulnerable to circuit abnormalities that underlie the various mental disorders. From a psychosocial perspective, especially regarding depersonalization, adolescence is a crucial time in development, and a difficult one, when people are challenged with the task of solidifying a sense of identity—who they are and where they are headed in life. Some of the highly stressful tasks of adolescence appear to trigger depersonalization in those vulnerable to it: separating from home, moving away to college, increasing performance demands, new socializing demands, and the first major romantic relationships and disappointments, to name a few. Although many people negotiate these highly stressful transitions with relative success, others, especially when faced with unexpected challenges or hampered by earlier developmental difficulties, find that these tasks are extremely stressful, even overwhelming, and can possibly trigger depersonalization.

Why does marijuana trigger depersonalization?

Marijuana undoubtedly triggers depersonalization; it was implicated in about 13% of all the people studied with the disorder in the U.S. series. We won't repeat here the lengthy explanations that can be found in chapter 6. Suffice it to say that chronic depersonalization can be triggered in some individuals even with sporadic or one-time use of marijuana, so the effect does not seem to be a dose-related or cumulative one. Also, it can happen without a "bad trip" or negative intoxication experience. All this suggests that the cannabinoid receptor in the brain (that receptor on which marijuana and other cannabinoids, including endogenous ones that our own brain produces) is a prime target for genetic studies of depersonalization. This so-called candidate gene has not yet been studied in DPD. In such a genetic study, researchers sequence the candidate gene and look for whether individuals with a particular disorder carry particular variants, or alleles, of that gene at a higher frequency than the general population. Such genetic variants could ultimately be one of the predisposing factors to the disorder.

Why does fluorescent lighting exacerbate depersonalization?

The short answer is that we do not know, yet this effect is terribly common for those with DPD. We discussed lighting above when talking about the sleep–wake cycle in depersonalization. Alternatively, depersonalized individuals are known to be unusually sensitive to all kinds of perceptual overstimulation (noise, crowds, busy streets, computer screens overloaded with information, new and unfamiliar environments, and even perceptually challenging cognitive tests), and the vulnerability to fluorescent lights could have something to do with this kind of perceptual overstimulation. A PET imaging study has documented that people with DPD have changes in brain activity in the sensory association areas of the temporal, occipital, and parietal cortex, which are responsible for processing and integrating incoming sensory stimuli.

How are seizures related to depersonalization?

For the most part, seizures are not related to depersonalization, meaning that individuals with DPD do not have a seizure disorder, and, by definition according to the *Diagnostic and Statistical Manual of Mental Disorders*, they cannot have a seizure disorder if they are diagnosed with DPD. If seizures are causing the depersonalization, as happens in a very small number of cases, then the diagnosis is one of seizure disorder, which is treated accordingly. Both temporal lobe epilepsy, as well as the rarer parietal lobe epilepsy, can exhibit depersonalization-like symptoms. Certainly, if there is any clinical suspicion that a person is having seizures, or even as a precaution, it is worthwhile to do a routine, or even an extended-time, EEG to exclude the presence of seizures. Similarly, a CT or an MRI may be indicated to exclude any kind of structural change in the brain that could be causing the depersonalization. In the vast majority of cases, these neurological work-ups do not reveal any abnormalities, and then the doctor can safely diagnose DPD. The temporal and parietal cortical areas that can be involved in seizures and can manifest depersonalization suggest that it is, in part, circuits in these areas that are dysregulated and underlie depersonalization even when it does not occur in the context of seizures. In the previous question we mentioned the PET imaging study that showed changed activity in the sensory association areas of the occipital, temporal, and parietal cortex in depersonalization.

How does LSD trigger depersonalization?

The general answer, as far as we know, is similar to the one described for marijuana. LSD and other hallucinogens are a particular type of serotonin agonist (i.e., they enhance certain serotonin-related activity in the brain). It may be that serotonin pathways are one of the pathways that modulate stress-related responses and in this way facilitate or trigger depersonalization. Ironically, however, there have been a few cases in which people self-medicated with LSD in an attempt to relieve their marijuana-induced deper-sonalization or agoraphobia. In these patients LSD did result in an improved sense of reality and ability to feel.[3] This practice is hardly recommended, however. So there are still many mysteries relating to this particular drug and its relation to chronic DPD.

If LSD and other serotonin agonists cause depersonalization, then why don't SSRIs also cause depersonalization?

The brain pathways and functions that control serotonin are complex and involve many types and subtypes of serotonin receptors. LSD and related sub-stances are specific serotonin agonists, which enhance serotonin-related ac-tivity. SSRIs (selective serotonin reuptake inhibitors), in contrast, are nonspe-cific serotonin reuptake inhibitors, and therefore acutely enhance serotonin transmission at all types of serotonin receptors. Over a few weeks, however, continued SSRI use actually decreases the sensitivity of serotonin receptors. In these ways SSRIs don't have a similar action to hallucinogens.

How does the drug ecstasy cause depersonalization?

A similar answer as for the other drug-related questions applies here and is discussed in chapter 6. Ecstasy has an effect on both serotonin and dopamine pathways in the brain, suggesting that these pathways may have particular alterations or vulnerabilities in those who become depersonalized after using ecstasy.

If a person has smoked marijuana many times, why does one time finally trigger chronic depersonalization?

It does not actually always happen with this kind of scenario. Some people have chronic depersonalization triggered by smoking marijuana once, twice, or three times. The phenomenon does not actually appear to be dose-related. Others may describe that their depersonalization was triggered on an occa-sion when the pot they smoked was unusually strong, or possibly laced, or when they were in a highly stressed state, or when they experienced a bad trip with overwhelming anxiety or a panic attack. From what we know, it seems that any amount of marijuana, however small or infrequent, has the potential to trigger chronic depersonalization in a person who is particularly vulnerable.

If depersonalization was triggered by smoking marijuana, does it mean there is irreversible brain damage?

No, there is no evidence that there is irreversible damage in marijuana-triggered depersonalization, nor in any other type of depersonalization. Indeed, the U.S. research program at Mount Sinai has compared in great detail the various characteristics of depersonalized individuals who had onset triggered by marijuana versus drug-unrelated triggers. No differences were found in any characteristics, such as age, severity and frequency of depersonalization symptoms, or particular types of depersonalization symptoms.[4] Thus, it seems that marijuana triggers a disorder that differs in no obvious way from other forms of the disorder. The fact that we have not yet found a medication that is effective in treating the condition does not mean that there is irreversible brain damage. It means that we have not yet discovered the particular neurochemical and brain circuitry abnormalities that subsume depersonalization and a medication that is able to correct these.

Is depersonalization some kind of spiritual awakening?

As a medical condition, the *Diagnostic and Statistical Manual of Mental Disorders*, 4th edition, is clear on this point, stating: "Voluntarily induced experiences of depersonalization or derealization form part of the meditative and trance practices that are prevalent in many religions and cultures and should not be confused with Depersonalization Disorder."[5] This said, depersonalization is sometimes referenced in various spiritual and meditative texts as a step on the road to enlightenment—the elimination of the self, as such. Some spiritual advisors of varying credibility have said that it is representative of having an "old soul." We explore these areas in some detail in chapter 7.

Depersonalized people find themselves in a kind of limbo, however, with one foot in this world and one in some other. This limbo may indeed involve a unique state of consciousness that is more attuned to how relative our perceptions of ourselves and the world are, the fragile division between being and not-being, the existential pondering of whether our lives are but a dream, and so on. However, it goes too far for most of those who suffer from it to label depersonalization a spiritual awakening. In contrast to what we usually think of as spiritual awakenings, it is not born from a life-altering spiritual experience, but is more likely to be born from very stressful and difficult experiences. It typically feels not enlightened and liberating, but confining and distorted. People who have it usually long to feel their usual selfhood, as they knew it with all its angst and earthly limitations. So, even though depersonalization can offer unique insights into the nature of human experience and of being, as other psychiatric and even medical conditions can, even in a transforming way, most would be happy to move away from it and go on with their lives and enjoy the pleasures of just being human.

There are some people however, who, as part of their adaptation to the condition, find ways of incorporating various eastern philosophies into the creation of their "new" self. This option is not for everyone, nor does it necessarily validate depersonalization as a spiritual awakening. Nonetheless, it is part of the depersonalization universe, which is why we chose to explore this area in chapter 7.

Is there a way to go in and out of depersonalization by one's own control?

For most that have the disorder, there is not. A few people report, especially early on in the course of their depersonalization, that they were able to turn it on and off voluntarily, to some degree at least. For example, children with traumatic childhoods of various sorts may describe moments in their early lives when they felt that they wanted to have no part in what was happening around them, and they somehow brought on a distance and detachment from their surroundings, leaving the scene or becoming immersed in some other aspect of their experience that was more tolerable. We have heard other stories in which a depersonalized state of some sort was coveted and sought after as a part of meditation practices. Some say that early on they could bring on a depersonalized state during meditation, but with time this state became autonomous and outside voluntary control and began to emerge spontaneously even outside of meditation. If depersonalization could volitionally be turned on and off, by will, it would not be classified as a psychiatric disorder, just as depression or anxiety or psychosis cannot be turned on or off. It does not happen this way.

Why is it so hard to find a single cure that works for depersonalization?

If we knew the answer, we would probably know the treatment. Still, we can speculate, and the most likely explanation may be that depersonalization affects unique brain circuits and their neurochemical pathways that are not extensively implicated in many other psychiatric disorders and do not respond to our usual medication arsenal. It is important to remember that effective medications for many psychiatric, as well as medical, illnesses were empirically or fortuitously found before the underlying biological abnormalities were elucidated. The same may come true with DPD, as by trial-and-error we test out all the new classes of central nervous system medications that are rapidly being developed. Alternatively, unique insights into the biology of the disorder, should these come first, could very well guide us to more effective treatments.

Why have so many doctors never heard of depersonalization disorder?

This is true, though it may seem hard to believe. Some patients with DPD encounter a well-informed professional and receive an accurate diagnosis quickly. But this is the exception, not the rule. More often than not, patients see psychiatrists and psychologists who tell them they are anxious, stressed, depressed, personality-disordered, or even psychotic without ever identifying depersonalization as their condition. This can be damaging and only perpetuates the patient's sense of feeling crazy, being misunderstood, or seeing themselves as an anomaly suffering from something that no one else has and no one else knows about. Depersonalization disorder, by our rough estimates, appears to be common and to affect 1–2% of the population, and although there is only limited comfort in numbers, it is better than suffering alone. Those with the disorder are becoming more informed and more able to search out and communicate with others suffering from the condition largely because of information and support groups created by sufferers themselves on the Internet. Among professionals, there has been greater recognition and appreciation for the disorder over the past decade, possibly in part because of a number of high-quality research studies that have put the condition on the radar screen for the mental health profession.

The British group has claimed that depersonalization is more related to the anxiety disorders, yet their research points to differences from those disorders. Can the anxiety disorder link be proved or disproved?

Paradoxically, the U.K. research program has reported a number of findings that contradict the notion that DPD is a kind of anxiety disorder. Sierra et al. reported that galvanic skin responses, which measure autonomic arousal, in response to negative stimuli were blunted in DPD but heightened in anxiety disorders. They also found in a functional MRI imaging study that depersonalized individuals had heightened prefrontal cortex activity and blunted limbic activity in response to emotional stimuli compared to normal participants, a pattern opposite from that in anxiety disorders.[6] In terms of cognitive processes, the U.S. research team has found that people with depersonalization have attentional processes very unlike those of people with anxiety disorders, in that they are not vulnerable to interference by disorder-specific anxiety-provoking stimuli but can effectively block them out.[7] To the best of our understanding, then, the relationship between depersonalization and anxiety is limited to the fact that extreme anxiety can trigger or worsen depersonalization, just like any other extreme state of mind can. This is, then, a nonspecific, stress-related response or trigger.

Certain drugs prescribed to treat depersonalization can actually make it worse. Can some of these drugs actually cause it?

There is no evidence in the literature that prescription medications can trigger or worsen depersonalization. There may be one or two such cases reported, and even those are dubious because of the other complex circumstances surrounding the onset of depersonalization. It is not uncommon for prescribed medications to cause a transient worsening of depersonalization, especially early on, if they have side effects that make people feel more drugged, sedated, or out of it in one way or another. However, this is different from any kind of lasting impact on the symptom.

Can hypnosis be used to treat depersonalization?

There are only a few cases reported or that we have encountered of people who attempted to treat their depersonalization with hypnosis, so the answer to this question is essentially unknown. There are two things, however, that we know for a fact. One is that that the more severe dissociative disorders, such as dissociative identity disorder and its milder variants, can benefit from hypnotic techniques as a part of their treatment, although this is not the mainstay of these treatments. We also know that individuals with these more severe dissociative disorders are often highly hypnotizable, and therefore can make good use of hypnotic techniques in treatment. Some researchers and clinicians have even put forth the theory that high hypnotizability is one of the factors that can predispose individuals to developing pathological dissociation if they are exposed to considerable adversity during their lives. However, the hypnotizability of depersonalized individuals is less clear and has not been studied. We do not, for a fact, know if hypnotizability is high for the group of people with DPD as a whole. Therefore, the word on hypnotizability, hypnosis, and its uses in depersonalization is still not out. Yet, for those with depersonalization who are able to be hypnotized, this could be a component of treatment that may be worth trying.

Notes

Chapter 1

1. Styron, W. (1990). *Darkness visible*. New York: Vintage Books, pp. 7, 38.
2. Dugas, L. (1898). Un cas de dépersonnalisation. *Revue philosophique, 55*, 500–507.
3. Amiel, H.F. (1882/1906). *The journal intime* (vol. 2). New York: MacMillan, pp. 304–305.
4. Freud, S. (1936/1964). *A disturbance of memory on the Acropolis. Standard Edition of Complete Works of Sigmund Freud*, vol. 22. London: Hogarth Press.
5. Noyes, A.P., & Kolb, L. (1939/1964). *Modern clinical psychiatry* (6th ed.). Philadelphia: W.B. Saunders, p. 84.
6. American Psychiatric Association. (1994). *Diagnostic and statistical manual of mental disorders* (4th ed.). Washington, DC: Author, p. 477.
7. World Health Organization. (1992). *International classification of diseases* (10th revision). Geneva: Author, p. 351.
8. Myers, D. (1972). A study of depersonalization in students. *British Journal of Psychiatry, 121*, 62; Noyes, P.R., Kupperman, S., & Slymen, D.J. (1977).
9. Depersonalization in accident victims and psychiatric patients. *Journal of Nervous and Mental Disorders, 164*, 401–407.
10. Hunter, E.C., Sierra, M., & David, A.S. (2004). The epidemiology of depersonalisation and derealisation. A systematic review. *Social Psychiatry and Psychiatric Epidemiology, 38* (1), 9–18.
11. Ibid.

Chapter 2

1. American Psychiatric Association. (1994). *Diagnostic and statistical manual of mental disorders* (4th ed.). Washington, DC: Author.

2. Simeon, D., Knutelska, M., Nelson, D., & Guralnik, O. (2003). Feeling unreal: a depersonalization disorder update update of 117 cases. *Journal of Clinical Psychiatry, 64*, 990–997.

3. Simeon, D., Guralnik, O., Schmeidler, J., & Knutelska, M. (2004). Fluoxetine therapy in depersonalization disorder: randomised controlled trial. *British Journal of Psychiatry, 185*, 31–36.

4. Simeon et al., "Feeling unreal."

5. Szymanski, H.V. (1981) Prolonged depersonalization after marijuana use. *American Journal of Psychiatry, 138,* 231–233.

6. Simeon et al., "Feeling unreal."

7. Ibid.

Chapter 3

1. Schilder, P. The treatment of depersonalization. *The Bulletin, Psychiatric Division of Bellevue Hospital,* 1939, p. 260.

2. Sierra, M., Berrios, G.E. (1997). Depersonalization: a conceptual history. *History of Psychiatry, 8,* 213–229.

3. Krishaber, M. (1873). *De la neuropathie cerebro-cardiaque.* Paris: G. Masson, 1873.

4. Dugas, L. (1898). Un case de depersonalisation. *Revue Philosophique, 45,* 500–506.

5. Krishaber, *De la neuropathie.*

6. Ibid.

7. Ribot, T. (1895). *Les Maladies de la personnalite* (6th ed.). Paris: Felix Alcan

8. Janet, P.(1903). *Les Obsessions et la psychasthenie.* Paris: Alcan, p. 106.

9. Dugas (n. 3), p. 457.

10. Ibid.

11. Dugas, "Un case," p. 458.

12. Ibid.

13. Janet, P. (1928). *De l'angoisses a la extase.* Paris: Alcan.

14. Amiel, H.F. (1882/1906). *The journal intime.* New York: Macmillan.

15. Janet, *Les obsessions.*

16. Ibid., p. 318.

17. Mayer-Gross, W. (1935). On depersonalization. *British Journal of Medicine and Psychology, 15,* 103–126.

18. Ibid., p. 118.

19. Ibid., p. 116.

20. James, W. (1902/1961). *The varieties of religious experience*. New York: Macmillan, p. 138.

21. Ibid., p. 67.

22. Mayer-Gross (n. 16), p. 118.

23. Freud, S. (1936/1964). *Standard edition of the complete works of Sigmund Freud* (vol. 22, pp. 239–248). London: Hogarth Press, p. 245.

24. Ibid..

25. Ibid.

26. Schilder, "Treatment."

27. Schilder, P. (1953). *Medical psychology*. New York: International Universities Press, p. 306.

28. Ibid., p. 305.

29. Wittels, F. (1940). Psychology and treatment of depersonalization. *Psychoanalytic Review, 27*, 57; Jacobson, E. (1959). Depersonalization. *Journal of the American Psychoanalytic Association, 7*, 581.

30. Sarlin, C.N. (1962). Depersonalization and derealization. *Journal of the American Psychoanalytic Association, 10*, 784.

31. Arlow, J.A. (1966). Depersonalization and derealization. In *Psychoanalysis: A general psychology* (pp. 456–477). New York: International Universities Press.

32. Shorvon, H.J. (1946). The depersonalization syndrome. *Proceedings of the Royal Society of Medicine, 39*, 779–792

33. Schilder, *Medical*, p. 310.

34. Roth, M.R. (1960). The phobic anxiety-depersonalization syndrome and some general aetiological problems in psychiatry. *Journal of Neuropsychiatry, 1*, 293–306.

35. Ibid., p. 299.

36. Torch, E M. (1978). Review of the relation between obsession/depersonalization. *Acta Psychiatria Scandinavia, 58*, 191–198, p. 194

37. Ibid., p. 195.

38. Noyes, R., Jr., Kletti, R., & Kupperman, S. (1977). Depersonalization in response to life threatening danger. *Comprehensive Psychiatry, 18*, 375–384.

39. Cattell, J.P., & Cattell, J. S. (1974). Depersonalization: psychological and social perspectives. In *American handbook of psychiatry* (pp. 766–799). New York: Basic Books, p. 768.

40. Ibid., p. 769.

41. Ibid.

42. Bettelheim, R. (1967). *The empty fortress*. New York: The Free Press [quoted in Cattell & Cattell (n. 38), p. 773].

43. Ibid. (n. 38), citing Laing, R. D., *The Divided Self.* Baltimore: Penguin Books, 1965.

44. van der Hart, O., Nijenhuis, E., Steele, K., et al. (2002). Trauma-related dissociation: conceptual clarity lost and found. *Australia-New Zealand Journal of Psychiatry, 38*, 906–914.

45. Holmes, E.A., Brown, R.J., Mansell, W., et al. (2005). Are there two qualitatively distinct forms of dissociation? A review and some clinical implications. *Clinical Psychology Review, 25*, 1–23.

46. Ibid.

47. Noyes et al., "Depersonalisation in response."

48. Sierra, M., & Berrios, G.E. (2001). The phenomenological stability of depersonalization: comparing the old with the new. *Journal of Nervous and Mental Disease,* 189, 629–636.

49. Ackner, B. (1954). Depersonalization: I. Aetiology and phenomenology. *Journal of Mental Sciences, 100*, 838–853.

50. Saperstein, J.L. (1949). Phenomena of depersonalization. *Journal of Nervous and Menal Disorders, 110*, 236–251.

51. Cappon, D., & Banks, R. (1965). Orientation perception. *Archives of General Psychiatry,* 5, 380–392; L'hermitee, J. (1939). *L'image de notre corps.* Paris: Nouvelle Revue Critique.

52. Mayer-Gross, "On depersonalisation."

53. Cappon & Banks (n. 50); Lewis, R. (1931). The experience of time in mental disorder. *Proceedings of the Royal Society of Medicine, 25*, 611–620; Shorvon (n. 30).

54. Amabile, G., Rizzo, P.A. (1966). Perdita della visione mentale: (contributo clinico). *Revista Sperimentale di Freniatria, 90*, 1156–1163.

55. Mayer-Gross (n. 15); Shorvon (n. 30).

56. Berrios & Sierra (n. 47), p. 635.

57. Ibid., pp. 629, 635.

58. Ibid., p. 635.

Chapter 4

1. Steinberg M. (1994). *Structured clinical interview for DSM-IV dissociative disorders (SCID-D), revised.* Washington, DC: American Psychiatric Press.

2. Steinberg, M. (2000). *Stranger in the mirror.* New York: HarperCollins.

3. Bernstein, E.M., & Putnam, F.W. (1986). Development, reliability, and validity of a dissociation scale. *Journal of Nervous and Mental Disorders, 174*, 727–735.

4. Sierra, M., & Berrios, G.E. (2000). The Cambridge depersonalisation scale: a new instrument for measurement of depersonalization. *Psychiatry Research, 93*, 153–164.

5. Ibid.
6. Radovic, F., & Radovic, S. (2002). Feelings of unreality: a conceptual and phenomenological analysis of the languare of depersonalization. *Philosophy, Pyschiatry, and Psychology, 9,* 271–279.
7. Ibid., p. 275.
8. Ibid., p. 276.
9. Ibid., p. 277.
10. American Psychiatric Association. (1994). *Diagnostic and statistical manual of mental disorders* (4th ed.). Washington, DC: Author.

Chapter 5

1. Simeon, D., Knutelska, M., Nelson, D., et al. (2003). Feeling unreal: a depersonalization disorder update of 117 cases. *Journal of Clinical Psychiatry, 64,* 990–997.
2. Baker, D., Hunter, E., Lawrence, E., et al. (2003). Depersonalisation disorder: clinical features of 204 cases. *British Journal of Psychiatry 182,* 428–433.
3. Dixon, J.C. (1963). Depersonalization phenomena in a sample population of college students. *British Journal of Psychiatry, 109,* 371–375.
4. Aderibigbe, Y.A., Bloch, R.M., & Walker, W.R. (2001). Prevalence of depersonalization and derealization experiences in a rural population. *Social Psychiatry and Psychiatric Epidemiology, 36,* 63–69.
5. Bebbington, P.E., Marsden, L., & Brewin, C.R. (1997). The need for psychiatric treatment in the general population: The Camberwell needs for care survey. *Psychological Medicine, 27,* 821–834; Bebbington, P.E., Hurry, J., Tennant, C., Sturt, E., & Wing, J.K. (1981). Epidemiology of mental disorders in Camberwell. *Psychological Medicine, 11,* 561–579.
6. Ross, C.A. (1991). Epidemiology of multiple personality disorder and dissociation. *Psychology Clinics of North America, 14,* 503–517.
7. Simeon et al., "Feeling unreal"; Baker et al., Derpersonalisation disorder."
8. Simeon et al., "Feeling unreal."
9. Baker et al., "Depersonalisation disorder."
10. Simeon et al., "Feeling unreal"; Baker et al., "Depersonalisation disorder."
11. Waller, N.G., & Ross, C.A. (1997). The prevalence and biometric structure of pathological dissociation in the general population: taxometric and behavior genetic findings. *Journal of Abnormal Psychology, 106,* 499–510; Jang, K.L., Paris, J., Zweig-Frank, H., et al. (1998). Twin study of dissociative experience. *Journal of Nervous & Mental Disease, 186* (6), 345–351.
12. Baker et al., "Depersonalisation disorder."

13. Medford, N., Baker, D., Hunter, E., et al. (2003). Chronic depersonalization following illicit drug use: a controlled analysis of 40 cases. *Addiction, 98*, 1731–1736.

14. Simeon et al., "Feeling unreal."

15. Baker et al., "Depersonalisation disorder."

16. Simeon et al., Feeling unreal."

17. Simeon, D., Guralnik, O., Schmeidler, J., Sirof, B., & Knutelska, M. (2001) The role of interpersonal trauma in depersonalization disorder. *American Journal of Psychiatry, 158*, 1027–1033 (2001).

18. Guralnik, O., Schmeidler, J., & Simeon, D. (2000). Feeling unreal: cognitive processes in depersonalization. *American Journal of Psychiatry, 157*, 103–109.

19. Allen, J.G., Console, D.A., & Lewis, L. (1999). Dissociative detachment and memory impairment: reversible amnesia or encoding failure? *Comprehensive Psychiatry, 40*, 160–171; Holmes, E.A., Brown, R.J., Mansell, W., et al. (2005). Are there two qualitatively distinct forms of dissociation? A review and some clinical implications. *Clinical Psychology Review, 25*, 1–23.

20. Simeon et al., "Feeling unreal."

21. Ibid.

22. Baker et al., "Depersonalisation disorder."

Chapter 6

1. Blanke, O., Ortigue, S., Landis, T., et al. (2002). Stimulating illusory own-body perceptions. *Nature, 419* (6904), 269–270.

2. LeDoux, J. (1996). *The emotional brain.* New York: Touchstone, Simon and Schuster.

3. Ibid.

4. Penfield, W., & Rasmussen, T. (1950). *The cerebral cortex of man: a clinical study of localization of function.* New York: Macmillan, pp. 157–181.

5. Sierra, M., & Berrios, G. (1988). Depersonalization: neurological perspectives. *Biological Psychiatry, 44*, 898–908.

6. Krystal, J.H. et al. (1998). The emerging neurobiology of dissociation: implications for the treatment of posttraumatic stress disorder. In Bremner J.D., Marmar C.R. (Eds.), *Trauma, memory and dissociation* Washington, DC: APA Press.

7. Kuhn, T. *The structure of scientific revolutions.*

8. Devinsky, O., Putnam, F., Grafman, J., et al. (1989). Dissociative states and epilepsy. *Neurology, 39* (6), 835–840.

9. Salanova, V., Andermann, F., Rasmussen, T., et al. (1995). Parietal lobe epilepsy: clinical manifestations and outcome in 82 patients treated surgically between 1929 and 1988. *Brain, 118* (3), 607–627.

10. Blanke et al., "Stimulating."

11. Ackner B. (1954). Depersonalization: I. Etiologyg and phenomenology. II. Clinical syndromes. *Journal of Mental Sciences, 100*, 838–872.

12. Vallar, G., & Perani, D. (1986). The anatomy of unilateral neglect after right-hemisphere stroke lesions: a clinical/CT-scan correlation study in man. *Neuropsychologia, 24* (5), 609–622.

13. Adolphs, R., Damasio, H., Tranel, D., et al. (2000). A role for somatosensory cortices in the visual recognition of emotion as revealed by three-dimensional lesion mapping. *Journal of Neuroscience, 20* (7), 2683–2690.

14. Simeon, D. et al. (2000). Feeling unreal: a PET study of depersonalization disorder. *American Journal of Psychiatry, 157*, 1782–1788.

15. Sierra & Berrios, "Depersonalization: neurological perspectives."

16. Matthew, R.J. et al. (1999). Regional cerebral blood flow and depersonalization after tetrahydrocannabinol administration. *Acta Psychiatria Scandinavia, 100,* 67–75.

17. Phillips, M.L., et al. (2001). Depersonalization disorder: thinking without feeling. *Psychiatry Research, Neuroimaging Section, 108*, 145–160.

18. Gorno-Tempini, M.L., Gorno, Price, C.J., Josephs, O., et al. (1998). The neural systems sustaining face and proper-name processing. *Brain, 121* (11), 2103–2118.

19. Lanius, R.A., Williamson, P.C., Boksman, K., et al. (2002). Brain activation during script-driven imagery induced dissociative responses in PTSD: a functional magnetic resonance imaging investigation. *Biological Psychiatry, 52*, 305–311.

20. Phillips et al., "Depersonalisation disorder."

21. Simeon et al., "Feeling unreal."

22. Ibid.

23. Simeon, D., Hollander, E., Saoud, J.B., DeCaria, C., Cohen, L., Stein, D.J., Islam, M.N., & Hwang, M. (1995). Induction of depersonalization by the serotonin agonist m-CPP. *Psychiatry Research, 58*, 161–164.

24. Southwick, S.M., Krystal, J.H., Bremner, J.D., et al. (1997). Noradrenergic and serotonergic function in posttraumatic stress disorder. *Archives of General Psychiatry, 54* (8), 749–758.

25. Simeon, D., Guralnik, O., Schmeidler, J., & Knutelska, M. (2004). Fluoxetine therapy in depersonalisation disorder: randomised controlled trial. *British Journal of Psychiatry, 185*, 31–36.

26. Anand, A., Charney, D., Oren, D., et al. (2000). Attenuation of the neuropsychiatric effects of ketamine with lamotrigine: support for hyperglutamatergic effects of N-methyl-D-aspartate receptor antagonists. *Archives of General Psychiatry, 57* (3), 270–276.

27. Simeon, D., Knutelska, M., Nelson, D., & Guralnik, O. (2003). Feeling unreal: a depersonalization disorder update of 117 cases. *Journal of Clinical Psychiatry, 64*, 990–997.

28. Ibid.

29. Walsh, S.L., Geter-Douglas, B., Strain, E.C., et al. (2001). Enadoline and butorphanol: evaluation of kappa-agonists on cocaine pharmacodynamics and cocaine self-administration in humans. *Journal of Pharmacology and Experimental Therapeutics, 299* (1), 147–158.

30. Bohus, M.J., Landwehrmeyer, B., Stiglmayr, C.E., et al. (1999). Naltrexone in the treatment of dissociative symptoms in patients with borderline personality disorder: an open-label trial. *Journal of Clinical Psychiatry, 60* (9), 598–603; Nuller, Y.L., Morozova, M.G., Kushnir, O.N., et al. (2001). Effect of naloxone therapy on depersonalization: a pilot study. *Journal of Psychopharmacology, 15* (2), 93–95; Simeon, D., & Knutelska, M. (2005). An open trial of naltrexone in the treatment of depersonalization disorder *Journal of Clinical Psychopharmacology, 25,* 267–270.

31. Griffin, M.G., Resick, P.A., & Mechanic, M.B. (1997). Objective assessment of peritraumatic dissociation: psychophysiological indicators. *American Journal of Psychiatry, 154* (8), 1081–1088.

32. Sierra, M., Senior, C., Dalton, J., et al. (2002). Autonomic response in depersonalization disorder. *Archives of General Psychiatry, 59* (9), 833–838.

33. PTSD is a complex disorder, and its complexity is not well captured in the current *DSM*. For example, some people have no major previous traumatic stress histories and may develop PTSD after a single adulthood trauma, like a car accident. Such people typically experience intrusive and arousal symptoms, but little in the way of detachment. Other people have PTSD of a more chronic and early-onset nature, for example, consequent to childhood abuse. Varying degrees of detachment, bordering on or comprising frank depersonalization, are more typical in these individuals. In other words, the presence and severity of dissociative symptoms varies greatly among individuals with PTSD. It may be that future editions of the *DSM* will take these complexities of PTSD into better account, by designating for example, a subtype of PTSD with prominent dissociation, or by designating a "complex PTSD" disorder characterized by both PTSD and dissociative symptoms.

34. Simeon, D., Guralnik, O., Knutelska, M., et al. (2003). Basal norepinephrine in depersonalization disorder. *Psychiatric Research 121,* 93–97.

35. Delahanty, D.L., Royer, D.K., Raimonde, A.J., Spoonster, E. (2003). Peritraumatic dissociation is inversely related to catecholamine levels in initial urine samples of motor vehicle accident victims. *Journal of Trauma and Dissociation, 4,* 65–79.

36. Coplan, J.D., Andrews, M.W., Rosenblum, L.A., Owens, M.J., Friedman, S., Gorman, J.M., & Nemeroff, C.B. (1996). Persistent elevations of cerebrospinal fluid concentrations of corticotrophin-releasing factor in adult nonhuman primates exposed to early-life stressors: implications for the pathophysiology of mood

and anxiety disorders. *Proceedings of the National Academy of Sciences, USA, 93,* 1619–1623.

37. Simeon, D., Guralnik, O., Knutelska, M., et al. (2001). Hypothalamic-pituitary-adrenal axis dysregulation in depersonalization disorder. *Neuropsychopharmacology, 25*(5), 793–795.

38. Ibid.

39. Unpublished data.

Chapter 7

1. Amiel, H.F. (1885/1906). *The journal intime of Henri-Frederic Amiel* (H. Ward, trans.). New York: Macmillan.

2. Ibid., p. xlvii

3. Amiel, *The journal intime*, p. 62. All subsequent quotations of Amiel in this chapter are taken from *The journal intime* unless otherwise noted.

4. Amiel, p. xlix.

5. Nemiah, J.C. (1989). Depersonalization disorder (depersonalization neurosis). In *Comprehensive textbook of psychiatry* (5th ed., vol. 1, pp. 1038–1044). Baltimore: Williams & Wilkins, p. 1042

6. Sartre, J.P. (1938/1962). *Nausea*. New York.: New Directions Publshing Corp. Subsequent quotations from the book are referenced by page number.

7. Camus, A. (1942 [1946]). *The stranger*. New York: Vintage Books, p. 1.

8. Dugas, L. Un cas de depersonnalisation. *Revue Philosophique, 45,* 500–507.

9. Ibid.

10. de Caussade, J.-P. (1731). Excerpt from a letter to Sister Mary-Antoinette de Mahuet.

11. Roberts, B. (1993). *The experience of no-self*. Albany: SUNY Press. All subsequent quotations of Roberts in this chapter are taken from this book.

12. Segal, S. (1996/1998). *Collision with the infinite*. San Diego, CA: Blue Dove Press. All subsequent quotations of Segal are taken from this book.

13. Huxley, A. (1954/1955/1956). *The doors of perception*. New York: Harper and Row. Huxley, A. (1954/1955/1956). *Heaven and hell*. New York: Harper and Row.

14. Huxley, *Doors*, p. 23. Subsequent quotes of Huxley are taken from this book unless otherwise noted.

15. Huxley, *Heaven*, p. 135.

16. Ibid., p. 135.

17. Janiger, O., & Dobkin de Rios, M. (2003). *LSD, spirituality and the creative process*. Rochester, VT: Park Street Press, pp. 27–63.

18. Ibid.

19. Ibid., p. 11.

20. Ibid., p. 55.

21. Ibid. p. 110.

22. Ibid. p.109.

23. Wilson, C. (1956/1978). *The outsider.* London: Pan Books Ltd.

24. Ibid., p. 24.

25. Watts, A. (1973). *In my own way: an autobiography.* New York: Vintage Books, p. 278.

26. American Psychiatric Association (1994). *Diagnostic and statistical manual of mental disorders* (4th ed.). Washington, DC: Author.

27. Newburg. A. Questions and answers online interview: www.andrewnewberg .com/qna/asp.

28. APA, *DSM-IV.*

29. Borges, J.L. (1960[1998]). *Everything and nothing, The Maker* (1960), *Collected Fiction.* New York: Viking Penguin, p. 319. All subsequent quotes of Borges are taken from this book.

Chapter 8

1. Schilder, P. (1939). The treatment of depersonalization. *Bulletin of the New York Academy of Medicine, 15*, 258–272.

2. Davison, K. (1964). Episodic depersonalization: observations on 7 patients. *British Journal of Psychiatry 110*, 505–513; King, A., & Little, J. (1959). Thiopentone treatment of the phobic anxiety depersonalization syndrome. *Proceedings of the Royal Society of Medicine, 52*, 595–596; Cattell, J.P., & Cattell, J.S. (1974). Depersonalization: psychological and social perspectives. In S. Arieti (Ed.), *American handbook of psychiatry* (pp. 767–799). New York: Basic Book; Harper, M., & Roth, M. (1962). Temporal lobe epilepsy and the phobic anxiety-depersonalization syndrome. *Comprehensive Psychiatry, 3*, 129–151.

3. Ambrosino, S. (1973). Phobic anxiety-depersonalization syndrome. *New York State Journal of Medicine, 73*, 419–425.

4. Simeon, D., Knutelska, M., Nelson, D., et al. (2003). Feeling unreal: a depersonalization disorder update of 117 cases. *Journal of Clinical Psychiatry, 64* (9), 990–997.

5. Simeon, D., Guralnik, O., Schmeidler, J., & Knutelska, M. (2004). Fluoxetine therapy in depersonalisation disorder: randomised controlled trial. *British Journal of Psychiatry, 185*, 31–36.

6. Hollander, E., Liebowitz, M.R., DeCaria, C.M., et al. (1990). Treatment of depersonalization with serotonin reuptake blockers. *Journal of Clinical Psychophar-*

macology, 10 (3), 200–203; Fichtner, C.G., Horevitz, R.P., & Braun, B.G. (1992). Fluoxetine in depersonalization disorder. *American Journal of Psychiatry, 149* (12), 1750–1751; Ratliff, N.B., & Kerski, D. (1995). Depersonalization treated with fluoxetine. *American Journal of Psychiatry, 152* (11), 1689–1690.

7. Simeon, D., Stein, D.J., & Hollander, E. (1998). Treatment of depersonalization disorder with clomipramine. *Biological Psychiatry, 44*, 302–303.

8. Anand, A., Charney, D., Oren, D., et al. (2000). Attenuation of the neuropsychiatric effects of ketamine with lamotrigine: support for hyperglutamatergic effects of N-methyl-D-aspartate receptor antagonists. *Archives of General Psychiatry, 57* (3), 270–276.

9. Sierra, M., Phillips, M.L., Lambert, M.V., et al. (2001). Lamotrigine in the treatment of depersonalization disorder. *Journal of Clinical Psychiatry, 62* (10), 826–827.

10. Sierra, M., Phillips, M.L., Krystal, J., et al. (2003). A placebo-controlled, crossover trial of lamotrigine in depersonalization disorder. *Journal of Psychopharmacology, 17* (1), 103–105.

11. Bohus, M.J., Landwehrmeyer, B., Stiglmayr, C.E., et al. (1999). Naltrexone in the treatment of dissociative symptoms in patients with borderline personality disorder: a open-label trial. *Journal of Clinical Psychiatry, 60* (9), 598–603.

12. Glover, H. (1993). A preliminary trial of nalmefene for the treatment of emotional numbing in combat veterans with post-traumatic stress disorder. *Israeli Journal of Psychiatry and Related Sciences, 30* (4), 255–263.

13. Nuller, Y.L., Morozova, M.G., Kushnir, O.N., et al. (2001). Effect of naloxone therapy on depersonalization: a pilot study. *Journal of Psychopharmacology, 15* (2), 93–95.

14. Simeon, D., & Knutelska, M. (2005). An open trial of naltrexone in the treatment of depersonalization disorder. *Journal of Clinical Psychopharmacology, 25*, 267–270.

15. Simeon, D., Gross, S., Guralnik, O., et al. (1997). Feeling unreal: 30 cases of DSM-III depersonalization disorder. *American Journal of Psychiatry, 154* (8), 1107–1113; Simeon et al., "Fluoxetine therapy."

16. Ibid.

17. Morgan, C.A., Rasmusson, A.M., Wang, S., et al. (2002). Neuropeptide-Y, cortisol, and subjective distress in humansexposed to acute stress: replication and extension of previous report. *Biological Psychiatry, 52*, 136–142.

Chapter 9

1. Quoted in Schilder, P. (1939). The treatment of depersonalization. *Bulletin of the New York Academy of Medicine, 15*, 258–272.

2. Ibid.

3. Cattell, J.P., & Cattell, J.S. (1974). Depersonalization: psychological and social perspectives. In S. Arieti (Ed.), *American handbook of psychiatry* (pp. 767–799). New York: Basic Books.

4. Fewtrell, W.D. (1986). Depersonalisation: a description and suggested strategies. *British Journal of Guidance and Counselling, 14*, 263–269.

5. Levy, J.S., & Wachtel, P.L. (1978). Depersonalization: an effort at clarification. *American Journal of Psychoanalysis, 38*, 291–300.

6. Frances, A., Sacks, M., & Aronoff, M. (1977). Depersonalization: a self-relations perspective. *American Journal of Psychoanalysis,* 325–331.

7. Hunter, E.C.M., et al. (2003). Depersonalisation disorder: a cognitive-behavioural conceptualization. *Behaviour Research and Therapy, 41*, 1451–1467.

8. Ibid.

9. Simeon, D., Guralnik, O., Schmeidler, J., Sirof, B., & Knutelska, M. (2001). The role of childhood interpersonal trauma in depersonalization disorder. *American Journal of Psychiatry, 158*, 1027–1033.

10. Hunter et al., "Depersonalisation disorder."

11. Hunter, E.C.M., Baker, D., Phillips, M.L., Sierra, M., & David, A.S. (2005). Cognitive-behaviour therapy for depersonalization disorder: an open study. *Behaviour Research and Therapy, 43*, 1121–1130.

12. Hunter et al., "Depersonalisation disorder."

13. Ibid.

14. Fewtrell, "Depersonalisation"; Fewtrell, W.D. (1984). Relaxation and depersonalisation. *British Journal of Psychiatry, 145*, 217.

15. Shorvon, H.J. (1946). The depersonalisaton syndrome. *Proceedings of the Royal Society of Medicine, 39*, 779–785.

16. Fewtrell, "Depersonalisation."

Epilogue

1. Anonymous posting, www.depersonalization.info.

Frequently Asked Questions

1. Simeon, D., Knutelska, M., Nelson, D., & Guralnik, O. (2003). Feeling unreal: a depersonalization disorder update update of 117 cases. *Journal of Clinical Psychiatry, 64*, 990–997.

2. Ibid.; Baker D., et al., (2003). Depersonalization disorder: clinical features of 204 cases. *British Journal of Psychiatry, 182*, 428–433.

3. Ludwig, A. (1966). Altered states of consciousness. *Archives of General Psychiatry, 15*, 225–233.

4. Simeon, "Feeling unreal."

5. American Psychiatric Association. (1994). *Diagnostic and statistical manual of mental disorders* (4th ed., pp. 488–491). Washington, DC: Author.

6. Phillips, M.L., Medford, N., Senior, C., et al. (2001). Depersonalization disorder: Thinking without feeling. *Psychiatry Research: Neuroimaging, 108* (3), 145–160.

7. Guralnik, O., Schmeidler, J., & Simeon, D. (2000). Feeling unreal: cognitive processes in depersonalization. *American Journal of Psychiatry, 157*, 103–109.

Index